NO BAR TO SUCCESS

To my darling Sally,
without whose inspirational, literary, intellectual and
computer skills, general enthusiasm and sheer hard work
this book would never have been written or published.

First published in Great Britain 2016 by
The Beautiful Publishing Company Ltd
of Wickham House, 464 Lincoln Road,
Enfield, Middlesex, EN3 4AH,
United Kingdom.

FIRST EDITION

All photographs reproduced in this work
are from the author's own collection,
except where credited otherwise.

This book is a work of non-fiction based on
the life, experiences and recollections of the
author. In some limited cases (particularly
in Chapters 23 and 24), names of people,
places, dates, sequences or the details of events
have been changed solely to ensure that no
confidential information about anyone the
author has ever represented or advised is used
or divulged and that in all cases the privacy of
such persons and others is totally protected.

Every reasonable effort has been made to
trace all copyright holders of material
reproduced in this book, but if any such
person has been inadvertently overlooked,
the publisher would like to apologise for
any such omission and will be pleased to
incorporate any such missing acknowledgement
in any future edition of this book.

A CIP catalogue record for this book is
available from the British Library.

ISBN No. 978-0-9564221-1-8

The Beautiful Publishing Company Ltd
Wickham House, 464 Lincoln Road
Enfield, Middlesex, EN3 4AH, UK

NO BAR TO SUCCESS

AN INSPIRING LIFE STORY

BY

PETER WHITEMAN QC

WITH

SALLY CARTER

CONTENTS

PREFACE

They all told me that, for an autobiography to sell, the author had to be a celebrity, a personality, preferably one who is well-known to television audiences. I am not such a person. You have probably never heard of me. I have never appeared on *Strictly Come Dancing*, or any of the TV soaps, or been a football manager. So why, despite all the 'advice' I received, did I still go ahead and write this book? Because I really believe, and I hope you will agree, that my life story is truly inspirational. My basic belief, and the essential theme running right through this book, is that nothing is impossible. But, of course, there is far more to it than that. It is a story of vicious cruelty, yet of kindness beyond belief; of heart-rending sadness, yet of the greatest happiness; of unbelievable success, and of abysmal failure; of intensely moving drama, and of death.

My aim is to excite you, entertain you and encourage you, in the hope that you will accept my basic belief. You may find such an aim surprising, given that I am a barrister and a judge – occupations that usually conjure up the image of a somewhat staid, conservative person. But that is definitely not me. Here you will find no tedious recitation of cases in which I have acted. Just the reverse. My unorthodox approach has been to draw back the curtain on the mystique of the legal establishment. It is an inside story, told by one who has been a barrister for some fifty years. No holds are barred, famous names are named, nothing is withheld, nothing is concealed. This is an amazing story, full of interest, told in a self-deprecatory and humorous way. So OK, I am not a TV star – but read this book and you will discover that my life has been fascinating and quite extraordinary. You may laugh, you may cry, you may be intensely moved, but I believe you will certainly not be bored.

ACKNOWLEDGEMENTS

I should like to express my sincere thanks to all those who have made possible the writing and publication of this book, particularly:

Sir Derek Jacobi (whose work I greatly admire), who enthusiastically agreed to write the Foreword. He has written eloquently in words I find most generous and touching, and has skilfully woven the similar characteristics of our two professions in a powerful and perceptive way.

Anthony Osmond-Evans of The Beautiful Publishing Company, whose unwavering support has continued from the moment he learnt of my book. His wise and thoughtful counsel has been a major influence on the shape and content of the book.

Pauline Lloyd, who has been the most superb, meticulous proof reader. Her attention to every last detail of the book was admirable.

Ross Gow, who has been a joy to work with, full of ideas and enthusiasm, positive and totally professional. It is no wonder he was the perfect person to publicise and launch my book.

George Metcalfe, for his editorial assistance, especially with the final shape and content of the book. Good-humoured, thoughtful, sensitive and patient, it has been a sheer delight to work with him.

Tony Barrett, whose thoughtful planning of the layout and framework of the book was undertaken with utter professionalism and sensitivity.

His Honour Judge David Paget QC, who kindly agreed to read significant parts of the book. His perceptive comments based on his considerable legal knowledge and experience have been of inestimable value to me.

And finally my darling Sally, whose enthusiasm, determination and encouragement have constantly inspired me. My autobiography is just as much a creation of hers as mine.

FOREWORD

BY

SIR DEREK JACOBI CBE

"Time present and time past
Are both perhaps present in time future,
And time future contained in time past.
If all time is eternally present
All time is unredeemable."
Burnt Norton from Four Quartets
T S Eliot

Photograph © Nobby Clark

It is a very great privilege that Peter Whiteman has asked me to write a foreword to welcome and celebrate his remarkable autobiography, *No Bar to Success*. He and I have been fortunate enough to have found an enjoyable level of success with our individual careers. We met recently at a dinner and we reminisced that we had both been pupils at the same boys' grammar school, Leyton County High School, in East London (Peter a few years after me). This wonderful school profoundly influenced both our lives and subsequent careers: I in the theatre, Peter in the law, where he has had an extraordinary career as one of the world's most distinguished tax barristers, a judge, a professor, one of the most influential legal authors on tax, and, at 34, the youngest QC in recent times.

His autobiography opens with the shocking and cruel death of his beloved wife, Kate, in a car accident in Argentina. Throughout his compelling text Peter shares with us his remarkable life, including the challenges, triumphs and tragedies that have brought him to today's eminence.

Actors and lawyers have many shared similarities. Actors must learn technique and study lines; lawyers have to master the intricacies of the law and absorb complex Briefs. We both have to face audiences, whether in the theatre, on the screen, in court or even before a judicial enquiry or parliamentary commission. We actors have to interpret a character in a world created by the dramatist or scriptwriter. The lawyer must be able to communicate what the client, whether private or corporate, would otherwise say, had he the skill or knowledge to do so. In addition, the lawyer frequently has to advise on complex, often international, issues, and this Peter has achieved with outstanding success.

Only recently Peter and I have mutually discovered that our lives share many other facets which have not ostensibly been part of our professional careers. Both of us came from relatively humble backgrounds in the East End of London. Both of us had supportive parents whom we wanted to be proud of us. Although my family background had what appeared to be some foreign aspects, Peter had to deal with the anti-Semitism that was endemic in the East End of London at that time. He writes movingly about running to escape bullies as a small primary school child, knocking in desperation on a stranger's door hoping for rescue, but then being taken by the ear by a pitiless housewife to his Headmaster, who caned him brutally.

The first big break for both of us came when we succeeded in winning our grammar school places at Leyton County High. In truth, it was touch-and-go whether either of us would actually be accepted there. Rheumatic fever kept me in bed for over a year. This forced me to do my Eleven Plus by correspondence course. I got into the school as a result of being interviewed by the rather fierce Headmaster and giving one of my most successful early 'performances'. For me the great revelation was the presence of the English master, Mr Bobby Brown. He was no disciplinarian, but he loved his subject and appreciated any student who responded. Being in London, we went with him on many school trips to theatres. He directed the school plays and obviously saw some spark in me that he fostered. It is greatly thanks to his early encouragement that I have gone on to have a very happy and fulfilling career as an actor.

Peter joined the same school a few years after me, so we did not actually know each other then. For him, as you will read, there was also a big question mark over whether he was going to be accepted by the school. He admits that his marks as a junior were at the very least disappointing until he was encouraged by the history master, Mr Paddy Clinch. It was Clinch who recognised Peter's latent potential to make a success of his academic career. Each year Peter rose to the challenges that Clinch set him and gained higher and higher marks so that he eventually emerged at the top of the school. It is partly as a result of the unselfish and generous encouragement by these two schoolmasters that both of us began to recognise that we were highly ambitious and capable of developing the talents we were born with. Peter won a scholarship to study law at the London School of Economics, while I went to St John's College, Cambridge, where once again I devoted myself to acting.

Throughout our lives Peter and I have somehow been granted the privilege of being championed and encouraged by wonderful mentors. Peter's mentors were distinguished legal academics, senior lawyers and judges; mine included great actors such as Sir Laurence Olivier, who was incredibly supportive in furthering my career for many years and who invited me into the National Theatre at its very start.

However intellectually accomplished, lawyers must from time to time recognise that they have to become actors. They must empathise with their audience. Much will depend on the evidence and especially the way it is presented. Sometimes the lawyer must play to the sympathy vote because he needs, just as actors do, to have the audience on his side. The defence lawyer needs the jury's sympathy, while the prosecutor has to convince them to loathe and detest the person or organisation in the dock.

Joint themes which Peter and I recognise in our separate but similar professions are as much of interest to lawyers as to actors. These include the powerful interpretation of words, being able to illuminate conduct and character to convey certain meanings; the ability to decode technical language in private contracts and in public laws; using the skills of rhetoric or persuasive speech to uncover the truth; and, finally, the necessity of being deeply sensitive to the relationships between law and equity and between justice and mercy. These are all enduring and timeless themes that are of course explored in *The Merchant of Venice*. It is very much a play about law and lawyers, and little wonder that it has become part of the canon of the growing law and literature movement in Law Schools. One of Shakespeare's finest quasi-legal speeches can be found when Portia says to Shylock, *"Though justice be thy plea, consider this, that in the course of justice none of us should see salvation: we do pray for mercy; and that same prayer doth teach us all to render the deeds of mercy."*

Not everybody has a good word either for lawyers or for actors. Mark Twain is famously quoted as asking, *"What chance has the ignorant, uncultivated liar against the educated expert? What chance have I…against a lawyer?"* On the other hand, Sir Laurence Olivier has commented, *"Acting is a masochistic form of exhibitionism. It is not quite the occupation of an adult."*

Our different professions of the law and the stage have given Peter and me enormous satisfaction, a good living and many memorable moments in our lives. I hope that, as you follow the story of Peter's brilliantly-told struggle to create an incredibly successful career from very humble beginnings, you will love this masterly and hugely enjoyable celebration of an outstanding life lived with grace and integrity.

CHAPTER 1

ACCIDENT

"'There's been an accident,' they said"
Ruthless Rhymes for Heartless Homes (Mr Jones)
HARRY GRAHAM

"It's going to be a perfect day!" I exclaim, as I throw open the curtains, letting in the sunlight. How wrong can you be? It is to be the worst day of my life. By far.

We have had a wonderful time in Buenos Aires, escorted by our guide, Alejandro, who three days later will play a role in my life that I could never have foreseen. It is going to be a beautiful day for our journey to the Argentinian Lakes – it couldn't be better.

Kate goes off to the bathroom to collect up everything and make herself ready for the day. I go and shower. Then all the last-minute preparations to ensure we have left nothing behind. I take two apples from the bowl as I pass it – they may come in handy if we get hungry when we are travelling.

Satisfied we have everything, we go down to the breakfast room situated on an elegant terrace. Even that early, the sun is very hot, so we find a nice shady corner. Alejandro is to tell me later that, whenever he walks by the table where we were sitting, he always stops and, because of what happened, he bows to it.

Breakfast over, it is then time for all the usual mundane checking-out formalities. When they are completed, we reflect that this has been a very good hotel to stay in – I don't know it then, but I shall never come back to this hotel, ever again in my life.

The journey to the airport is uneventful, but I know there will be a problem when we arrive there because our luggage is, as usual, massively over-weight. But Kate will be in her element, convincing the person at the check-in desk that the scales are incorrect, that the luggage didn't weigh that much on the way out, that, as we are foreigners and love Argentina, surely the airline could make a concession and so on and so on. It will be aggravating for everyone except Kate. She really thrives in that type of situation. She enjoys it. It is a challenge for her. And if she should succeed today, she will have a warm glow for the rest of the journey.

We chat all the way to the airport – I suppose in forty years we have never stopped chatting. We are very excited about seeing the Argentinian Lakes. When we were planning our holiday here, it was a close call whether we visited the Lakes from the Argentinian or the Chilean side of the Andes. We had originally decided to go to Chile. But the travel agent who arranged our holiday to include visiting Chile had really annoyed Kate because he misquoted the cost of the holiday. It was such a stupid argument to have. So incensed was Kate that I was persuaded by her to change to another firm of travel agents, who recommended visiting the Lakes from the Argentinian side. No argument could have had more appalling consequences, but such is fate. Such is life – and death.

We arrive at the airport to catch our plane to Bariloche. And yes, we do have the usual run-in at check-in, but this time, despite all Kate's blandishments, we do have to pay excess baggage. A defeat for Kate's charms and persuasive powers of argument, but she takes it well – as I have said, it is something of a game to her. At least today she hasn't threatened to unpack and repack her suitcases on the airport floor, transferring as much as possible to her hand-luggage. That is usually her ultimate weapon if she hasn't succeeded up to that point. She has used it many times, holding up the entire line of people waiting to check in, and possibly for that reason she has achieved total capitulation. Today, however, I am spared that dramatic flurry of activity and (to me) consequent indignity.

After that, check-in goes normally and we arrive at our allocated seats on the plane. Now Kate and I have always had an understanding. On trains she always gets her choice – the seat facing forwards, as she feels sick if she travels backwards. On planes, we agreed a long while ago that I should have the window seat as, having no sense of balance at all, my feeling of orientation is better if I can see the horizon. I slide across to the window seat.

Kate looks at me ensconced there. She hovers thoughtfully next to 'her' aisle seat. "You said the view of Buenos Aires from the air as we flew in from London was fantastic." Indeed, I had said exactly that – the view was stunning. "So can I sit next to the window to get the view of the city this time?" I say, "Sure," and, on reflection, I have always been so pleased that I gave that immediate and positive response. I am certain I have not got everything right in life, but on that occasion, in response to Kate's question, I certainly did. I can't even bear to think how I would have felt if I had said "No." I would always have regretted it. I think it was the very last thing she ever asked of me – her very last wish – and, although it may have been a tiny thing, I'm so glad I said "Yes." It was something so small and so insignificant, but now my response means the world to me. And that, in the event, Kate had the view that she was so keen to see.

The view from the plane as we left Buenos Aires is great and Kate adores it. Looking out of the plane window, she asks, "What is that land down there?" I look many thousands of feet below us, at the ground bathed in unbroken sunshine. "The Pampas," I answer. Kate queries this. "But I thought the Pampas were mountains." "Not quite," I say, and I give her a quick geographical overview of the Pampas. Kate has always been somewhat geographically challenged – she once went to Israel for a holiday on the basis that she didn't want to go as far afield as Greece!

The plane journey is uneventful, as there is no turbulence on this beautiful clear summer's day. We both feel fine and are very excited. Kate has done all the planning for the holiday and has chosen a brilliant itinerary. As we chat on the plane about the wonderful sights in store, little did I know that I wouldn't be seeing any more of the itinerary planned for the days to come. I also didn't know at that time that I would be travelling back on the very same plane to Buenos Aires the following day with an empty seat next to me and a coffin in the baggage hold.

We land at Bariloche and are met by our tour guide, Martha. Poor Martha, who that day is going to shoulder a burden that no one should ever be asked to bear. She introduces us to our driver, who was to change our lives forever – but I can't (maybe for psychological reasons) even remember his name. It is early afternoon and by now it is oppressively hot. I look at my watch. It is 2.15. It is the last occasion that day I am aware of the time. Martha and the nameless driver take charge of our luggage and stow it in the boot of the car. So now we are all set, full of excitement, ready to drive to Angostura and our hotel for the next three days. We get into the car provided by the tour company. Kate chooses to sit behind the driver, another fateful decision by her that day. If I had sat there … But there is no point in agonising over something which is done and cannot be undone. I get into the car and sit behind Martha. I notice that Kate has not put on her seat belt. There is a good reason for this. Since she had a breast cancer operation in 1994, Kate has found wearing a seat belt very uncomfortable. She would wear a seat belt in the front seat, but never in the back. I know that, if I had suggested she wear a seat belt, she would have refused outright, as she had done some ten days previously in London.

The car starts moving and we are off on our visit to the Lakes. On the journey Kate and I ask Martha a whole series of questions. Martha said to me afterwards, "The two of you never stopped talking to each other, and you were so excited about the rest of your holiday. You were obviously at ease in each other's company. You talked so much. I can tell you that I meet lots of tourists and it is rare, very rare, to see two people so happy and talking so much in each other's company."

The journey to Angostura is supposed to take 2–2½ hours. Soon after we leave Bariloche Airport, we come to a beautiful lake and drive along by the side of it for a while. The day is perfect – scenery, weather, company – and there is everything to look forward to.

We leave the lakeside and continue on a fairly straight road which has only one lane in each direction. Very little traffic in sight. There is gravel by the side of the road and, next to this, a wide grass verge. Beyond the verge, and so further from the road, are clumps of trees every so often. All very pretty and most peaceful. The car is moving along at about 60 miles per hour, not particularly fast, and indeed some cars overtake us. As a passenger I am always quick to notice when a car is being driven badly. This car is not. But then I hear gravel at the side of the road being kicked up by our tyres. The car hasn't seemed to swerve and, except for the scrunching sound of the gravel, I wouldn't have noticed what must have been a slight change in direction. Certainly there is nothing dramatic, and although I am a little concerned, I am not frightened. We continue along the road, and although there are some curves in it, it is basically straight. The driver continues at the same speed, about 60 mph. He is silent (I assume he doesn't speak English). He doesn't even speak to Martha. There is nothing strange about his behaviour. There is no indication at all that he is drunk, or driving erratically. Only the drift onto the gravel has heightened my awareness. Martha tells us that the driver has driven a couple of hours to pick us up at the airport. I don't think then, but reflect later, that he may have been tired, possibly overtired, particularly as Martha tells us that he has been driving long distances recently. In any event, although the drift onto the gravel has unsettled me, Martha seems totally relaxed while she chatters away. Possibly she didn't notice it or, if she did, thought it to be of no consequence.

But then it happens a second time. The car drifts slightly, not dramatically, onto the gravel again. As before, I feel a little concerned, but not frightened. Kate notices nothing. Nor do I mention it to her – she would probably have thought that I was overreacting.

We continue driving along, entering a new, somewhat different stretch of road. It is built on an embankment; the ground on the right is level with the road surface (and we are, of course, being driven on the right-hand side). However, to our left, beyond the other lane, the ground drops steeply away.

And then something happens. I don't know what, but something is definitely happening. The car goes eerily quiet. The sound of the car tyres travelling along the road surface ceases. It is so strangely quiet. And then a new sensation. The world is being turned upside down, or that is how it feels. Our world IS actually being turned upside down. I then realise with horror what is happening. The car is somersaulting. In the air. It has somehow, by some force, been catapulted into the air – it is doing somersaults over the ground and that is why there is no road surface noise. We are in the air. Turning over and over. This explains why, as yet, there is no sound of any crash, no sensation of any collision. I am not able to focus on anything or anybody. Not Kate, not the guide, not the driver. Everything is an enormous blur. And then I understand why. Because I am being tossed around in the car like a rag doll – crashing against the roof of the car, then the floor, then the seat. Still no noise, although ludicrously I think that I must be covered in bruises. Although I didn't appreciate it at the time, that was the least of my problems.

BANG! The most almighty ear-splitting sound breaks the silence. The car has crashed into the ground. The whole vehicle shakes at the collision of metal on earth. I realise afterwards that that must have been the first time the car had hit the ground after 'taking off' from the road and somersaulting into the air. The sensation of being in a vehicle that is rolling over and over continues for what seems an eternity. The car hits the ground several times. BANG, BANG, BANG! Maybe the car crashes into the ground as many as five or six times. One ear-splitting sound follows another as the car shudders at the repeated impacts. I realise by now that the car, having come off the road, must be rolling down the embankment. We have crossed the left-hand lane of the road and rolled down the steep incline of the embankment. As the car rolls over and over, I continue to crash around inside it. As I do so, I have one thought which recurs again and again. "We will only be safe when the car comes to rest. We will only be safe when the car comes to rest. We will only …". Eventually it does and I am on the car floor in front of my seat. I don't know how I feel. I don't even think about how I feel. My first thought is for Kate. I look to my left – her seat is empty, but the car door is wide open. I can see a clump of trees through the open door. There is no sign of Kate beyond that open door. I see blood. It is on me. All over me. I don't stop to inspect it or to discover if it is mine. I can't feel anything. The only thing to be done is to find Kate and discover how badly she has been injured. I turn my body over, raise myself onto my seat. More blood there. I try to get out through my door to see where Kate is. I can't. It is jammed closed. So I have to ease myself across to where Kate was sitting. More blood there. I then try to get out of the car through the open door. Afterwards I realise it must have been then that my trousers became stained with Kate's blood. I get out of the car through the open door. I feel very weak. Putting my feet to the ground, I realise that my legs have turned to jelly and I feel totally dazed. Standing upright, I feel very strange and dizzy. I look around. The car has come to rest at the bottom of the embankment, near a gully. I stagger to the gully. Totally disorientated. No Kate. I call out her name. Several times. No answer. I don't know what to do. I just have to go on searching. No Kate. No sign of her. No sound. I call out. Again and again. "Kate, Kate." All to no avail. I just don't know what to do. I turn around. I see the car. Or what remains of it. It is a complete wreck. Where is Kate? I somehow manage to get round the back of the car, using it as a prop to take my weight as I make minimal progress. And then I see her – about 30–40 feet away, lying on her back, motionless, on the steepest part of the embankment, not that far from the road. She is lying at an angle, on the steeply sloping grass, facing the sun.

I realise afterwards that she must have been thrown out of the car soon after it left the road. Possibly when I heard the first bang. I move up the embankment as fast as my jelly-legs will take me, to the most appalling of sights. She is motionless. There is blood all over her body. I fear the worst but still hope she may be alive. But what would her injuries be if she is still alive? Almost certainly horrendous. And then suddenly Kate's lips move. Not much, but just a little. Maybe she is still alive – but no sound comes out. And then her tummy moves in slightly. Yes, maybe she is coming round from unconsciousness. Maybe she will move some more. Maybe she will talk to me. Maybe. But all these faintest of hopes are to be dashed very soon. Clutching at such small movements in the hope that there might be life in this inert body is doomed. No more movements. There is nothing more. Now no sound from her at all. The movements are probably the involuntary ones of a dead body. But still I hope. Ludicrous but true. There is no life. There is no hope. I have lost her.

Later I am told she must have died instantly; probably as a result of her neck being broken. But I don't know this now. And then I look more closely at her face; her injuries are horrific. There is a great flap of skin on her forehead, the length of a hand, that has been ripped open and torn back on itself. But it has not been totally torn off, so gently I fold it back and put it where it should be. I do this with great love and an overwhelming sense of grief, and as though it will achieve something. Of course it won't, but I have to do it. And then I see the worst horror of all – like some grotesque Braque or Picasso painting. Her left eye and left ear have somehow become mangled up together and have become one. It is horrific and I can't bear to look at it. This beautiful woman, so grievously injured, so appallingly disfigured. I put my arm round her back and gently lift her towards me. I put my other arm around her. I cradle her in my arms. I am distraught. How can I comfort her? How can I help her? What can I do? I go on holding her, cradling her for some time. Of course I didn't think of it at the time, but we must have made the most tragic sight. I am on my knees, cradling her body, with my arms around her. At the scene of the accident I keep on thinking, "I only hope she knew nothing about it and that she hasn't suffered." How I hope she hasn't suffered. How I hope the car didn't fall on top of her – crushing her after she had been thrown out of it.

I then realise I never heard her scream. I don't know how I could have borne it if I had heard her scream. But I have no recollection of any sound from Kate during the course of the accident. Indeed, I have no recollection of her in the car while the accident took place. But fortunately she never screamed or made any sound of any sort at the accident. If she had, that would have haunted me for the rest of my life. It would have meant that she did know what was happening and that she was terrified. I couldn't bear that thought. I couldn't have lived with that, knowing that she realised what was happening. So when I am told later, in Argentina and in London, that she died immediately and knew nothing about it, that is everything to me. If it weren't so, I don't know if I would have kept my sanity.

By now I know she must be dead, but irrationally I still hope. I just don't know what to do. I stagger around in my totally demented state and eventually finish up at the top of the embankment. I go up to a crowd of onlookers who have gathered on the road above the site of the accident. They look aghast at what has happened. They are like dummies in their state of shock. They don't move. They are silent, even in the sight of this accident. They stare at me blankly. I shout at them. "Get an ambulance, NOW! Please get an ambulance! Please!" There is no sign of the police, just the group of onlookers. Some of them, together with Martha (whom I have not seen at all while the accident took place), try to comfort me. I am totally inconsolable. I cannot believe it – suddenly, out of nowhere, on this beautiful day, a tragedy occurs which has killed my wife and will totally destroy me. In seconds, everything that is my life has gone – gone forever.

In my disorientated condition I drag myself over to the driver of the car as though this will achieve something. Martha tells me he is distraught because the car, which he owns, is a total write-off, damaged beyond repair. I say to Martha hysterically, "He's lost his car. So what? I've lost my wife." I feel totally out of control. I am crazy. I run over to the driver and shout furiously at him. "You killed my wife. You killed my wife. You killed my wife." My shouting is pointless. He won't even understand because he doesn't speak English. And I think, as far as I am able to think on this tragic afternoon, it must have been the driver's fault, as no other car was involved. Is he drunk? Is he overtired? I shall never know. But what does it matter, nothing will change the fact that Kate is dead. Death coming out of the sky on a sunny afternoon, in the middle of nowhere, by Kilometre Post 34. But at least Kate died doing what she liked best – travelling in exotic locations. She loved that, as did I. Not now though.

I go back and sit by Kate. I look at her. It is the most appalling sight. I stroke her injured head. I don't know where to look. It is all so horrendous. Still no movement. Still no police. Martha comes over to me and says, "You mustn't sit in the sun. It is very hot today. Come and sit under the trees, it will be cool there." I think and mumble, "What does it matter whether I sit in the sun or not? Kate is dead, nothing matters, why should I care whether I sit in the sun or not? Nothing will ever matter now." But Martha and the others help me to my feet and take me over to the shade. I stumble across the long grass. They hold me up. I have no idea what is happening. This cannot be true. It must be a nightmare. When will it end? I cannot take in what has happened. And in the space of seconds. And those seconds have extinguished Kate's life, and mine as well.

I sit in my shady place, under the trees, where I have been taken. And then I look at Kate's body lying in the sun. The most horrible realisation hits me. I must be mad. How can I leave her lying in the sun uncovered? Why haven't I thought of it before? I am so stupid, I am so uncaring. How could I possibly leave her baking in the sun, unprotected? I get up shakily. Despite Martha's entreaties to stay in the shade. "You can't go there. Stay here in the shade. You can't do anything." I push away her arm, which is trying to restrain me from moving to Kate. She repeats, "You can't do anything." I mumble, "I can. I can. I must. I must go to her."

"I must cover Kate. I must cover Kate." I repeat it like a mantra. I order myself to go over to her. To help her. I stumble back across the long grass. As I go, I keep saying, "I must cover Kate." Everything I say that afternoon I repeat over and over again.

I cover Kate's body, but not her face, with my bloodstained jacket. Now I feel I have done what had to be done. I should have done it earlier, much earlier. I know she has gone now, but before I cover her face, I must say farewell, farewell forever. She has to hear my parting words.

"Goodbye, my darling. I love you. Thank you for everything. And thank

you for giving me Victoria and Caroline. I love you. Goodbye, my angel."
I know I will never see her again, my friend for forty years, and I don't.

I kiss her forehead – that poor, wretched, devastated forehead – and cover her face with my jacket. I am led off to the ambulance, which has at last arrived, to be taken to what and to where I have no idea.

CHAPTER 2

HARD TIMES

*"It's not easy for people to rise out of obscurity
when they have to face straitened circumstances at home."*
Satires III
DECIMUS JUVENAL (60–130 AD)

There's that noise again. I don't like it. I never do. It hurts my ears and Mummy tells me it hurts people as well. I am 2½ and I am always the first person to hear it. But now I'm off – running. I know where the best place is. I always go there when I hear that noise. Under the big kitchen table, that's the best place. I run with my toy Pluto and I sit there with my hands over my ears to keep the noise out. When I am under the large table, I feel safe, and when I dash there, everybody knows there is going to be a terrible noise. So they get up and start moving around; and then they start running. I know where they are off to. Mummy picks me up from my sanctuary under the table. I don't want to go. I want to stay. It's safe here. Mummy carries me and Pluto under her arm and off we go to the garden outside. Running, we soon reach the steps down to our little house under the garden. We go down. Inside it is cold and damp. It is not a friendly place, but at least I have Pluto with me. He will look after me. I know it. From inside we hear the noise getting louder and louder. Now it is very loud. Is it on top of our house? The noise doesn't stop. It gets worse. It is like the sound of a huge car engine but much, much louder. But then, after a little while, silence. Nobody moves. And then there is a big bang, a very big bang. It hurts my ears. I jump. We all jump. I am frightened. But Mummy and Daddy look happier now. They even smile. Daddy says, "That one didn't have our name on it then. I think we can go back to the house now."

Now there is no noise. It is quiet. No noise at all. We walk back to the house, with Mummy carrying me. I hope that horrible noise doesn't return. It frightens me. It hurts me. And everyone looks so worried.

That is the only memory I have of my earliest years. The noise I heard, and remember all too well, was the sound of a rocket, pilotless and flying automatically. The family, apart from my father (who basically remained in London), lived in Southend, having been evacuated from our home in the East End of London (Walthamstow) at the start of the Second World War. The rockets launched from German-occupied Europe flew across south-eastern England on their way to other targets, especially London. Southend being on the Essex coast, many flew directly over the town on their way elsewhere. Some, however, did land on the town, either by accident or design.

My father, David, confirmed many years later that I was always the first to hear a bomb or a rocket coming and, when I scurried under the table, they knew something deadly was approaching. They took their cue from me and literally ran for cover. That must have been my first valuable contribution to my family's well-being.

The other memories I have of my early years fall into the category of family stories I heard so often, particularly from my mother, Betty, that I cannot be sure whether I can really remember them or whether their telling and retelling has led me to believe that I do in fact remember them. I cannot distinguish between the two – a familiar phenomenon.

My maternal grandmother, Jesse Coster, did not figure in my life at all. She died in 1940, before I was born. My maternal grandfather, George Coster, died in 1946 and I have only very hazy memories of him. He was said by my mother to be a jovial man with a wonderful sense of humour. He was also, according to my mother, a kind, thoughtful, considerate and loving family man. My maternal grandfather was a furrier by trade, but his business, like so many others, suffered severely during the Second World War and eventually it collapsed.

What then of my mother? She was a charming, delightful, loving person, who only lived for her family. She was the product of a generation which has long since disappeared. A generation which, in the main, believed that

Top, left: My parents on honeymoon in Bournemouth, April 1935; *top, right:* The Author aged 1, 1943; *bottom, left:* The Author aged 1 with Alfred and Jill, and *bottom, right:* My father as an officer in the Fire Service, 1941

an unmarried daughter should stay at home, cosily ensconced in the family home. To go out to work would not have been regarded as appropriate or 'nice'. It meant, in the case of my mother, born in 1911, that she never worked for a living. 'Appropriate' or not, 'nice' or not, such an old-fashioned approach had severe financial repercussions for us when, after the war, the family's finances hit rock bottom and an income produced by my mother would have been a lifesaver.

Turning to my father's family, my paternal grandfather, Alfred, was an autocratic and essentially unpleasant man, who never spoke of his family history. To this day it remains a bit of a mystery. If my father ever had the temerity to ask his father about his family, I am sure he would have received a very sharp rebuff. Indeed, as far as I can recall, my grandfather never seemed to engage in any type of conversation with his son or indeed anyone else. Certainly I disliked both my paternal grandparents, who were totally lacking in warmth, affection, humour or encouragement – an unusual situation, given that they were Jewish. For example, I never remember a single instance of them taking me or my siblings on a family outing. I am sure it never crossed their minds to do so. When, many decades later, Kate and I took our children out for a fun afternoon at the cinema, the theatre or wherever, I often caught sight of children and their grandparents having a great time together. I envied them because it was something I never experienced.

My dislike of my paternal grandparents intensified when they came to live with us in the late 1940s. The family circumstances had continued to deteriorate and my grandparents, having nowhere else to live, announced to my parents that they were coming to live with us. It was not a request but a statement indicating a decision THEY had made! There was no question of consultation or discussion with my parents. It was announced as a fait accompli. My mother for once was very angry, but my father somewhat meekly agreed. This despite the fact that our home was cramped anyway, and having two more people living there would make it feel very overcrowded. In the event, it certainly did. It also created a good deal of tension and friction, particularly for my mother who had to share the tiniest of kitchens with her demanding and autocratic mother-in-law. It also meant that I saw my grandfather at close quarters. Not a pleasant experience, which did not endear him to me at all. Indeed one event seemed to justify my conclusion that he was really not a nice man. It was a trivial incident but, as often with trivial incidents, it showed the real nature of the person. One day, while my father was out at work, a large ink stain appeared on the floor of our living room. My mother knew my father would be furious about this desecration of our home and she made repeated unsuccessful attempts to remove it. My father duly arrived home, duly saw the stain and was duly furious. He demanded an explanation. Who was the culprit responsible for this outrage, he asked? My grandfather said it was me – that, whilst playing on the floor, I had spilt a bottle of ink from my drawing set. This was a lie. It was a pathetic attempt to exculpate himself from any blame. Fortunately, my sister, Jill, had seen what had occurred, namely that, while my grandfather was doing a crossword puzzle, he accidentally knocked over a bottle of ink. Jill immediately came to my rescue and told my father what had happened. He was extremely angry, not only because of the stain on the floor, but because his father had lied to him. My grandfather, having been caught out lying – he did not seek to contradict Jill – swept out of the room and slammed the door shut. He regarded the incident as over and it was never referred to by anybody in the family again. But it was a very disillusioning experience. It had a devastating impact on me because I had been accused by my grandfather of being responsible for something I simply had not done. It was despicable for my grandfather to lay the blame at the door of his little grandson. However, that was the man's nature and I never, ever trusted him again.

As I have already mentioned, I never learnt anything about the history of my paternal family from my paternal grandfather. However, my niece, Laura, who is very interested in genealogy, has searched through various public records. She discovered that one branch of my paternal family lived in Prussia as long ago as 1772 and were tailors by trade.

And so to my paternal grandmother, Bessie, née Levy. What information did she impart to us about her branch of the family? Well, here there was a rich vein to be mined. She told us that for many generations there had been a tradition of London taxi driving in the Levy family. That tradition continued down to my father, and to my brother, Alfred. As Laura discovered from the Public Census of 1841, a direct ancestor of my father owned fifteen 'hackney carriages' in that year.

So far I have not written in any detail about my father, quite deliberately, because, being a complex person, he was, on reflection, easily the most interesting member of my family. He was also a highly intelligent man. He was born in 1908 and I have no doubt that, if he had been born a few decades later, he would have gone to university and become a professional man. In fact, he did pass the Preliminary Examination of the Institute of Chartered Accountants and everything was in place for him to become articled to an accountancy firm. However, as was the custom at that time, a clerk had to pay a 'premium' to become articled. In my father's case, the premium required in 1926 was £100. His father refused to pay the necessary premium because he wanted my father to work for nothing in the public house he managed in Hackney. A promising career thus ended before it had even begun because of my grandfather's selfishness.

As a result, the obvious thing for him was to follow in the family footsteps and become a London taxi driver. However, before I write about his life as a 'cabbie', I must mention that from 1933 until 1945 he was an officer in the Fire Service.

At first he was a part-time officer, but during the entirety of the war he was a full-time firefighter. Although the family continued to live in Southend, he was based at the Whipps Cross Drill Hall, Walthamstow. Being based there meant that, as and when necessary, his unit was called in to assist with controlling and putting out fires in the East End of London during the Blitz. At the height of the Blitz, this was a daily occurrence. The conditions in which the members of his unit fought such appalling fires, with bombs dropping all around them, would have been quite horrendous. My father suffered from vertigo, a condition I have inherited, and one of the most difficult tasks he had to undertake was to climb an extension ladder 50–80 feet in the air, either to direct water to the centre of a fire or to rescue people trapped in a building. "Dad," I asked him on one occasion, "how could you climb all the way up such long ladders high into the sky when you suffered from vertigo?"

"I did it because I had to do it, and I never looked down. That helped enormously." And often, and indeed on the night in question related below, he had to climb the ladder to the top, rescue an endangered person, sling him over his shoulder and finally carry him all the way down. No mean feat for a man who suffered from vertigo.

But even that was not the worst part. Although hardly known or recorded, the most frightening aspect of fighting fires in the Blitz was, as he told me, that quite often, the main part of the raid being over, a lone German plane would return to the scene of devastation the Luftwaffe had created to machine-gun the firemen below. Firemen at the top of extension ladders when this occurred were totally isolated and completely exposed. My father told me this was the most terrifying aspect of all, being entirely at the mercy of the machine-gunner in the German plane, who could pick off the firefighters at will.

On one occasion my father told me a deeply disturbing story about his time in the Fire Service. One evening when the Blitz was particularly appalling, with huge fires raging all around them, my father and his colleagues were allowed a short respite from their firefighting duties. They went down below into a makeshift bunker to shelter from the bombs. The night had been terrifying, even by Blitz standards, and several members of the unit had been injured. A rebellious mood among the firemen had started to develop. "Why should we go up there again, we have done enough for one night," and similar mutterings of discontent. The break over, the senior fire officer ordered them to go above ground to resume their duties. The bombs were falling thick and fast and a large number of fires were burning – many, if not most, out of control. The risk to life and limb was enormous and the noise must have been terrifying. The men, despite the order, refused to go up. They had simply had enough. The senior fire officer asked them a second time and sought to reason with them. But the men were adamant. The senior officer fell silent and, with a stony look at the men, retreated from the shelter and went above ground. He soon returned, but this time with a very determined-looking Guards officer, who had already drawn his revolver from its holster and was holding it at elbow level. It was clearly ready for use. The Guards officer slowly and sternly said, "You will go up there and resume your duties now, or else." No attempt to reason or cajole; the Guards officer was not there to plead with them but to order them to go on fighting fires "or else". My father said he never knew what the Guards officer would have done if his unit had refused to obey the order. But none of the men was prepared to run the risk and, very grudgingly and with much cursing under their breath, the men went up to face the further horrors of that night. Would the Guards officer have used his revolver on the men, and if so, to what effect? None of the men could possibly have known, but clearly the unit believed that this tough-looking, experienced Guards officer – my father described his face as looking as though it had been carved out of granite – might well have used his revolver. Certainly his demeanour and his tone of voice left them in no doubt he was on a mission: to get the men back to their vital work – however terrified or rebellious they might be. It was a frightening experience, in addition to the usual horrors of the Blitz. The whole incident was always vividly recalled by my father – more than any other he was involved in during the war.

Apart from serving as a fire officer, my father pursued his work as a cabbie throughout his life. In referring to his career, I must begin at the beginning. His recollections of London when he started driving a taxi were fascinating. They went back to the days when taxis (hackney carriages to give them their proper name) were pulled by horses. At that time the driver sat up front, perched on a bench seat, exposed to all the elements. The driver sat in the open air and, however unpleasant the weather, it had to be endured alone and without any protection. Even later on, when the hackney carriage was motorised, the driver still sat up front, alone and unprotected from the weather. My father recalled his grandfather going out to work looking like the Michelin man because he was wearing so many sweaters, scarves, gloves and pairs of trousers. In the early part of the twentieth century it was an incredibly harsh occupation to pursue.

My father's grandfather was called by his colleagues 'Sugar Levy'. Why 'Sugar'? Apparently, he was a kind man who was extremely grateful to the animals who enabled him to make a living, albeit a modest one. So, because of his love for them, he always carried masses of sugar lumps in his pockets, which he generously bestowed on his own horse and other horses driven by his colleagues.

Those insights into my father's early working life were fascinating, but the reality of being a taxi driver, even in the 1940s and 1950s, was grim.

It was a tough, relentless and difficult occupation to follow, producing little income at that time. Of course, whatever my father earned in a day was partly luck, but it was also heavily dependent on the time of year. June to September were the best times for my father (when we were poor) and

January to March the worst (when we were often very poor). And as the seasons changed, so did his mood. On days in winter he could earn as little as £1 for a whole day's work and he would return to the house in a black mood. And, as children, we were apprehensive about his return home; had he had a good day or a bad day? A bad day meant a bad mood, which would certainly last until dinner. But, to be fair to my father, he was always worried whether he would earn enough to, as he put it, "keep food on the table."

As far as poverty was concerned, the worst time of all occurred in the winter of 1954–1955. My father had to go into hospital to have a rare skin complaint investigated. None of the doctors seemed to know how serious it was or whether it might spread internally. He became a patient in Guy's Hospital, which is a very long way from Walthamstow – about 1½ hours by bus. (There was of course no question of going by car – my father didn't own one.) I went with my mother every day after school to see him. It may be that, because those times were so bleak for us, when I speak of the daily journey, my mind has dramatised it. However, my memory tells me (apart from one matter concerning rain falling every single day, which cannot be right) that everything I am about to relate is true.

The journey by bus, the Number 35, seemed to take forever in the most depressing circumstances – a seemingly endless bus ride in the cold winter weather. There was no heating on the bus and there was an open platform at the back for access and egress, which allowed the wind to sweep through the whole vehicle. When we boarded the bus, we always made for the front seat, or as near to it as possible, where we both sat in wet raincoats, huddled together on the seat for warmth. Despite being so worried about my father's illness, my mother tried to be cheerful, no doubt for my sake. But I knew that her heart was breaking – she not only adored her husband, but she was also totally dependent on him in every way.

My recollection is that, every time we went on that wretched Number 35, the rain was lashing down on the bus and everybody and everything in the street. It cannot have been like that every day, but that is how my mind, so depressed at the time, chooses to remember it. Those visits to Guy's carry some of the bleakest memories of my childhood. But it was not just the visits to hospital that caused my mother, and indeed the whole family, to be so distressed by those anxious times. The other overwhelming concern for us was having enough money to live on and particularly enough money for food. The source of family income had disappeared while my father was in hospital. Apart from my brother's meagre wages, there was no money coming into the household at all. My father had never been in a position to make provision for a time when he might be unable to work, whether because of illness or otherwise. I do not recall any money being made available through the State sickness or unemployment schemes. So my brother decided he would do some part-time work to eke out the family finances. He took a job pushing advertising leaflets through letter boxes. The pay was abysmal. It was particularly noble of him to undertake such a tedious activity because it was hard tiring work, which he usually had to do after a long day at his normal workplace. And of course he was exposed to all the elements while he was earning his pittance. But however little, it provided some desperately needed money. (When he worked at weekends, I went with him, and I think he was grateful for the company and someone to help him share the job of distributing those tawdry leaflets.)

My father left hospital eventually. However, it was an extremely unsatisfactory discharge because the doctors could not provide any cure or treatment for him. They simply did not know the cause of his complaint after all the investigations they had carried out. As for the future, they could provide no reassurance. An unhappy and very worrying period of my life in so many ways, caused by a medical condition with a disappointing outcome. For my mother it was even more distressing. She and I felt, perhaps unreasonably, somewhat let down. We had endured so much without having anything to show for it.

Closing that episode, I start to think of my father in more general terms and in particular his role as the head of the household. What was he like as a family man? He was certainly not an easy man. Although he could be described as a good family man, in that his life revolved around his wife and children, I have often wondered whether that was really because at the end of the day he was essentially anti-social. He rarely mixed socially with people outside his immediate circle and, for example, I can never remember my parents entertaining family or friends, although my mother could have coped easily and, being an excellent cook, would have provided a superb meal. This is a source of regret for me because my father could converse very intelligently on any subject of significance and he was a fascinating raconteur. On the rare occasions when he and I would be at the same social gathering and he was in 'full flow', he would have his audience in the palm of his hand. Indeed, afterwards people would say what excellent company he was. The fact that my parents did not mix socially, and in particular that outsiders very rarely set foot in our home, plus the rabid anti-Semitism at both my primary and secondary schools, made me at that time a cripplingly shy person. That lasted throughout my teenage years; the subconscious thought was that home was a place where I was safe, and that being with others was 'foreign territory' where I felt exposed. This is something anyone who knows me now may find hard to believe, but it is absolutely true and not exaggerated for the purposes of this autobiography.

I return now to my father's personality. One of his most endearing characteristics was his great pride in his children. Despite what had happened to his attempt to enter the accountancy profession in 1926, he was clearly never jealous of the success I later achieved at the Bar. He revelled in it. I recall my mother telling me many, many years later that, as they walked past the Sweet & Maxwell legal bookshop in Chancery Lane, the entire shop window being devoted to a display of my books, my father turned and asked my mother rhetorically, "Well, what do you think of our son now, eh?" According to my mother, he was glowing with pride.

Such pride was equally in evidence when he attended my LLB and LLM degree ceremonies, and perhaps even more so when I was admitted to the Bar in 1967. The latter was possibly the most gratifying moment of all to him. Given his occupation, he had only ever seen Lincoln's Inn from the outside, when he took 'fares' there; to be admitted to its illustrious interior was something which not only left him in awe of the grandeur of the place, but also gave him the greatest joy, given the occasion.

And talking about my educational progress, I have to mention that my father was always prepared to make the sacrifices necessary to enable his children to make educational and career progress. Money was always short in our house, and encouraging his daughter and younger son to pursue their chosen paths did mean making sacrifices; not only finding, to the extent he was able, the necessary funding, but also by sacrificing the income that would have been produced for the household by sending his children to work at the earliest opportunity. Those sacrifices my father accepted very willingly, despite his own treatment at his father's hands. I am sure no other course of action crossed his mind. It showed a wonderful selfless side to his character.

In the course of many years as a cabbie, my father accumulated a wonderful fund of stories. There were two in particular he liked to tell, and indeed he retold them many times! The retelling of both stories gave him great pleasure and filled him with pride. The first started in the normal way – he was hailed in the street and stopped for a group of people. So far so very normal, but then everything changed when he was told to go to Queen Elizabeth Building, where my Chambers were located at the time. Of course he could not resist enquiring who the passengers were going to see. When he was told it was me, he was absolutely thrilled. He told them Peter Whiteman was his son, and I think at that moment he was as overjoyed as any proud father would be. He related the whole incident to me with the most enormous smile on his face; he relished it, as well he might.

The second special story my father regaled his audience with filled him with even greater pride because of the identity of the fare. The story went as follows. As the passenger in question, an elderly and, according to my father, very distinguished-looking gentleman, got into his cab, he asked to be taken to Lincoln's Inn. My father was intrigued – he was very curious to find out who he was 'carrying'. He could not restrain himself from engaging in conversation with someone he assumed to be a legal luminary and possibly a judge. Given my connection with Lincoln's Inn, he was itching to find out who his fare was, and possibly even more important to my father, whether he knew me. But first he felt he should engage in small talk before he said what was in his mind. As he did so, he said he found his fare to be both interesting and utterly charming. Sufficiently emboldened, my father felt he could raise the first question that intrigued him. "My son is a member of Lincoln's Inn; his name is Peter Whiteman. May I ask yours?"

"Of course you may; I am Lord Justice Stamp. How interesting that your son is Peter Whiteman."

"Oh, do you know him?" said my father.

"Indeed I do. We think very highly of him and we are keeping a close eye on his career. He is very promising and we think he will go a long way."

"Thank you for telling me this; it is such a wonderful thing to hear," said my father, who was bursting with pride at this unsolicited comment from such an eminent judge. He couldn't wait to tell me what had been said.

My father was extremely well-informed and full of common sense, so that his advice was, at any stage of my life, much appreciated and respected by me. His enquiring mind manifested itself in many ways. In the 1940s and 1950s he subscribed to the American publication, *The Saturday Evening Post*; he purchased a French newspaper once, often twice, a week to improve his knowledge of that language; and in the 1960s he began learning German and started buying *Die Welt* regularly. All of this represented a pretty enlightened approach to life, given the age in which he lived, and his background.

His interests were wide-ranging. He was, as I am, passionate about opera. He had a large collection of operatic recordings, including many complete sets of LPs. My father was also fascinated by art and extremely keen to improve his knowledge of artists and paintings. He occasionally purchased books on art and enjoyed rereading them at leisure. Obviously he was only able to augment his collections of records and art books as far as his limited funds allowed. But, as a taxi driver, he knew where to buy such things second-hand and very cheaply, often in markets – although the records, as he subsequently found out, were often scratched or marked in some way.

And now to an aspect of my father's interests which very much appealed to me then, and still does now. My father took a very keen interest in football and cricket. Football meant following Tottenham Hotspur Football Club ('Spurs'), and by following I mean attending every home League and Cup game. Occasionally we even went to away matches in London, with all the passion and rivalry that such 'derbies' produced.

My father and I were also great cricket fans. At county level we supported (unsurprisingly) Essex. We went to some county games, but our support was never as regular or enthusiastic as our commitment to Spurs. However, we did go to Test Matches at Lords and The Oval, particularly when the Australians were the opposition. For that reason, I especially remember the 1953 and 1955 Test Series.

As I have already indicated, my father was not only supportive but also a source of sensible and practical advice. He was very insightful. It was he who saw that I would be ideally suited to follow the career of a lawyer.

He was encouraging in that regard but never sought to pressure me into that decision. He was quietly persuasive but left it at that.

Now to my siblings. My brother Alfred, whom I have already mentioned, is six years older than I, and my sister Jill, three years older. Because of the age gap, I have very few shared childhood memories with my brother, apart from going to see Spurs and, of course, family 'days out' (my father was not able to afford holidays). In my childhood, Alfred was always kind, thoughtful and considerate. He was interested in everything and would try anything within reason. He was also a very generous person. For example, determined to leave school at the age of 15, one of the very first things he did was to give me weekly pocket money. At that time, and even now, I imagine that was an unusual thing for an elder brother to do. He also saw the very best in people and never suspected the worst.

My sister Jill, to an extent both physically and generally, took after my father, as I do. She is a highly intelligent, generous, adaptable, hard-working and determined person, who was and is very proud and protective of her family. She is a really lovely person and, quite rightly, is totally adored by her entire family, including me.

But I conclude this chapter by recalling the saddest memories of my father. I became much closer to him as his life drew to a close. In 1978 he had been diagnosed as having colon cancer and, despite treatment over the years, he eventually succumbed to that disease. On two occasions he was admitted as an in-patient to Barts Hospital, where he received excellent treatment. Every day he was in hospital, I went to see him, and on workdays I walked at lunchtime from the Temple to Barts. I remember so well walking there each day, and I treasure the memory of our lunchtime conversations. Of course, he knew he was dying and, when asked how he was, he always said, "Hoping for the best but prepared for the worst." One day I went to see him and he had received some very grim news. My mother had been to see him earlier and he said, "Mum walked in this morning looking as pretty as a picture and I then had to give her my bad news. I felt so guilty." Indeed, my mother was always very pretty and I have no doubt he always adored her, and she him. I have no doubt that my parents remained deeply in love until the very end.

But to return to my lunchtime conversations with my father at Barts, they remain very precious to me. We were alone, as all the rest of the family came in the evening. It was so obvious to me that my father, knowing he was dying, wanted to talk about his life. As I have said, the treatment my father received at Barts was superb. Whenever I asked him, "Are you in pain?" he always said, "No." And I assumed, erroneously, that by 1986–1988 medical science had advanced so much that pain from cancer was a thing of the past. I was long ago disabused of that notion, but I shall be ever grateful to Barts Hospital for securing my father's pain-free exit from this world.

My father died on 5 March 1988. It was, as one would anticipate, one of the most emotional and upsetting experiences of my life, seeing my father dead in his hospital bed, and then, with my brother, taking his wedding ring and watch from his body. What was my reaction? At one of my sessions with my psychiatrist, Dr Islam, in 2009, he suddenly asked me what my reaction to my parents' deaths had been. (My mother had died in January 2003, aged 92). I was totally lost for an answer. In my father's case, I hadn't thought about it for some time and I simply could not answer Dr Islam's question. I was completely lost for words. I fell silent. I couldn't respond to Dr Islam's question then, and seven years later I still find it difficult. Some questions cannot be answered. At least, not by me when the pain is so deep. On reflection, the response I should have given was that I felt totally bereft, absolutely devastated and numb with grief.

The person whose advice I could always seek, knowing it would be wise, was no more. My loss was immeasurable.

CHAPTER 3

"CREEPING LIKE SNAIL UNWILLINGLY TO SCHOOL"

As You Like It (Act II, sc. vii)
WILLIAM SHAKESPEARE

It is a grey day. A grey winter's day. It has been raining. It is only just beginning to get light. A dismal, depressing and damp day. Not a day to lift anyone's spirits. I know I won't enjoy the day. I don't enjoy any day at my primary school. I am never happy there. I don't really have any friends in that soulless, forbidding place. Not wanting to reach my destination, I walk at a desultory pace. I walk alone. I always do. Neither parent ever takes me to school. All this emphasises my feeling of isolation in my world of crushing loneliness. Of always being alone. Alone with my thoughts as I walk wearily to a destination that brings me no enrichment, no pleasure and no hope. Of anything. Drab school, drab walk, drab life.

I have now reached Shernhall Street, Walthamstow E17, on my 1½-mile walk to school. My feet feel leaden and I drag one foot in front of the other. I think, "Is everyone unhappy at school, or is it just me?" But then there is nothing to make me happy there. I tell myself to stop thinking about school. About what nasty tricks Douglas Green, Keith Davis or some other delightful villainous devil will play on me today. I continue to crawl along at my snail's pace.

Nothing on this miserable trek is calculated to lighten my mood. I look to my right. It is a scene of complete devastation. Why did the gods take such vengeance on Shernhall Street? The whole area is so bleak. No proper rebuilding after the war has taken place yet. After all, it is only 1947, so the landscape is bereft of any features. Or at least of any meaningful features. There were buildings here. But they have all gone now. Bombed, flattened out of existence. There is the occasional wall left half-standing. Its chimney stack almost demolished, pointing jaggedly into the sky, the remains of a fireplace, but nothing else. Except the steel railings cut off just above ground level so that the severed metal could be taken to assist the war effort. And that is all there is to be seen in this godforsaken place. Other than the all-pervading tall dead grasses and wisps of chickweed wafting in the breeze with each gust of wind. What a depressing and distressing wilderness. It holds out no hope for the future. That typifies the times. What a testimony to the stupidity of war. The stupidity of man. So many buildings, homes, shops, all destroyed by the Blitz, which obliterated our world as we knew it. And worst of all, so many lives destroyed in that relentless bombardment of our cities by the Luftwaffe.

I look to my left. There again is another bomb site – my daily excursion to school is punctuated with one bomb site after another, but the worst are in Shernhall Street, on both sides of the road. However, the desolate landscape on the left gives way to a small area of habitation. In an attempt to rehouse the population dispossessed of their homes by bombing, the government has erected basic prefabricated units, allocating one to each family. These grey boxes are totally featureless. But they do provide shelter for those who have lost everything, and the occupants are very grateful to have them. And for me they do provide relief from the endless sequence of bomb sites which line my route to school.

On a day like this everything I see around me is grey. And as for me? I am grey too. Not only in mind, but the way I am kitted out from top to toe in the school uniform – grey, of course. Grey school cap, perched crookedly on the back of my head, barely keeping my hair in place. Then there is my grey school blazer, with its Essex County Council insignia as my badge of belonging. Ironic that, as I never felt any sense of belonging to this impoverished, wretched little seat of so-called learning. Short grey trousers, of course. Socks, grey as well, with one pulled down to languish around my ankle, to comply with the 'dress code' of my peers. The one sock pulled down in accordance with 'tradition' made me one of 'them', or so I misguidedly thought. 'Misguidedly', as the rest of the day at school nearly always disabused me of this foolish notion. Even so, I still want to 'belong'. But I never do. A figure of fun. A 'Jewboy' in Walthamstow. The others would never see me as 'belonging' or indeed even acceptable. Just someone to abuse, mentally or physically, or both, whenever the mood took them. Particularly when they were bored. With that prospect each day, no wonder I cut a drab, solitary figure as I trudge my pathetic way to school.

My legs are aching, as it is a long walk, uphill all the way. But I have now arrived at my destination, as the chipped, faded sign on the entrance gates informs the world that on this hallowed land stands Maynard Road Primary School. Another day at my private torture chamber is to begin. And horror of horrors, as I pass by the sign, my first sighting in the school playground is of a motley bunch of my regular tormentors. They are lurking in a corner by the side of the playground. They are shouting and fooling around. The noisiest ones, as usual, are Green and Davis, both of them big for their age, making me more vulnerable. The members of the gang call themselves 'The Green Gang'. I know them so well and I can see they are looking to inflict 'cruel and unusual punishment' on some poor unsuspecting, vulnerable soul. Immediately I see them, I try to fade into the brickwork of the school so they will not notice me. Too late. These villains with such eagle eyes have spotted me almost as soon as I have seen them. This is it. Let the misery begin. They amble over towards me in a loutish, cocky, 'we rule the playground' type of way. How I hate them and their vile, spiteful, brutish behaviour. They will scar me for life. I know it. As they near me, their first words confirm my worst fears. "Whiteman, we're going to 'ave you. We are going to give you a real hiding!" Green says in his loud oafish tones. For what, I have no idea. But then they never needed a reason. They just enjoyed handing out a thorough beating to anyone they disliked and who was unable to defend himself against this pack of wild animals thirsting for blood.

There is only one thing to do. Run, run as fast as I can. Say it is discretion being the better part of valour or simply being a coward, but it really is the only thing to do. So I take to my heels and pelt across the playground. But the 'pack' immediately picks up the challenge and is in hot pursuit. I run faster. I don't look back. I daren't look back. In the chase my school cap flies off the back of my head. Where do I run to? I decide immediately. I tear out of the other school gates. I hear their footsteps getting closer. I reach the exit just ahead of them. I dash out. Strictly forbidden by the school rules. In desperation I hurtle across the road outside. Strictly forbidden. They are in hot pursuit. And they are getting closer. To run after me this far and at this speed, they are in deadly earnest. They obviously want to give me a real thrashing. For what? Probably nothing at all. But where do I run to now? On the other side of the road there are houses with steep steps leading up to their front doors. As they are gaining on me, I have nowhere to go but up – up the steps – and knock on a front door in the hope that it will be opened by some kind lady who will protect me from these thugs. A vain hope, but what else can I do? If I go on running, they are bound to catch me. I fling myself up the steps, almost tripping on one of them, and, gasping for breath, I hammer desperately on the door. No sooner have I tried to summon help than they are upon me. They push me down and start punching and kicking me. Hard. It hurts. They mean it to. They are having fun. Green and Davis are to the fore, inflicting as much pain as they can. Even though I am protecting my face with my hands, I can still see them. They are shouting all sorts of obscenities at me, but my focus is trying to avoid the vicious punches and kicks.

And then suddenly, apparent salvation. The door opens. Except this does not look like some kind old lady. She looks an evil-tempered, nasty and very angry harridan who bitterly resents being disturbed. Particularly by a group of young thugs from the school across the road. If this is salvation, it could not wear a more furious face. She is livid with all of us. And that includes me. Almost as soon as the door is opened, my tormentors stop hitting me and shoot off at great speed down the steps of the house, across the road and back into the playground. They vanish like snow on the first sunny day of spring.

They made a speedy getaway because they were standing while they were attacking me. I couldn't because I was crouched, cowering on the steps to avoid punishment, elbows and hands protecting my face. Moreover, as I thought redemption was at hand, I made no effort to beat a hasty retreat – even assuming I could, after my beating.

"You 'orrible little rascal!" Hatchet-face shouts at me. "I'm fed up with all of you knocking on my door and then running away. I've had enough of you lot. You're all thugs and spivs. Well, I'm going to do something about it. You really are going to regret it!" And with that, in the best tradition of Dickens' writing, she grabs me by the ear and, holding it, yanks me to my feet.

I am totally devastated. I thought she was going to save me. I was the one who was beaten up, but now I'm the one who is going to suffer even more.

In what way I know not. However, it is clear that the perpetrators have got away scot-free. They have gone and melted into the throng of those milling about in the playground. My hoped-for rescuer has become yet another tormentor, whilst the others have fled – unpunished – back to the playground, where no doubt they are laughing their heads off. The innocent will suffer and the guilty will go free. I will be treated as the perpetrator of the whole wretched episode. And punished accordingly, particularly as the Headmaster is so keen to have good relations with the local residents. Life is so unfair, so bloody unfair.

Hatchet-face is still grabbing me by the ear. She is pinching it and it hurts. "You are going to get what you deserve!" And with that she drags me down the steps of her house, castigating me the whole time. She pulls me across the road and the playground and then into the school building itself. All the time wrenching me by the ear so that I am in real pain. We arrive at the door to the Headmaster's study. She has been here before, as she clearly knows the way. She knocks and, when bidden, enters, dragging in the miscreant to demand that he should be punished severely for his outrageous behaviour. She explains what has happened to the Headmaster, although she makes no mention of my tormentors. Their participation in the whole fracas is excluded. As she must have seen them, the omission is clearly deliberate. When she is asked if there were any other boys involved, she says, "No." She is lying. Why should she lie? But whatever the reason, I am dumbfounded. This is the first time I have heard an adult lie. I am so shocked because, being naive, I assumed that everyone tells the truth. Stupid assumption. So another horrid outcome of the morning's events. I have done nothing wrong, I have suffered at the hands of others, and yet there seems to be a conspiracy against me to ensure that my life is made a misery – unbearable. Hatchet-face finishes recounting her distorted version of events, the Headmaster apologises for my behaviour, orders me to do likewise and then dismisses this loathsome woman from his study, promising her I will be caned. Caned. For what? The chase, the thrashing, the ear-pinching, the hauling off to the Headmaster's study, the lying and now the cane. I have nowhere to go and no one to seek comfort from. I have not even been asked for my side of the story. This is so unjust, so unfair and so unbearable. How can I, as a 5-year-old, cope with this?

Somehow I do, not even crying when I am caned on my bare bottom. So indignity is now added to the litany of my suffering today. The unfairness of the whole episode is something I know I will never forget. And for a short while the bruises inflicted by the attack and the welts left by the cane bear testimony to the whole ghastly episode. How could anyone allow this to happen to me? The Headmaster dismisses me, admonishing me yet again, and I go to the quiet of the adjacent school cloakroom. Finally by myself, I sit down gingerly and start to cry. First a little and then, as I recall the events of the day, I burst into floods of tears. No one sees me. At least that is a blessing. At least I can weep alone. No one to chastise me further.

The rest of the day passes uneventfully. I do remember to go to the lost and found cupboard to retrieve my school cap, but all I can really think of during that long day is getting back home to safety. However, even this comforting thought is blighted by the possibility that the Gang may set upon me when I leave school. I leave school fearfully at the end of the day, alone of course. Except that I take with me a huge sense of grievance against the world in general. I know the viciousness and the lying have had an impact on me that I shall never forget. I have been hurt in so many ways today, not merely the bruises and welts.

The walk home is totally different from the walk to school. It is not a walk into the fear of the unknown, but a walk to safety, security, sanctuary and protection from those 'vile bodies'. Even now, going home always relaxes me, comforts me and gives me a warm feeling that I shall soon be in my sanctuary, protected from the world. That heart-warming emotion will always be mine and no one will be able to take it away from me.

On my way home I think it was not only my body that took a beating that day. My mind took a hiding as well. My faith in human nature, the essential goodness of people, was shattered. The unprovoked violence, the lying, the deliberate infliction of severe pain, the cruelty. Once again I think it's so unfair. I knew then, as I know now, that this terrible series of events happening to me as a 5-year-old on a single day would scar me for life. It did. As a result, I have always been passionate about eliminating unfairness and injustice wherever it has been within my power to do so. Possibly this played a part in my subsequent decision to become a lawyer, as few roles in life could have given me greater scope to right such wrongs.

Although very different, another incident involving unbelievable behaviour (at least to me) occurred some five years later and that too involved my schoolmates. Although not as severe, its ramifications were far more fundamental and resulted in yet more suffering, and this time for two years, not just one day. But more of that later.

CHAPTER 4

HOME, SWEET HOME!

"Creep home, and take your place there"
Young and Old
CHARLES KINGSLEY (1819–1875)

On the way home, despite my worst fears, there is no sign of the Gang. Perhaps they feel they have done enough for one day. Certainly I am hurting in so many different ways. The abuse, the attacks and the caning. And the feeling that I have done nothing to deserve any of this. It all seems so unfair that I should be nursing the bruises, the pain and, worse, the vilification that I have suffered.

But at least I am nearing my home – one last turn right and I will get my first sighting of it. My home is my sanctuary. There I will be safe, protected from everything. The Gang can't reach me there, or torture my body or my mind any more. There I will be safe. I attach so much importance to what is a very ordinary small house. However, it is not the external characteristics that are of any consequence to me. It is the warmth of my family and the security within that are so crucial to me.

So I drag my weary, sore, bruised bones towards my comforting objective. It is a quiet street. So no noise or disturbance to distract me from my miserable reflections on the day's events. There have been many bad days at school, when I have been abused, one way or another, and nearly always anti-Semitism features prominently. I have learned to live with that. But today was the worst by far because it culminated in a caning. That was not only painful but so unjust. I feel I shall nurture this grievance all my life. Still no sign of the Gang and, in any event, I am so near home that I could dash the last few steps and reach safety before they could inflict any further suffering on me. So I start to relax – a little.

But only a little because I am now worrying about what I am going to tell my parents about the day's events. And I have to make my decision now because I shall soon be at the front door and my mother will be there to greet me. She is always there. She is always at home in the afternoon. No doubt my return from school is an important moment in a life that is very uneventful. So my story, if I have one to tell, must be sorted by the time my mother opens the door.

I arrive. I have no key. There is no need. My ever-present mother will let me in. My father will be at work, but even so I must have my story straight now because my mother always asks me about my day at school.

She opens the door and greets me with a big smile. This is part of her daily routine, just as much as waving goodbye to me in the morning, when she waves and waves to me until I disappear out of sight. She adores her children and lives for them and her husband. She couldn't bear the thought of any of us suffering.

It is partly for that reason that I take an instant decision, as I look at my mother's very pretty smile, that I will not mention the horrors of my day. She will be so terribly upset. Why should I upset my mother, the kindest and most caring of people? And then I think of the bruises I must have. She will see them and ask about them. I just have to hope there are none on my face, and as far as I can recall, the Gang concentrated their vicious punching on my body. Any bruises there I can keep from my mother, as I am now old enough to bath myself. I must just be careful not to let her see me undressed at any time. All these thoughts cross my mind as I reach home, standing there looking at my mother.

And the inevitable question comes, as it always does:

"How was school today, dear?" With as much conviction as I can muster, I reply, "Fine." My mother doesn't have the slightest clue what that one word covers up. Provided I am careful, she will not see the bruises the Gang inflicted on me, or the welts from the Headmaster's caning. She would be so distressed and would not know what to do about the horrid beating I endured. In any event, she wouldn't decide anything until she had spoken to my father. She always defers to him. So I will tell my mother nothing and keep my fingers crossed, hoping my body does not belie the story of my "fine" day at school.

Nor is there any question of telling my father. At school we just don't do that. That is for wimps. Anyway, with his strength of character, if I do tell him, he will be off to the school, demanding appropriate action be taken against the miscreants. His complaint will be made in loud, vociferous and forceful terms. But if the Headmaster did take action – a big 'if' because the Headmaster is a pusillanimous creature – one way or another the Gang would find out that I had 'squealed' on them. The beating I have taken today would be as nothing compared to the revenge they would then mete out to me. So I decide to take a vow of silence on this appalling episode in my life.

For the time being I relax into the comfort and security of home, my refuge from the harsh realities of life.

CHAPTER 5

THRUST INTO A
BARREN WASTELAND

*"Hath not a Jew eyes? Hath not a Jew hands, organs, dimensions, senses,
affections, passions? … If you prick us, do we not bleed?"*
The Merchant of Venice (Act III, sc. i)
WILLIAM SHAKESPEARE

"When the going gets tough, the tough get going."
JOE KENNEDY
Appointed US Ambassador to London 1938

Five years have passed since the vicious 'Green Gang' beating. The whole episode has left me with a deep and abiding sense of grievance. That sense of injustice is soon to be followed by another. I am now 10 years old. There is a real crisis in my life. The dreaded Eleven Plus examination looms ever larger with each day that passes. In those days the Eleven Plus was the most significant event in a child's educational journey throughout the school years. It provided the most fundamental separation of schoolchildren in the educational system at that time, as it determined the type of schooling a child aged 11 would receive for the rest of his school life. Known universally as the Eleven Plus, it was a test which streamed final-year primary pupils for secondary education. If a child passed the examination, he would be offered the chance to go to a grammar school, but if he failed, he would be consigned to a secondary modern. There was a third category, a technical school, but there were only a few of these. Passing the Eleven Plus and going to a grammar school held out the prospect of a good academic future. The standard of teaching would be high and thereafter such education would lead to Ordinary Levels (O levels, the rough equivalent of GCSEs now), Advanced Levels (A levels), and possibly university. For those who didn't go to university, there was the alternative prospect of entering one of the professions or following some other worthwhile career path. Those who failed the Eleven Plus would be obliged to attend a secondary modern school, where there was only the faintest of nods in the direction of an academic curriculum. The educational standards in secondary moderns were generally accepted to be pretty low, or at least they were in East London. The emphasis in such schools was on 'preparing a child for life', which often provided an excuse not to teach history but woodwork, not geography but 'arts and crafts', and for girls, not science but domestic science (a euphemism for cookery). All such secondary modern courses were justified on the basis that they constituted 'practical skills'.

So failing the Eleven Plus meant attending a school where there was no real chance of obtaining any meaningful educational qualifications, nor any worthwhile instruction, for some four years, as the school leaving age was then fifteen. At the time many took the view that, effectively, the State system gave up on those who failed the Eleven Plus, providing minimal education for those it regarded as 'no-hopers'. It was a harsh, ruthless and uncaring system of streaming.

I am so anxious to pass the Eleven Plus because I want a grammar school education with the possibility thereafter of going to university or entering a profession. But it is more than that. I am not only desperate to grasp a positive that is being dangled in front of me, but also to avoid an extremely unattractive negative. That is, the local secondary modern school. Joseph Barratt (JB), to which I will be consigned if I fail the Eleven Plus. Both my brother and sister have attended JB and loathed it. Not only are the teaching standards abysmal, but it is a school where bullying, fighting and anti-Semitism are rife. There are numerous gangs who roam the school playground, devoting their time and energy to devising the most horrible ways of inflicting cruel and unusual punishment on those unfortunates to whom they have taken exception. Usually there is no reason for picking on a classmate. As far as the gangs are concerned, anti-Semitism is an excellent reason to beat the living daylights out of someone. At present there are no black or Asian schoolchildren at JB and so Jews provide the prime target for the gangs' vicious attacks. Alfred and Jill have related the tactics of their tormentors to me in great detail. The very idea that I might end up at JB, with all the unpleasantness that would await me there, is horrific. So to me it is essential that I pass the Eleven Plus; I am determined to avoid the dreaded JB.

I am approaching the most critical phase in my educational career, but I am not at all hopeful of passing the examination. Indeed, just the reverse. Over the years I have bumped along term-by-term at the bottom of the class. Not one teacher has encouraged me to believe that I will pass the Eleven Plus, or in any way expressed optimism of my chances of going to a grammar school.

But what makes my crisis of the looming Eleven Plus worse is that my parents expect me to pass it. Really without question. I know the overwhelming majority of schoolchildren fail the Eleven Plus, which makes me even more depressed. Fail and there is no way out. Fail and my parents will be devastated.

I duly take the examination and duly fail. No surprises there for me, nor apparently for my teachers. But it is a huge and unwelcome surprise for my parents, who are desperately disappointed by my failure. They are truly shocked and my father goes 'silent' on me. It is a horrible eerie silence that for a while makes my life at home unhappy.

However, I am granted a reprieve from being branded a failure for the rest of my life and banished to the educational wasteland of the secondary modern. The reprieve takes the form of being invited to sit an oral examination. This is an interview designed to see whether borderline candidates, who would otherwise be classified as failures, should nonetheless be given the opportunity of attending a grammar school. In my case, the Oral, as it is familiarly called, is to provide the third occasion when my faith in human nature suffers a severe blow. In particular, it leaves me convinced, sadly, that honesty is not always the best policy.

The Oral takes place some three weeks later. Three weeks of anxiety for me, increased by the fact that my parents once again expect me to pass, even though I receive no guidance from my school as to how I should prepare for the interview. So, bereft of support, I am left once more to fend for myself at this critical time in my life.

I attend the interview. I am petrified. I have no idea of the questions I will be asked, or by whom. Or of the answers that will be acceptable. My future depends on the answers I give. Obviously I consider there is no other course of action than to answer the questions honestly. So I sit there, before five people I have never seen before at my school, terrified by the experience that is about to befall me. I am shaking with fear.

The questions start. I can hardly articulate my replies.

"How do you spend your evenings?" asks one interviewer.

"I watch television."

"Every night?" asks a disappointed-looking interrogator.

"Yes," I reply.

These and all the other answers I give are truthful, what else? But they are not the responses that the panel find appropriate. This I discover when I duly fail the Oral and am relegated to the category of Eleven Plus failures. My parents are bitterly disappointed. But no more than I am.

There are six other candidates from my school, who are all interviewed on the same day as I am. After all the interviews have been concluded, we cannot resist discussing the questions that were asked and the replies we gave. In particular, we discuss the question as to how we spend our evenings. The answers the other six gave were all broadly to the same effect. They read every evening, books written by such authors as Dickens, Hardy, Thackeray and the like. Truthful answers? Of course not. They were lying through their teeth. They never read in the evenings, as they candidly admit to me. The names of the authors whose books they allegedly read were all 'manufactured' for the occasion – they have been coached very thoroughly by someone (at school?) to give the appropriate responses. Of course, eventually they ask me what replies I gave to the 'evenings' question.

I tell them. They fall about laughing.

"You chump! How on earth do you think you can pass the Oral if you give answers like that? You have to give them the answers they want to hear. You have to fool them."

"So you lied?"

"Of course we did, dimwit!"

Then they start laughing at me again. I am a figure of fun. This time for telling the truth! I have been honest and I am now being ridiculed for it. They know the rules of the game and how to play it. At least in their eyes. I am too straightforward, too naive, to play by those rules. Result? I fail the Oral, while the other six pass. They pass by lying. I learn a very hard lesson today. I discover the serious consequences of this over the following years.

I attend JB. It is an appalling institution. Even by the standards of Walthamstow, it is a very tough school. The educational standards are dire. All of my classmates can't wait for the moment when they leave JB. They are just killing time, with no interest in learning at all. Many of them are looking for fights before, during and after school. Green and Davis have preceded me to this institution and are still determined to be as horrible to me as possible. As at Maynard Road, they lead a group of thugs who patrol the playground during breaks, determined to make trouble. And if possible, to inflict pain and suffering. They recruit new gang members from those coming here from other schools. These thugs are equally determined to give anyone they dislike a beating or at least to 'rough them up', as they delightfully put it. For me it is more of the same as at Maynard Road. All of those who don't know are soon informed by Green that I am Jewish. This puts me at the head of the queue to be picked on, to be beaten up, during school breaks. Anti-Semitism is rife and violent at JB, even more so than at Maynard Road. For many of the Gang it is just another excuse to give someone a beating, and Jews are particularly vulnerable because, as I have mentioned, there are no other ethnic minorities.

Nor is the violence confined to the school playground. Inside there is considerable aggression. On one occasion I ask to be excused from class to go to the lavatory. The request is granted. As I approach the cloakroom, I see a Jewish boy on the ground, being savagely attacked by members of the Gang, using not only their hands but also their feet. They are kicking their victim on the ground with shocking viciousness. The sound of shoe hitting flesh still haunts me to this day. As I am particularly vulnerable to a similar attack, I beat a hasty retreat before they see me. I never ask to be excused again!

The only other break-time activity I am aware of occurs behind the bicycle sheds. JB has both a boys' and a girls' section, separated by a fence which is easily climbed. So, although I don't look forward to break times, there are many others, on both sides of the fence, who do, with eager anticipation! This is the only sex education on the curriculum and possibly it is the only subject that is taught well!

I have another distressing memory of my time at JB. Upon my arrival at the school in 1953, I am summoned by the Headmaster to his study. His first words take me aback and I wonder what misdemeanour I have committed.

"You shouldn't be here," he says succinctly. I am not sure what, if any, answer he expects. I say nothing and wait for him to explain. He continues, "I have been looking at your Eleven Plus results – they were good and you should have gone to a grammar school. You shouldn't be here!"

I am lost for words. Even now I am not sure why the Headmaster imparted this information to me. There was nothing I could do about it. Apparently there was nothing he could do about it either. Of course it increased my sense of injustice about the fate that had befallen me. First I had endured the fiasco of the Eleven Plus and now I am being told that I should have been awarded a grammar school place. The whole episode has condemned me to this ghastly school completely unnecessarily. What keeps me going through this unhappy time is to recite to myself, "I'll show them!" Even when blows rain down upon me, I repeat this mantra and stiffen my resolve to come out on top one day. Easily said, but how am I to achieve it? There is only one escape route open to me to reach that objective. The Thirteen Plus examination. "The Thirteen Plus, the Thirteen Plus," I recite to myself each night, as I try to go to sleep and forget the horrors of the day. There has to be some justice in life. There must be. The Thirteen Plus.

CHAPTER 6

I ENTER A NEW WORLD

"In this life we get nothing, save by effort …
Far and away the best prize that life offers
is the chance to work hard at work worth doing."
Address 1903
THEODORE ROOSEVELT – US President 1901–1909

"The dream begins with a teacher who believes in you,
who tugs and pushes and leads you to the next plateau,
sometimes poking you with a sharp stick called 'truth'."
DAN RATHER

When a Jewish boy reaches the age of 13, he becomes a 'bar mitzvah'. The event is usually marked with a religious ceremony in a synagogue and a celebration afterwards. Although not technically correct, many Jews regard a bar mitzvah as 'becoming a man'. It is not completely accurate, as a bar mitzvah is not regarded under Jewish law as becoming an adult, but rather as acquiring many of the rights and responsibilities of a Jewish adult. But, whatever the strictly accurate religious significance of becoming a bar mitzvah may be, it is clear that a Jewish boy, when he is bar mitzvahed, enters a new world. He leaves his past world behind him, and he enters a new world full of his hopes and aspirations. Hence it is an occasion of the greatest importance to any Jewish boy and thus a time for celebration. He has arrived and his future lies before him. So in reality the popular notion of a bar mitzvah has much to commend it.

In seeing a bar mitzvah as entering a new world, the Jewish religion could not have been more prophetic or more accurate in my case. As I turned 13 years of age, I did enter a new world with all its religious connotations. But I also entered a new educational world. As far as my religion was concerned, although I did not come from a particularly religious home, I had been preparing for my bar mitzvah for several years. First by being instructed in the religion by the rabbi of my local synagogue, and later by learning the appropriate portions of Jewish law that I would have to read in synagogue on the day of the ceremony. That day was 13 August 1955. Everything went well in synagogue and my parents held a small celebration with a few close relatives at our home. No occasion for a lavish celebration in a grand hall, as so often happens today. Indeed, not only was I happy to have a celebration at my 'blessed home', but also my parents were not able to afford a large party.

The day of my bar mitzvah came and went, but the new world that I was entering, the one that mattered just as much to me, was my new educational world. It coincided with the year of my bar mitzvah, itself the sign of a new life with limitless hopes and aspirations. But their fulfilment, indeed any form of realisation, was not immediate. How could it be? Two years passed before that was to occur.

In entering my new world, my most fervent hope was that all the bullying, all the tormenting, all the physical and mental attacks on me, largely motivated by anti-Semitism, would come to an end. My hope was that they would be a thing of the past. Well, that was my hope, but as I subsequently relate, I was in for a very nasty initial shock.

The new educational world opened up to me because I had taken and passed the Thirteen Plus. That examination mirrored the Eleven Plus in that success ensured advancement to a grammar school. The Thirteen Plus was, however, the 'last chance saloon'. Failure meant that there was no further opportunity to escape the horrors of the secondary modern and one was condemned to spend two more years marking time.

But pass I did. No dramas this time. A straightforward pass on the written examination meant there was no Oral to take, with all its problems. I left JB with enormous relief and apparently I had passed the Thirteen Plus very well. The Headmaster of JB, Mr Maxwell, who had said, "You shouldn't be here!" in 1953, was able to tell me two years later:

"I said to you, all that time ago, you should have been in a grammar school and you have proved me right. All credit to you, as you have passed the examination very well. I wish you every success in the future."

He seemed to be delighted that I was now going to what he regarded as the right educational establishment. And, indeed, I was crossing my scholastic Rubicon. It is impossible to overstate the tremendous boost that passing the Thirteen Plus examination gave to my self-confidence. Until that time I had always regarded myself as a failure and, after the debacle of the Eleven Plus, always doomed to be both a loser at school, and in life thereafter. Passing the Thirteen Plus, particularly as I had passed it very well, changed all that. My vision of the future was now totally different and I could look forward to achieving some success at school and pursuing a worthwhile career afterwards. I was starting to believe, after the Headmaster's kind words, that, if I applied myself, anything was possible for me, and this was to become my mantra for life.

When I entered the portals of my new school for the first time in September 1955, I could have had no idea that I had embarked on a journey that would give my life purpose and meaning forever. When I arrived at the main entrance of the school, I looked up to see carved in stone above my head 'Leyton County High School', words which to this day resonate with me in the most positive way. It was only subsequently that I was to realise and appreciate that LCHS was one of the finest examples of the English grammar school system as it existed at that time.

After passing through the impressive entrance, I was shepherded with others into the School Hall to be 'inducted'. We were the so-called 'late developers', who had that year passed the Thirteen Plus examination. All the other pupils had been there for some two years, having passed the Eleven Plus.

On the stage one of the seated figures rose and came forward to stand at the lectern. He looked a stern man; he was tall and well built, and as I looked at him I thought he cut a formidable figure. Then he addressed his audience:

"I am Mr Cummings, the School Headmaster."

His words resounded round the School Hall. He had a deep, rich voice, further reinforcing my initial conclusion that this was a very impressive man. He delivered a short introductory talk about the school, of which, with one important exception, I remember nothing, partly because I was still taking in my new surroundings. I was in awe of them. Affixed to one wall was a very large Honours Board, headed 'State Scholarships', which listed in luminous gold characters all those pupils who had been awarded the most prestigious national scholarship. Even at that very early stage, I determined that one day my name would be added to that illustrious roll call of outstanding scholars. The fact that this thought could even cross my mind indicates how much my self-confidence had been boosted by passing the Thirteen Plus examination and moving to this grammar school.

Mr Cummings continued with his address to us. One part of this, which I do remember, was directly relevant to me.

"On the basis of your results in the Thirteen Plus examination, you will all be put into the B stream. That is, except for four of you, whose results were particularly good, and they will go into the A stream." He then named the four and, to my amazement and delight, I was one of the elite group.

We four were then taken to our very first class at LCHS. It was that class that was to provide a very nasty initial shock for me. I was full of optimism, but my balloon was about to be punctured in a dramatic way. It would reawaken the horrid memories of my earlier schooldays. It was an insensitive question that stirred up everything that I was so keen to put behind me.

Up the stairs, along the corridor to Classroom 13, Dr Hermus' room. I am bouncing along the corridor. New school, great results, and a brave new world ahead of me. I have every reason to be happy at the outcome of events that day.

We are shown into Room 13 by a prefect. Of course we arrive late in class because of the induction process. Everything is new to us. The school, the classroom, the classmates and not least the teacher, Dr Hermus. He hardly looks up at us as we enter the room. He then raises his eyes and glowers. Possibly because we have disturbed the class, which, of course, was something for which we were not responsible. Hunched over his desk, clearly displeased, and looking over his half-moon glasses, he says in stentorian tones to me, "Sit there." He waves vaguely into the middle distance of the room. I make my way gingerly to the allocated desk, feeling vulnerable in my new classroom surroundings. Dr Hermus' eyes follow my every step with evident displeasure. Is he waiting for me to make a mistake, bump into a desk, or trip over something? My discomfiture and feeling of isolation are increased by my new classmates, who are staring at me and also no doubt hoping that I will commit a faux pas. Somehow I navigate my way to my desk without incident. I sit down. For the first time Dr Hermus sits bolt upright and stares me straight in the eye. His first words take me totally by surprise and astound me.

"Are you Jewish?" he barks out. I am startled and also shaken by his question. It is so unexpected – indeed it is the first question I have been asked at LCHS – that I stammer out, "Yes." What a bizarre question to ask. What is the relevance of it? Even if it is relevant (and no reason has occurred to me in the subsequent sixty years as to why it should be), what an insensitive question to ask of a pupil who has just arrived in a new school. Why he asked the question I shall never know. What I do know is that it had the most enormous effect on me. At the start of my LCHS life I was singled out in front of my classmates as being somebody who was different. It made a deep impact on me. I was left wondering, did Dr Hermus' question indicate that I was in for another bout of anti-Semitism in my new school? At the time I thought, "Oh no. I can't face the prospect of more years of being bullied because of my religion." So the fear now was of the unknown. What was Dr Hermus' question leading up to? What did it indicate? And even worse, what would his next question be? This most unattractive and bad-tempered man had instilled fear in me at the start of my very first lesson at my new school. In the event, there is no second question. That first question to me stands alone, and Dr Hermus – as I learn subsequently, a very sour man – moves on to question others.

Even at the end of the lesson I am still trembling, worried about the significance of the question. I am so distressed by it that I can think of nothing else. It is so disturbing that for a while it completely obliterates the earlier memories of the day, and particularly the excellent results of my Thirteen Plus examination.

Now, so many years later, I can be relaxed about the incident because actually the question from Dr Hermus indicated nothing of any consequence. Neither he, nor any of the other teachers at LCHS, ever asked me a similar question again. It did not indicate that there was anti-Semitism at LCHS. Indeed there was none. Nor was there any bullying. LCHS turned out to be the educational institution that I had hoped for, and it more than fulfilled all my scholastic aspirations.

LCHS made the most enormous impact on me. Indeed, one of the teachers there became the second greatest personal influence on my life. The school made me the person I am. Without LCHS and its wonderful team of teachers, I would not have achieved in my lifetime what I have done. It has left me with a thirst for knowledge, which will be with me forever, and a profound love of the many subjects I studied there, particularly history and geography. And how well they were taught. To me, as I have indicated, LCHS at the time I was there (1955–1961) epitomised the very best of the State school system.

There were two reasons in particular for this. First, as I have mentioned, the teachers were outstanding. They did instil in us such enormous enthusiasm for the subject they were teaching. They were totally dedicated to their work and also completely committed to doing the very best they could for their students, frequently taking extra classes in their own time after school hours.

The other reason why LCHS stands out in my mind as such an excellent school was the enormous range of subjects that were taught there. French was compulsory, as was a second language, German, Spanish or Latin. In addition, modern Greek, classical Greek, Russian and Portuguese were taught after school hours; again demonstrating the dedication and commitment of the teaching staff. In my experience at LCHS, any interest in a subject was encouraged and nurtured as far as it could be.

That brings me to the second greatest personal influence on my life; for it was under his guidance that I was awarded a State Scholarship. Mr Clinch (always known to everyone as Paddy) was the senior history teacher at the school. He was a passionate Welshman, enthusiastic about everything, and particularly if it was Welsh. He encouraged me to think that anything was possible and that I should always aim for the stars. He made me believe that one's background and circumstances should never be a bar to future success. An inspirational person as magical as Paddy is very rare, and I was so lucky he was a teacher at LCHS. He changed my life forever. He was a superb teacher. He lit the flame of my love for history which will never die.

Despite all my hopes when I arrived at LCHS in 1955, my school record in the next two years was abysmal. I scraped along at the bottom of the class during that period; unfortunately a situation I had become familiar with at school. There were thirty-five members of the class and I usually managed to finish bottom or second from bottom. It is true that I did manage to do a little better each term in history under the supervision of Paddy Clinch.

As an outstanding teacher, he of course encouraged my interest in his subject and gradually my marks in history started to become quite respectable. (My marks in all the other subjects remained pretty appalling.)

Then, however, came the big breakthrough which would change my school life. In 1957 I had to go into hospital for an operation which was likely to keep me away from school for three weeks. I was very concerned that I would fall behind during this time, so I approached Paddy to ask for his advice. He responded very positively and soon afterwards presented me with a reading list and details of essays he wanted me to write. During my absence from school I worked diligently on the tasks I had been set, and as a result that term I obtained a mark of 76 per cent (absolutely unheard of for my scholastic efforts in any subject) and was placed fourth in the class in history. So now history in my school report was like a beacon shining in the dark, in contrast to my other customary poor results.

Bless Paddy for his unique decision to award me that mark; that was the complete turning point in my school life, and indeed in my life generally. I never looked back. I started to work very hard in all my subjects. Paddy had taught me that enthusiasm, hard work and dedication could produce results, really good results. From then on it was onward and upward all the way. I was, as so often in my life, fired up by a particular incident. But none was more important than this. From then on I was never to be found languishing in the murky backwaters of the 'thirties' in class. They were banished forever. Paddy had shown me what I could do under his outstanding guidance. I was much enthused by his knowledge, interest and passion but, most importantly of all, I made the vow that I was going to justify the fourth place he had given me.

The next term, instead of being thirty-fifth or thirty-fourth in class, I reached the dizzy heights of sixteenth. Not only did this bring the obvious joy of having made real progress, but it also meant that, if I achieved the same results in future, I would not have to worry about being relegated to the B stream – that was the Sword of Damocles that had hung over my head since I arrived at LCHS. Two terms after my '76–4', I rose to sixth in the class and occupied similar rankings throughout the rest of my school career.

Two other memories of LCHS are worth recording. The first, although very annoying at the time, taught me a valuable lesson for life. The second relates somewhat humorously to schoolboys being schoolboys, that is, puerile and immature.

At LCHS we were taken from time to time to a residential youth centre in North Essex, the purpose being to build our characters. One day, when I was 14, we had an initiative test. The structure of the test was simple. We were given a list of questions which had to be answered and that could only be done by visiting nearby villages (e.g. what is the name of the main street?) or a church (e.g. in whose memory is the pew in the third row at the far left end dedicated?) or a war memorial (e.g. how many names are listed of soldiers who were killed in the Second World War?) and so on. With my usual enthusiastic approach I set off from the hostel on foot at a cracking pace. Almost running, I dashed straight out of the driveway of the hostel, past the pillars which marked its entrance, and over the deep moat just beyond those pillars. And my luck was in. As I emerged onto the road, I successfully hitched a lift in a car to visit a village which would provide the first answer on the questionnaire. In due course I went to each of the villages which would yield up the required answers. And, as far as I could tell, I was well ahead of all the others. Having completed all the answers on the questionnaire, I decided to return to the hostel. As I approached the entrance, I believed that I was the first home and accordingly would duly cover myself in glory. However, as I reached the moat, out of nowhere sprang the LCHS equivalent of Green and Davis, Blount and Biggs, known at school as 'the two Bs'. They were standing there provocatively, cans of beer and cigarettes alight in their menacing hands.

Blount started what was clearly going to be a deeply intellectual conversation, "Have you got all the answers to the questionnaire?"

"Yes," I say, not knowing the storm that is about to beset me. In fact, I reply with a certain amount of pride, in the belief that I am the first one home. "What have you been doing for the last two hours?" I enquire a little foolishly, knowing their reputation as lazy thugs who dwell in the wilderness of the C stream. "We've been sitting here, drinking and smoking all the time," says Biggs aggressively. "Anyway, we want your list of answers," he adds. I respond, "No way! I worked hard to be the first one home with them and you've just sat on your bums drinking and smoking! If you want the answers, you go and do what I did."

"Well," says Blount, "either you give us the answers or we will duff you up." My mood changes. The feeling of pride has departed and I am now worried about what Blount and Biggs are going to do to me. "Here we go again!" I think, and all those painful memories of what occurred at Maynard Road come flooding back. I suppose they never really went away. So I try a different tack. I attempt appealing to their better natures. A pointless exercise.

"But that's not fair. I do all the work and you get all the credit."

"Well," says Biggs, "you can't complain; it's an initiative test, ain't it, and we're using our initiative!" And although I don't think so at the time, Biggs has a point. They have used their low cunning to good effect. They become even more menacing when Blount issues his ultimatum, "Your choice: your list or you get duffed up." I look around in the hope that assistance might be forthcoming from some unexpected quarter, but there is no possibility of help or escape. I know they have won; I give them the list, but life being what it is, they still 'duff me up'. Even now I have a vivid recollection of what occurred that day; no doubt in large part because it revived memories of the beatings I had suffered at the hands of Green and Davis.

The second memory, a light-hearted and amusing one, relates to the testosterone level of young lads as they reach puberty. We had had a male French teacher who was old, bald, fat and very boring. He impressed no one, including, so we believed, his colleagues. He was then replaced by a luscious young woman, who was appointed to guide us through the intricacies of the French language – Miss Le Boeuf. She was, to us panting, inexperienced, pubescent and pimply teenagers, a vision of loveliness; the epitome of a 'French mistress'. Most of my lovesick classmates would follow this gorgeous, perfectly-proportioned vision of beauty and grace just to catch a glimpse of her nyloned legs. Almost everyone in the class lusted after her with a totally insatiable appetite. Miss Le Boeuf sat at a desk with two sets of drawers on each side and a space in the middle for her delicious legs. The delectable Miss Le Boeuf wore short skirts and, every time we had a class with her, there was an almighty rush to get through the doors of her classroom to sit in one of the two rows that had a clear view of her desk, or, to be more realistic, of her legs. Indeed, there became a market in what City traders would now no doubt term 'Le Boeuf futures', that is, pupils who had acquired the best 'viewing' seats of Miss Le Boeuf's legs would sell their privileged viewing position that day for money or some other favour. These poor, possibly somewhat pathetic 15-year-olds seemed to think of, and indeed look at, nothing else. Such is the behaviour and approach of sex-starved and frustrated teenagers. But what was certainly true was that the arrival of Miss Le Boeuf made our class a much more exciting place to be. And as for me, my schooldays were certainly 'looking up'!

And then something happened which set the school alight with rumours buzzing everywhere. But first, let me put things in context. At the beginning of term, we were asked what sport we wanted to play: the choices were football, rugby, hockey, athletics, gym or cross-country running. Football was voted for by a few; rugby, hockey and gym got 'nul points', and cross-country running an amazing 90 per cent of the vote. In my innocence, I was staggered by the popularity of cross-country running. A more approachable and far less naive friend of mine enlightened me. "They only vote for cross-country running so they can go off into Epping Forest and have a smoke for an hour or so. You don't think they run, do you? Wise up!"

Well, it so happened that one day, as the cross-country runners were setting off from school for their weekly 'exercise', they saw Legs Le Boeuf walking along with Mr Van der Pant, one of the maths masters at the school. (You can imagine the schoolboy comments that were made about his name.) Anyway, shock, horror, the runners could not believe their eyes, or indeed their luck. They decided to follow this romantic couple, who were heading for the forest. Thereafter there was a daily lunchtime routine at the school of following the couple (some with binoculars) to see how the school tryst was developing. I think, to their great disappointment, however, any furtherance of their sex education never took place and we never did discover if the relationship blossomed further.

Light-hearted interludes aside, I was pursuing my school career with renewed vigour, and as a result, as I have mentioned, I was placed around the top six in class every term. Eventually I passed eight O levels with good grades, three A levels (the approximate equivalent under the current marking system of five A* passes) and two S levels (Scholarship levels) at Grade A.

As a result, I was awarded one of only two State Scholarships conferred that year on pupils at my school. At that time a State Scholarship was the mark of outstanding scholastic achievement (carrying with it a grant of £240 per year to meet subsistence costs, and a further grant to meet all tuition fees at university). Another advantage was the cachet attached to being the holder of a State Scholarship, which marked one out, both at school and at university, as being a member of a highly regarded scholastic elite. But for me there was also the personal joy of seeing my name, in glowing gold letters, added to the list on the Honours Board that I had noticed and aspired to on my very first day at LCHS – a dream come true! And quite frankly, without such a grant, it would not have been possible for me to go to university because my father could never have afforded the fees and other expenses involved.

I left LCHS in 1961. The school and its wonderful band of teachers had been brilliant to and for me. I can remember nearly all of their names to this day. They had enthused me, stimulated me, given me a thirst for knowledge, which would continue throughout my life. I am indebted to them more than they will ever know, and nothing gives me more pleasure than to publicly acknowledge that and thank them for their dedication and commitment to the school, their pupils and their subjects. And all of that in an atmosphere where they conveyed real warmth and taught with such good humour.

Ultimately, after a really inauspicious start to my LCHS schooldays, I left school on a high. The last few years were happy and rewarding, and my final school results were all that I could have hoped for. The eventual pride and delight of my parents and siblings, particularly after the earlier setbacks, was considerable, especially as I was to be the first family member ever to go to university.

POSTSCRIPT

The contrast between the scholastic wasteland that was JB and the vibrant educational institution that was LCHS could not have been greater. My relief at leaving JB was enormous. Obviously I left there with no regrets whatsoever, and, because of my unhappiness there, I made no further attempt to remain in touch with the school. But even from that 'place of wrath and tears', I have carried through life a fond memory. It relates to the Headmaster, Mr A A Maxwell, and that memory was brought to the forefront of my mind some twenty-two years later. Mr Maxwell, on the two occasions that I had seen him in his office, had been both pleasant and, as far as he could be, given my school record, encouraging. Indeed, on reflection, I consider that a fair way of regarding his role as Headmaster was that he was attempting to do the best he could in a most difficult educational environment. Be that as it may, twenty-two years after I left JB, a missive came out of the blue which both surprised and touched me. When the fact of my appointment as a Queen's Counsel was published in 'The Times' in April 1977, Mr Maxwell must have seen it because soon afterwards I received a card of congratulation from him. I hope he felt that his view of my ability had been vindicated and, moreover, that he could take some credit for helping me to embark on a path which would lead to considerable success. I have kept the card Mr Maxwell sent to me and shall treasure it always.

CHAPTER 7

YOU'RE IN!

"One of the greatest pleasures of life is conversation."
Essays (1877). Female Education
REVD SYDNEY SMITH

"That is the happiest conversation where there is no competition,
no vanity, but a calm quiet interchange of sentiments."
The Life of Samuel Johnson (Vol II, diary entry 14 April 1775)
JAMES BOSWELL

Where to go? What to study? Who could I turn to for advice? Major decisions which would determine the path I would follow for the rest of my life. It was amazing how quickly my time in the Lower and Upper Sixth had passed. Going to university seemed a long way off when I started studying for my A levels in September 1959, but the time passed quickly and by late 1960 I felt I really had to focus on the university I wanted to attend and the subject I would study there. (The idea of taking a one-year break, or a gap year from education, was unknown at that time.) October 1961 seemed to be approaching rapidly and I was receiving inconsistent advice about what I should do. One of the very few defects of LCHS was the lack of careers guidance; the only information available consisted of cardboard boxes filled with glossy brochures distributed by the professions and other prospective employers. In those circumstances I felt very much at sea. I was drifting along in a very unfamiliar world.

As so often before, it was Paddy Clinch who came to my rescue. With his guidance, the choice of subject was narrowed down to two, history (unsurprisingly, given his and my passion for the subject) and law. For the shy boy I then was, the thought of appearing in court with all eyes upon me was daunting; however, the process of logical legal analysis was very appealing. So, despite the fact that I was fascinated by history, the decision

I made was to study law at university.

The decision having been made, Paddy said he would make enquiries to discover which universities were regarded as the most outstanding for the study of law. As a result of his researches, I concluded that I should apply to the London School of Economics (LSE) and Trinity Hall Cambridge.

So, in due course, I applied for and was granted an interview in law at the LSE. I was very apprehensive about the interview before arriving in Houghton Street (the home of the LSE). Eventually I found the room of Professor J A G (John) Griffith, where the meeting was to take place. As I knocked on the door, I felt a knot in the pit of my stomach – my whole future depended on the next fifteen minutes or so. In this short space of time it would be up to me to convince Professor Griffith that I was a worthy candidate to be accepted by the Law Department of the School, and again I was determined to succeed.

I enter the room. John Griffith motions me to sit down on his red leather sofa. As I sit down, John Griffith's first words dispel my worst fears and I feel all will be fine.

"Well, there is obviously no point at all in discussing your CV, or indeed asking you any formal questions. Obviously you're in. Indeed, you are probably far too good for this place."

It will not be the last time in my life that I cannot believe my ears. It is not just John Griffith's relaxed and friendly manner. In a way, although it takes me by surprise, that is the least of it. It is what he said – "You're in!" The words ring in my ears – they will resonate with me forever.

I have literally not said a word, but after only a few moments I have been accepted as a student into one of the most prestigious Law Departments in the country. All my fears have been dispelled by three small words. Those words are still crashing around my head as I try to come to terms with this wonderful news. I hear somewhere in the distance John Griffith say:

"I don't want to talk about law or this place. I want to have a conversation about something far more interesting, where you will not be under any pressure to convince me of anything. I see from your CV you are very interested in fishing. Let's talk about that." And we do, for about half an hour. Throughout this whole time, while trying to talk intelligently about fishing, I am making a supreme effort to absorb the news which I know will shape my future life. Our relaxed and stimulating exchange of views on fishing comes to an end and I bid John Griffith the fondest of farewells; not surprising, given the news he has conveyed to me.

I leave his room walking on air. I am deliriously happy but also completely bemused. Can there ever have been a more bizarre interview than the one I have just experienced? No questions about law. No questions about my CV. Indeed, no real questions at all. Not for the first time in my life, I am unable to grasp what has happened to me. Euphoria sets in in a big way. And I ask myself why I have had so many unusual, indeed unique, experiences in one short lifetime?

Shortly afterwards, Trinity Hall invites me for an interview, but that one is on very traditional lines. Nothing like my relaxed fishing conversation with John Griffith. But the result, as I discover later, is the same. I realise I am in a very fortunate position, being able to choose between two such well respected Law Faculties. But which one? I deliberate for some weeks. The more I think about it, the more I am disinclined to go to Cambridge. At that time I was left-wing in my political thinking and, the more I thought of Cambridge, the more I thought I did not want to go to a bastion of privilege, elitism and exclusivity, or that is how I saw it then. How times change!

A second not inconsiderable reason for choosing the LSE was that, if I went there, I could continue to live at home in Walthamstow. Even taking my State Scholarship grant into account, financing three years away from home at Cambridge would have put an intolerable strain on my family's resources. The more I discussed it with my father, the more it became clear that there was simply not enough money available to fund studying away from home.

Anyway, in the event, the LSE clearly became my front runner as the choice of academic institution, a decision put beyond any doubt by Paddy Clinch's further researches on my behalf. He had discovered that the Law Department at the LSE was truly outstanding, with so many professors who were the leading authorities in their chosen fields. The decision was made, my left-wing conscience was satisfied, and I looked forward to three years of being on the receiving end of academic excellence. I was not to be disappointed in any respect, and I never regretted my choice of the LSE. It bestowed on me benefits far beyond anything I could have reasonably expected. It formed and informed my life. Like LCHS, it totally and fundamentally changed it forever. In the best possible way.

So, in October 1961, I set off for Houghton Street. I was full of anticipation. Full of hope. Full of excitement. Eager for the challenge ahead. There was a brave new world before me and I was going to enjoy it to the maximum.

The first item on the agenda the day I arrived at the LSE was the induction lecture. There is only one aspect of that lecture that I remember, and that came close to its conclusion. An eager group of about eighty 'freshmen' (of whom about a third were female) was told that each student would be placed under the supervision of a member of the Law Department, who would be his or her personal tutor. The undergraduates' names were read out in turn and the tutor assigned to each student was announced. The roll call continued, and at last it reached 'W'. "Peter Whiteman. Professor Wheatcroft."

We had been informed that the allocation of students to tutors had been carried out on a totally random basis. I was only to discover subsequently how very lucky I had been in having Professor Wheatcroft named as my tutor. It was to prove to be the most amazing stroke of luck. This all as a result of a totally random allocation, which no doubt took only a few minutes. Fate?

After the induction lecture, we were instructed to make contact with our personal tutor, so I went to meet him in his room in the East Building of the LSE, Room E305. That was the first time I met Professor Wheatcroft and my initial impression was of an utterly charming, very distinguished man. I thought during our conversation that I had found my 'Paddy Clinch' figure at university. Again I would be in very safe hands. Quite fortuitously, I had been allocated by the Department to a man who was to be the mentor who would guide me through university and later my professional career. He was to shape my life forever. Lucky, lucky me!

CHAPTER 8

THE BRIDGE

"I am prepared for the worst, but hope for the best."
The Wondrous Tale of Alroy (Part X, Chapter III)
BENJAMIN DISRAELI

It is now September 1964, and I have been at the LSE for three years. I am approaching the end of my days there, or so I believe at the time.

I look down. It is quite a long way down. But then I am on the third floor. On the bridge that links the main building with the East Wing of the LSE. There is no reason to pause on the bridge. I may be quite high up, but there is no real view. Nothing to see except taxis and cars way below, using Houghton Street as a short cut to Lincoln's Inn or places further afield. Nothing fantastic about this view. I turn and walk a few paces to the other side of the bridge. More to see now, but nothing exciting. Just students milling around, entering or exiting the main entrance of the School. In the distance Bush House, the BBC's World Service headquarters, looms up. Hardly thrilling. I have stopped on the bridge because I am worried about what I have to do next. My career, my life, is going to turn on what I am told in the next ten minutes or so. Thus I stand on the bridge, marking time. Very apprehensive, and I notice my hands are shaking.

Other students pass over the bridge. Some I know. They say, "Hello," but I am really totally lost in my own thoughts. There are certain defining moments in one's life. I am just about to experience one and I fear the worst. But then, defining moment or not, I always do. I realise that I have prevaricated long enough. Anyway, to delay my exit from the bridge any longer would result in a rudely late arrival for the appointment with my tutor, the person who has so thoughtfully guided my fortunes at the LSE over the last three years. My initial impression of Professor Wheatcroft as a marvellous man has been totally vindicated over the three years I have been at the LSE. How do

I describe him? Kind, caring, thoughtful, generous and considerate. I can go on listing his personal qualities for a long while. The word 'urbane' might have been invented for him. And I have not even mentioned his intellectual abilities and his professional career. He was a practising solicitor, then became a Master of the Supreme Court, and finally Professor of Revenue Law at the LSE (the first Professor of Revenue Law in the country, and still the only one when I was at university). A man, therefore, with the most dazzling curriculum vitae, huge professional, judicial and academic knowledge, and enormous practical experience. An exceptionally wise man who, as I have indicated, was so generous in every possible way, and particularly with his time and contacts. I held him in the highest esteem. To say he was my mentor at university is a gross understatement. He had taken me under his wing from the first moment I met him after the induction lecture.

So, enough of marking time, enough of looking at taxis far below, enough of putting off the inevitable, it is time to make my way to Room E305. It is a few paces from the end of the bridge. Walking on the faded linoleum beneath my feet, I arrive at my destination. Full of angst. Full of anticipation of the news that Ash Wheatcroft (always called Ash because of his second name, Ashcombe) might convey to me. I knock softly on the door.

"Enter" comes from within.

I have been in this room several times before. A large room, as befits the Convenor of the Law Department. It even has a little balcony outside, although it has no view of any consequence. But, Ash being a lawyer, it is hardly surprising that the most memorable aspect of his room is his library. Shelf after shelf on every wall, except for window space, is filled with law reports and learned legal tomes. A massive library accumulated during his long professional and academic career. And then this huge desk, which dominates the room. Behind it? Ash Wheatcroft sitting there with the most welcoming smile on his face, occasionally puffing on his pipe. Because of his charming manner, I start to relax a little, but I cannot do so too much when I know the purpose of this interview is to receive my keenly-awaited LLB results. On this interview, I feel, depends my entire future. If my results are good, there is no limit to what I can hope for. But there is darkness within me, which has prepared me for the worst – failure, which will reawaken traumatic memories of that Eleven Plus fiasco.

Ash motions to me to sit down opposite him. He then takes another puff on his pipe. Smoke slowly rises towards the ceiling.

"Peter, I have some very good news for you!"

I relax. The tension disappears. A little. I notice the shaking of my hands has stopped.

"Well," Ash says very slowly, with profound effect, "your final-year results are extremely good. They are very impressive. What is even more important is that each year your examination results have improved. This year, markedly so. If you had achieved the same results in your first two years that you have obtained this year, you would have been awarded a First Class Honours. Even so, your overall result is an extremely high Upper Second."

I had been so concerned as to whether I had passed the final examination at all. If I failed it, what would I do? But all such thinking was now consigned to oblivion. I had obtained my degree and justified the hopes of all those who had placed so much faith in my future. I was so overjoyed by the news that, although I could see his lips moving, I was not really listening to a word Ash was saying. A degree, a very good degree, and my future as a solicitor (my professional career choice at that time) seemed to be assured.

I started to believe that a great future might lie ahead of me. But my slow realisation was well behind the thoughts and aspirations Ash had for me, which he must already have been contemplating since receiving my results. What he was now about to impart would change my thinking as to my future career and professional life from that day on.

"Peter, what I am saying is that your results are so good that I think you should stay on at the LSE and take a Master's Degree. And if you were to specialise in Revenue Law, I could continue to keep you under my wing and do my best to ensure that your Masters was the success that we would both hope for."

"… we would both hope for" were words I could scarcely believe I had heard. This was the ultimate authority, the 'king', if you will, of Revenue Law, talking to a 22-year-old and linking my hopes for my career with his. But there was more, much more, to come.

"I have also been thinking that, instead of becoming a solicitor, you should become a barrister." This was so much for me to absorb in one interview. My only thought then was, "How could I become a barrister?" The prospect terrified me. I was still a painfully shy young man and the idea of standing up and addressing a judge in open court was daunting. I simply could not do it. It was impossible. I felt sick, even at the thought of it. But how could I inject a negative response into a conversation which Ash had so carefully thought about beforehand? I said nothing. I listened to my oracle and showed no emotion. Any problems as to appearing in court or, indeed, before that, how I was to finance my entry into the profession, were matters for another day. However, unbelievably, there was even more to come. As he expressed his further thoughts, I realised how carefully he had considered my future.

"Peter, as far as the Bar is concerned, perhaps I could be of assistance there. When the appropriate time comes, I could introduce you to my very good friend, a leader of the Revenue Bar, Hubert Monroe." I knew Hubert Monroe QC to be one of the outstanding tax specialists practising at the Bar. "I am sure I could arrange a pupillage in his Chambers at 4 Pump Court." I did not know at that time that 4 Pump Court was one of the most prestigious sets of Revenue Chambers.

The articulation of Ash's planning during the course of our conversation is so much for me to absorb in a relatively short period of time. I am struggling to do so. But his kindness, thoughtfulness and generosity of spirit are not lost on me. In a few minutes I have been told so many things which overall, I am sure, will change the direction of my life forever. No wonder I am so lost in my own thoughts that, although Ash is still talking, I am only hearing snippets of what he has to say.

"As to the immediate future … The LLM course … So overall I think the best way forward … So you would then study three Revenue subjects and, as to the fourth, possibly …".

I am now drifting in and out of this conversation, if it could be so described. It is more of a monologue as to how Ash sees my academic and professional life unfolding in the future. At this stage, however, and possibly so as not to overwhelm me, he does not mention some other wonderful plans he has in mind for my career. They are to be disclosed later.

More comments from Ash, but they waft over me like the smoke that is drifting from his pipe towards the ceiling. I hardly appreciate that Ash has concluded his comments and that it is time for me to make my exit. I rise from my chair, somewhat dazed and confused, but nonetheless I am fully aware that this is a momentous day for me. I am grinning from ear to ear. I am absolutely over the moon about all the wonderful plans that Ash has for my future. He is beaming. Thanks to him, we are two people with a single common objective that is thrilling.

I say goodbye and close the door gently behind me. A few paces onward, away from E305, and I am back on the bridge. My perch above Houghton Street. But now I am a very different person pausing on the bridge to peer down on the black cabs busily conveying their passengers to wherever. How could so much change in such a short period of time? When I paused here before on the way to E305, I was full of doubt, apprehension and real anxiety. Then I was shaking with fear as to what the future might bring. My legs did not want to carry me where I knew I had to go. They seemed to be leaden. Not now. All the worries and all the fears have gone. I have walked from Ash's room to the bridge with a real spring in my step. I am happy beyond measure. I am full of joy and excitement. The world is wonderful. With Ash guiding me, I know anything is possible. This and my new-found confidence know no bounds. Nothing is impossible. Now I would really "show them!"

And then, as I take my last few paces towards the Main Building, the blindingly obvious occurs to me. The bridge I had walked over an hour before in such trepidation had become in that short space of time my pathway to a potentially glittering career. The route which I had feared would lead to the mediocre was now my personal stairway to the stars. That meeting in September 1964 was the first of many with Ash where, over time, he would guide me along the path he had chosen for my future. In the next chapters I describe what took place at those meetings, and taken together they leave one overriding question that occupies my mind. The question is not "What did he do for me?" but "Why did he do it for me?" After all, there were so many other very bright students at the LSE who were worthy of similar attention and whom he presumably could have taken under his wing in the same way. In other words, why did he select me, out of all my peers, as his protégé?

POSTSCRIPT

The written words of Benjamin Disraeli quoted at the beginning of this chapter are not only appropriate to the content that follows, but they are also particularly poignant for me. They are the very words my father spoke to me as he lay dying of cancer in Barts Hospital, when I asked him one afternoon how he felt. His hope was not to be realised. He died that night.

CHAPTER 9

THE MASTER('S) PLAN IS REVEALED

*"In all things, success depends upon previous preparation,
and without such preparation there is sure to be failure."*
Analects
CONFUCIUS (c.550 – c.478 BC)

*"Spectacular achievement is always preceded by
unspectacular preparation."*
ROBERT H SCHULLER

My interview with Ash, as I realised at the time, had been a life-changing event. I was to study for the LLM degree (something which had not crossed my mind previously) and, even more importantly, I was going to the Bar. What a fantastic future to contemplate! Clearly he was determined to further my career as far as he possibly could. And as Head of the Law Department, he was in a position to do so. In 1962 he had completed writing the *British Tax Encyclopaedia,* a massive work in five volumes, which was the definitive treatise on the subject. He had also written a number of other books and was founding editor of the *British Tax Review.*

Following my meeting with him in September 1964, I registered for the LLM degree. Three of the subjects I chose for the degree (following Ash's advice) were aspects of Revenue Law, all of which were taught by him. The fourth subject I chose was Monopolies and Restrictive Practices. The degree was extremely demanding, requiring total dedication to the subject matter of all four courses. As a result, during that year I worked extremely hard because I was determined that I would be thoroughly prepared for the approaching LLM examination. I regarded time spent in preparation as being essential if I was to obtain a good degree that would justify the faith Ash had shown

Above: My graduation degree ceremony, 1964

in me. The detailed preparation in all four subjects was no hardship, as I found each of them fascinating. In particular, Revenue Law appealed to me enormously. I was absorbed by the intellectual challenge of mastering the intricacies of Tax Law (I still am) and analysing the principles to be distilled from the established case law. The LLM was a one-year course and for the whole year I was excited and stimulated by what I was studying. I also felt, in a very minor way, that I was at the cutting edge of the establishment of Revenue Law as an academic subject.

While I was busily working away on my LLM course, I was not to know (or even contemplate) that Ash was busy on my behalf. He was making more plans to advance my career. So one day there is a tap on my shoulder by Ash's secretary, saying he would like to 'have a chat' with me. Once again I made my journey across the bridge to Room E305, although this time I was not feeling anxious or tense about the possibility of receiving bad news.

"Peter," Ash began as I sat down, "I have been thinking about your future career. In addition to becoming a barrister, perhaps you should consider teaching at a university. At the very least, I think it is an option worth exploring." I said nothing because there was nothing I felt I needed to say. If Ash suggested anything, I knew it was after giving the matter the most careful consideration. I had put my career, my future, in his hands and, as those hands were so safe, it was only logical and sensible to follow his advice.

"However, if you are to teach at a university one day, I think you should obtain a part-time teaching position so that you can show that experience on your CV."

Of course, I agreed, and then I was about to discover that he had been even busier on my behalf than I realised.

"I have had a word with the Principal of Willesden Polytechnic and he has agreed to appoint you as a part-time lecturer in Land Law." So, apparently, it was all settled to my enormous advantage.

Every week I accordingly made my way to a nondescript building in Willesden. I enjoyed teaching Land Law at the Polytechnic and I believe I established a real rapport with the students. This was to be my first experience of teaching and, if I had to 'cut my lecturing teeth' anywhere, then Willesden provided a very pleasant place to do it. Although, as one might expect, at times it was a steep learning curve for me, albeit a worthwhile one. It was my first tentative step on the ladder if I was to become a university lecturer. After my year's teaching at Willesden finished, I received yet another invitation from Ash to see him in his room. Coincidental timing? I think not. Ash had a master plan and another part of it was about to fall into place. I now looked forward to being 'summoned' by Ash to his room, as I lived in the hope that something exciting would transpire from any meeting with him. After all, the precedents were very encouraging.

I am in Room E305 yet again. Ash is behind his vast desk and, with a very avuncular expression, he starts talking:

"The teaching at Willesden was fine, but you need something more solid on your CV as a progression from that post. If you are hoping to become a university lecturer, you must have a full-time teaching appointment behind you. Now it so happens that the Dean of the Faculty of Laws of the University of Manitoba is in London, staying at the Strand Palace Hotel, and he is seeking to recruit full-time members of staff. I think, if you were successful, that would be a very appropriate appointment. So here is his telephone number in London. Why don't you give him a call?"

Well, if that's what Ash thought, who was I to do anything else? So I phoned the Dean (Professor Edwards) and we arranged to meet for tea at his hotel. Now I am not very fond of afternoon tea – food which I don't want to eat and which (in such circumstances) has to be eaten very delicately. Whiteman and formal tea simply don't go together. Although I use a napkin on such occasions, I can guarantee that, wherever I place it on my lap, I will always manage to drop some delicacy onto a part not covered by a dainty piece of linen. Formal tea is the worst of all. All those little 'fancies' with cream, chocolate, toppings of all sorts – for me it couldn't be anything other than a disaster waiting to happen. So there's the Dean, and there's Whiteman, with the pastry trolley trundling towards us. Now, somebody smarter, knowing my terrible record on such occasions, would simply wave the trolley past. But what do I do? I take a pastry. First mistake. Second, and worst of all, is what I take. What could be the worst possible pastry to choose? A millefeuille. Nonetheless, not thinking, I take one of those tempting darlings. Even I can't imagine what is to follow. Having some rudimentary idea of the 'polite way' to consume such a treasure, I try to cut it with the side of my dainty pastry fork. First I try gentle persuasion, carefully nudging the fork down the millefeuille. All that achieves is to squash it and send the cream oozing out of the creature. Who on earth invented such a fiendish delicacy? It has to end (at least for me) in disaster. And it does. And in a way even I could never have foreseen. Gentle nudging having failed, I think the direct approach might be better, so with considerable force I slam the edge of the fork onto this object from hell. And it works – sort of. The fork goes straight through the pastry and divides it neatly into one-quarter and three-quarters in size. Good so far as the one-quarter is concerned. However, the other three-quarters has a life of its own and is winging its way at great speed across the table, into the Dean's lap, and lands plumb centre on his flies. I don't know who is more taken by surprise. The Dean just simply looks as the great dollop of cream on his zip and seems to be (maybe not unreasonably) totally mesmerised by it.

I feel action is required. The Dean seemingly frozen to the spot, I reach across the table and delicately remove the demented millefeuille from his lap and put it on my plate. The Dean can't believe what is happening. It is so bizarre. And then I raise my fork with the intention of eating this much-travelled millefeuille. However, even I think to myself, "You can't eat it, you don't know where it's been!" and then I think immediately, "It's even worse than that, you can't eat it because you do know where it's been!" At last I show some sense and put this creature of my torment to one side. I have never had a formal tea since.

I cannot recall a single word of my conversation with the Dean as the millefeuille was winging its way to and fro across the tea table. I was hypnotised by the flying object. Anyway, my somewhat crass behaviour did not prevent the Dean from offering me an Assistant Professorship of Law at the University of Manitoba. In the event, for reasons I will explain later, I did not take up the offer.

However, before I could accept, in September 1965 there was another invitation to cross the bridge to see Ash. As with my LLB results, Ash was keen to tell me in person the results of my LLM examination. They were due to be published very soon, but Ash wanted to impart his news right away. Unlike the anxiety I felt about my undergraduate results, this time I was more hopeful that the news would be good. So, as I knocked on the door of E305, I was not fearful about my fate and my mind was reasonably relaxed; no trembling this time. What I could not anticipate was that Ash would unveil one item of fabulous news after another.

"Peter, first, your LLM results." This was the moment of truth upon which so much would depend. Suddenly, apprehension had taken over from excitement. Ash looked me directly in the eye and there was a huge smile on his face. I knew everything was going to be fine, probably more than fine.

"Well, you have obtained your LLM, but that's hardly surprising. But I am really delighted because you have been awarded a Distinction, one of only two conferred this year."

I try to take in this wonderful news. My mind is jumping with joy. Ash simply says:

"I am so pleased." But there was more, much more, to come. I had thought that I had come to E305 'just' to be given advance notice of my LLM results. But I am soon to realise that I am many steps behind Ash's plans for me.

"The results justify all I have in mind for you."

I am intrigued. What does he have in mind? I do not have to speculate for long because Ash continues:

"Peter, I am about to write a book on the new Capital Gains Tax" (which had become law in the Finance Act 1965) "and I would be very grateful if you would assist me in writing it."

In the last year or so I had received so much good news in this room, but this request for 'assistance' in writing a book with Ash was of a totally different order. This was to me the most fantastic news. I had hoped for a long time to write a book with Ash, although I believed it was a somewhat unrealistic ambition. There were so many academics and practitioners with considerable tax experience he could call upon to assist him in writing a book which would no doubt become, given his eminence, the authoritative work on the subject. Hitherto, the thought that he would actually ask me, someone with no practical experience of Revenue Law, to write a book with him was an unrealistic ambition. In any event it was a long-term hope and I could never have expected it to happen as soon as this. Another dream was becoming reality and I felt this man's ambitions for me knew no bounds.

Collaborating with Ash and the third author, Andrew Park, on the book on Capital Gains Tax in the following months was a sheer joy. I learnt so much from being involved for the first time in writing a book which was to become the definitive work on the subject. The learning curve for me in co-authoring a major textbook on a completely new tax was very steep. However, vitally, it laid the foundations for my future career as an author of books on Revenue Law. I loved the informative discussions with Ash and Andrew in Room E305 and I found them immensely stimulating. And actually writing (of course, in longhand at that time) the material to be incorporated in the book gave me the greatest pleasure. To me then, as now, being creative and producing a work of real substance is one of the most fulfilling experiences life can offer.

After that fast-forward about my first writing experience, I return to my meeting with Ash in September 1965. The news that Ash had already disclosed to me was wonderful. But he was not done yet.

"Peter, there is something else I want to discuss with you. In suggesting that you should teach at Willesden and apply for a position at Manitoba, I mentioned in general terms the prospect of your becoming a university lecturer. Now is the time to mention what I have been planning for you for quite a while. It was not merely to become a university lecturer. It was to teach <u>here</u> at the LSE. To become a full-time member of staff so that you will be in the best possible place to work with me."

It was, however, too late for me to be appointed to the full-time staff for the academic year beginning the following month. But, as Convenor of the Law Department, it was open to Ash to offer me the post of Professorial Assistant to him, which he did. He then added:

"Your appointment will be with immediate effect, and very importantly, it will help you when, later this term, you apply for the post of Assistant Lecturer."

In the event, it certainly did.

The term beginning in October 1965 became very busy for me, collaborating on the book and teaching at the LSE. However, my appetite for work was boundless. To succeed in my application for a university lectureship, I had to write something in my own name. I had to write well, write now, and be published as soon as possible. The Capital Gains Tax book would only serve my writing ambitions in due course. I wanted my name as an author on the printed page before my interview at the LSE later that term. So, in October 1965, I started to write for the *Modern Law Review,* a publication regarded as LSE's legal house 'journal'. The *MLR* was published bi-monthly and I decided to write for every issue. Even more ambitiously, I decided to spread my wings by writing not on Revenue Law, but on Monopolies and Restrictive Practices, the 'fourth' subject I studied for the LLM.

I had loved the Monopolies course for the LLM. I was fascinated by it, and here again another professional mentor stepped into my life. Not a lawyer, but an economist, Professor Basil Yamey. Basil was, and is, eminent in his field. He had taken the course on Monopolies for my LLM and he was not only a most talented teacher, but also a delightful, kind, self-effacing man. I liked him enormously. I asked him to oversee my articles for the *MLR*. He immediately and enthusiastically agreed. And I desperately needed his advice.

The articles I wrote for the *MLR* included economic thought and theory, so to have the guidance, and eventual approval, of Basil Yamey was critical. He gave of his time willingly and generously. We had numerous discussions on the drafts of articles I had written, and his invaluable comments were very thoughtfully and tactfully expressed. Yet another person to whom I owe an enormous debt of gratitude. The final versions of the articles I wrote were infinitely better than the original drafts. The economic analysis relevant to the legal issues was, after our discussions, far more perceptive and soundly based. Thanks to his considerable help, all my articles were published (never a foregone conclusion) and were very well received. I am delighted not only to record my sincere thanks to Basil in this book, but also to mention that he is, at the age of 97, still alive.

Soon after I started teaching as a Professorial Assistant, I applied for the post of Assistant Lecturer at the LSE. This led to another trip across the bridge.

"I've been thinking," Ash began, "about your interview, that is. The Board will consist of three. The Director, Sir Sydney Caine, me and one other professor of the Law Faculty, probably Professor Toby Milsom. The Director only ever asks four questions of any candidate on these occasions, so it is vital that I tell you those four questions now so that we can prepare the answers you should give. That preparation will entail much thought but very little actual work. Sir Sydney might not ask the questions in the following order, but they will all be there one way or another. He will certainly ask you whether you are writing a PhD. If yes, he will then ask you whether you have decided on the title of your thesis. Then the next question will probably be whether you have started work on it. Finally, he will enquire whether you have carried out any research on the subject matter of your thesis.

"Now, these are not difficult questions, but it is vital that you say yes to all of them." So then and there Ash and I started to discuss the answers I should provide to Sir Sydney when the inevitable questions came. It was, of course, crucial that, in addition to giving affirmative answers, I could, if necessary, provide further information so that my overall response was entirely convincing. In outlining the questions that he believed Sir Sydney would ask, it was clear that Ash regarded preparation for all aspects of the interview as absolutely essential.

Come the day of the interview, I was obviously apprehensive. I was determined to be on the teaching staff of the LSE so that I could work with Ash in all the ways he had outlined to me. That was my dream for the future.

I went to the room where my immediate future would be decided. I was shown into the Board Room, a cavernous place with a huge semicircular table in the middle. No doubt the table, on many occasions, would accommodate, say, 25–30 dons. Today, however, there were only three people seated there. Such a small number of people at a huge table looked faintly ridiculous. Almost like the Mad Hatter's Tea Party, without the tea. But instead of someone shouting, "No room, no room!" Sir Sydney beckoned me to sit down. I was dreading the possibility of being asked questions for which I had not prepared. I was particularly concerned about the participation of Professor Milsom, as Ash had warned me that his questions were unpredictable.

Sir Sydney began and, unsurprisingly, his questions were as Ash had anticipated.

"Now first I want to know, as I regard it as most important in the context of teaching at the LSE, are you writing a PhD?"

"Yes," I confidently replied. (On Ash's advice I had registered at the Graduate Office of the LSE to write my PhD thesis only one week earlier.)

"Excellent, excellent!" came the enthusiastic response. "Have you started work on it?" That enquiry threw me a little because that was meant to be question three, not two. (To paraphrase Eric Morecambe when he appeared with André Previn on TV many years later, the Director was asking all the 'right' questions, but not necessarily in the right order.) Not daunted, I answered in the affirmative; after all, I had decided on the subject matter of my thesis, and indeed I did have a title for it. That was the topic to which Sir Sydney turned next.

The Director seemed very pleased and looked at his two colleagues in turn, showing quiet approval and complete satisfaction on his face. I felt very encouraged; the play was being acted out precisely in accordance with the script which had been provided (by Ash!).

Sir Sydney moved on to his next question. "Have you decided on a title for your thesis?"

"Yes." Well, that was true. Never afraid to be a little grand when the occasion demanded, I told the assembled trio that the title of my PhD would be *A History of the Taxation of Income in the British Commonwealth of Nations.* No false modesty there.

"Excellent, excellent!" the Director said for a second time.

The final, or what I hoped would be the final, question was whether I had done any research for my PhD. "Yes," I said very proudly. Well, that was true as well. In a sort of way. One afternoon the previous week I had gone all the way from Houghton Street to visit Rhodesia House (as it was then called) some five minutes away along the Strand. As it was during the frenetic days of UDI (the Unilateral Declaration of Independence), Rhodesia House was extremely busy trying to cope with all the many varied and sensitive issues current at that time. My request for a copy of the Rhodesian Income Tax Act in such circumstances was greeted with astonishment. So astonished were they that such a banal question could be asked in the midst of an international crisis that they, without thinking, supplied me with a copy of the said Act (after a slight delay in locating it). As I had read a part, possibly only a small part, of the Act, I could answer Sir Sydney's question truthfully, in the affirmative.

"Excellent, excellent!" said the Director for a third time, adding that he had no further questions of "this most suitable candidate." Sir Sydney then turned to Ash and enquired whether he wanted to ask me any questions. From my perspective the response could not have been better.

"I know this candidate extremely well, so there are no questions that I need to ask of him. I do not propose to prolong the interview further," looking somewhat sternly at Professor Milsom.

Thus it fell to the said Professor to complete the interview. His questions were so convoluted, arcane and simply unintelligible to me that I found myself struggling to provide a sensible response. One such question followed another. However, soon thereafter the "Excellent, excellent!" Director came to my assistance and said, cutting across Professor Milsom, "Well, I think we don't need to go on with this interview. I don't think we need to ask any further questions of this most able candidate." This time the Director did not use the word 'excellent'. No matter. Sir Sydney had acted decisively in bringing the interview, which had followed its predicted path, to a conclusion.

Any residual doubts I had as to the outcome of the interview were soon removed. The following week I received a letter from the LSE, stating that

I had been successful in my application and, extremely encouragingly, that, as I was already on the teaching staff of the School, I could assume the duties of my new post immediately. Ash's carefully-laid plans had come to fruition, exactly as he had envisaged. I was overjoyed at being appointed to the teaching staff of the LSE. Another dream, of enormous consequence to me, had been realised. A dream it was, but a touch of reality was injected into my thinking. It was the salary for the said post. It certainly would not make me rich for life. It was a meagre £1,050 plus £60 weighting allowance! But the amount of the salary was not the point. It paled into insignificance, given the exciting future that now lay ahead of me. The LSE was right at the top of the list of Law Faculties in the country, with a teaching staff that was truly outstanding. Competition for places in the Law Faculty was intense, and to be appointed a member of staff there was a true accolade.

No doubt, in Ash's grand scheme of things, another objective having been achieved, he moved on to the next. To put what happened at the following meeting in Room E305 in context, I should mention that I had for a long while nursed one particular ambition. To write a book with Ash on Income Tax. My collaboration with Ash on the Capital Gains Tax book had gone extremely well. It had been published in November 1966 and the sales of that volume far exceeded the publisher's expectations. It was, as anticipated, very soon regarded as THE practitioners' textbook on the subject. Its success was extremely gratifying. However, Income Tax was my burning interest. Writing a book with Ash on the subject would, I appreciated, happen, if it happened at all, in the distant future.

At that next meeting, softly, slowly, Ash uttered the words which were pure music to my ears.

"Would you like to write a book on Income Tax with me?"

Outwardly I tried to maintain some aura of calm, possibly even gravitas. With such a momentous question, however, and at my age (24), not an easy thing to do. So I replied in what I hoped was a dignified way.

"Yes, of course. I would be honoured and delighted to do so."

Behind what I hoped was a serene facade, I was in a totally euphoric state. Mentally I was doing furious cartwheels. Firecrackers were going off all over my body. I was deliriously happy.

At this time Ash was 61. The book he had written on Income Tax in

1962 (*The Law of Income Tax, Surtax and Profits Tax*) was the acknowledged practitioners' work on the subject. It had no rival. As we discussed the matter further, what, in fact, Ash was offering me was the opportunity to write a totally new book, which would replace his 1962 magnum opus. It was only some fifty years later that the thought occurred to me (as it had done with the Capital Gains Tax book), "Why did he ask *me* to write this new encyclopaedic work, and not an established practitioner or academic?" So many people with far more experience than I had would have jumped at the opportunity.

We then discussed the details for writing the book and its general structure. Very soon thereafter I embarked on this, the most exciting of all the ventures that had come my way under Ash's auspices. It took me four years to write the book, called in the event *Whiteman and Wheatcroft on Income Tax*. It eventually ran to some 1,500 pages and cost on publication £12.75. It is still being published almost fifty years later but at the somewhat higher price of £409.

In 1971, on publication, the book was well received and once again sales far exceeded the publisher's expectations. But the aspect of this magnum opus which touches me more than any other was the Preface to the First Edition, which Ash wrote without my asking. When I read it, I could not have been more moved. That Preface showed the generosity of spirit and the graciousness of character of the man who was Ash Wheatcroft. The Preface read as follows:

"*In 1962 Messrs Sweet and Maxwell Ltd published my book 'The Law of Income Tax, Surtax and Profits Tax'. Changes in Revenue Law thereafter meant that book needed to be rearranged and rewritten and in 1967 I asked Mr Whiteman, then my colleague at the Law Department of the London School of Economics and a former pupil of mine, to undertake a major revision – a decision I have never since regretted.*

The present book, although based on my old one, has been completely rearranged and rewritten by Mr Whiteman, with only limited assistance from me. At my suggestion, it therefore appears with his name above mine on the title page, as in my opinion it is now a much better book than mine was.

G.S.A.W."

CHAPTER 10

THE EXCITEMENT
OF BECOMING
A BARRISTER
AND BEING WITH
THE PRINCESS

"When I, good friends, was called to the Bar …
I was, as many barristers are,
an impecunious party."
Trial by Jury
W S GILBERT AND A SULLIVAN

At my momentous meeting with Ash in September 1964, his advice had been very clear: I should be called to the Bar. But being advised to become a barrister and actually doing so were two very different matters. First, to become a member of the Bar, I had to join one of the Inns of Court and at that time the admission fee was £200. The problem was that I simply had no money. In 1964 I was still at university and there was no question of my family funding me. So there was only one option: to go cap in hand to each of the four Inns of Court to see if they would waive the admission fee or award me a bursary or scholarship.

To me, the Inns of Court were completely unknown territory. I did not know anyone who was a barrister and who could, therefore, provide me with an introduction to the rarefied world of the Inns of Court. There was nobody to take me around the Inns, explain anything about them to me, let alone accompany me to the various Treasury Offices, their respective administrative headquarters. It was something I had to do, and there was no option – it had to be done alone. So a few days later I set off to make the short journey from the LSE to the Inns of Court. Although it was still September, it was a cold, windy, bleak day. I certainly felt cold inside as I embarked on my fateful journey.

As I walked along Fleet Street and Carey Street on the edges of the 'mysterious' Inns of Court, they seemed very remote and forbidding places. A world unto themselves – clubs very much reserved for their members. So I walked around the Inns with a great deal of trepidation. I was treading the path apprehensively, as I was entertaining real doubts about becoming a barrister at all. As I have said, as a very shy young man, the idea of appearing in court, with all those present hanging on my every word, simply terrified me.

Despite all my reservations, I had to put them aside if I was to pursue the path which Ash had advised me to follow. So I made my uncertain way to the four institutions on that September day with my metaphorical begging bowl. Sad though it may seem, I was really left with no choice but to join the Inn which would provide me with the financial support I so desperately needed. Each time I arrived at a Treasury Office, I had to screw up my courage just to enter the impressive buildings, and then I agonised as to how I should phrase my request for money. Not easy. I was terribly diffident about doing so. I felt that I was entering these august offices of the Bar asking (to adapt the words of Oliver Twist), "Please, sir, may I have some money?" So embarrassing.

When I enquired about the prospects of being awarded a bursary or scholarship at the Treasury Offices of the Inner Temple and Gray's Inn, they were perfectly polite but refused to give me any encouragement as to the prospects of financial assistance being made available. At Middle Temple there was no question of that Inn awarding me a bursary or scholarship, as they were, in those days, only awarded to graduates of the Universities of Oxford and Cambridge. I was, accordingly, very downhearted when I set off for the Treasury Office of the last Inn of Court, Lincoln's Inn. I need not have been. After all these years, I still remember my surprise at the warmth of the welcome I received there. I was greeted by Mr Pilkington in the Treasury Office, a silver-haired, dapper man of real charm. After I had explained my circumstances to him in some detail, he made it quite clear that, although he was not authorised to commit the Inn to anything, he anticipated, on the basis of my curriculum vitae, that the Inn would be prepared to assist me financially. Although Mr Pilkington reserved the Inn's position entirely, I anticipated, perhaps a little too optimistically, that the Inn would relieve me of the financial burden of becoming a member and that possibly, in due course, I might even be awarded a scholarship. Now there seemed to be real hope, after what had been, up to then, a very daunting and depressing experience. Mr Pilkington had been extremely helpful and had welcomed me to Lincoln's Inn. I had no doubt that in an unfamiliar world I wanted to make this Inn my legal home; a decision I have never since regretted – to put it very mildly. As I walked back the short distance to the LSE, I felt I had achieved a great deal that day. I had entered a forbidding world and in some way, solely on the basis of my own efforts, I had cracked it. My self-confidence had received an enormous boost. And in Mr Pilkington I felt that, if ever I had a problem at the Bar, there would be someone I could turn to for help. And, indeed, my perception was to prove absolutely correct. In the following years, whenever I presented myself at the Treasury Office, Mr Pilkington was there to assist me, exuding his charm and warmth. As time went by, I was left in no doubt that he was taking a real interest not only in my progress at the Inn but also in my career generally. He seemed to be absolutely delighted first when, soon after my meeting with him, I was awarded a Sir Thomas More Bursary, which paid for all my fees to the Inn, and then subsequently when I was awarded the Hardwicke Scholarship, the Mansfield Scholarship and the Kennedy Scholarship. My faith in Lincoln's Inn had been totally vindicated. My belief in Mr Pilkington was completely justified. The fondest memory I have of Mr Pilkington is of an event that occurred some three years later. But I must not run ahead of myself, for there is much to be written about those three intervening years.

After I joined Lincoln's Inn, I was never in any doubt that my future was at the Bar. I loved the atmosphere and I was excited by the scope it would give me to develop the passion of my professional life, Revenue Law. But, at the same time, I was very occupied by teaching at the LSE. As a result, I found it very difficult to make the time to study for the Bar examinations. If I wanted to follow the path that Ash had mapped out for me, obviously I would have to take the examinations – one day. But I seemed to find an endless series of excuses to defer taking them. Procrastination was the order of the day. Each time I thought about sitting the Bar examinations, I would convince myself that I couldn't spare the time for the necessary preparation. But even I couldn't convince myself that I had any justification for not undertaking

the other requirement laid down by the Bar Council to become a barrister
– quaint as it might be.

In 1964 there were two essential qualifications for becoming a barrister.
First, obviously, passing the Bar examinations. Secondly, not so obviously
relevant, eating thirty-six dinners in Hall over a three-year period. The
philosophy underlying the requirement to eat thirty-six dinners was that
students would become acquainted with their future colleagues at the Bar.
The intention was that such dining together would create a friendly and
fraternal atmosphere amongst those who would practise alongside each
other at the Bar in future years. But there was no question of the occasion
of 'dining' being used by the Inns to increase the student barristers' knowledge
of the law, or of the English legal system. Thus there was no instruction by
a judge, barrister or academic before or after dinner, nor a talk delivered
by a distinguished legal luminary. That happens now, but not then. It was
purely a matter of eating a three-course dinner and so ticking off another one
of the required thirty-six.

The compromise I reached with myself was that, although I would defer
sitting the Bar examinations, I would immediately dedicate myself to the
pleasurable task of sampling the gastronomic delights produced by the
kitchens of Lincoln's Inn. So on another cold autumnal day in 1964 I set off
from the LSE to make my way to the Inn, and more specifically to the New
Hall of the Inn where the 'dinners' are served. It is called 'New' Hall because,
although it was built in 1845, there was already in being another Hall which
was constructed in 1483–1485. That, unsurprisingly, is called Old Hall. But
back to New Hall, which stands proudly overlooking, on one side, the gardens
of the Inn and, on the other, Lincoln's Inn Fields. From the outside it can be
seen to be a magnificent, indeed awesome, building, as befits an Inn of Court,
indeed the oldest Inn of Court. Inside it is equally impressive, first because
of its ceiling and the numerous colourful panels containing the coats of arms
of members of Lincoln's Inn who have become judges; also because it is very,
very large. Indeed, it might be described as cavernous. To a new member of
the Inn on a first visit it is absolutely stunning.

That evening, when I made my way to the Inn, it was not the first time
that I would sample the delights of eating in Hall. Not the first time that
I had seated myself at the inordinately long highly-polished wooden tables

that seemed to stretch from here to eternity. Indeed, as soon as I had joined the Inn, I had been to New Hall regularly for lunch. The formality that existed in the Inn in those days, even at lunchtime, was, I found, somewhat intimidating. On a more light-hearted note, I recall that, when I first started eating in New Hall, some of the oldest barristers were still wearing spats. When I first saw them, it took me a while to realise what they were. When I did, I really felt, particularly given my surroundings as well, as though I was living in Dickensian times.

But the memories of those early days and the formality that went with them were sometimes unappealing. For example, the older barristers not only had their regular tables for lunch, but also their regular seats at those tables. Woe betide any young barrister who, in ignorance, sat in the dining chair that was used daily by an older member of the Inn. He would, of course, be evicted, and not necessarily in the most polite way. On one occasion I witnessed a senior member of the Inn standing over the chair he used every day at lunch and becoming puce in the face because a young barrister was sitting in 'his' chair. The 'green' barrister soon realised his error – indeed, it was forcefully pointed out to him – and he disappeared elsewhere with his tail between his legs. He looked, and no doubt felt, very embarrassed. He had become acquainted with one of the most important customs of the Inn at that time in a most unfortunate way.

Despite the fact that I was dedicating myself to the gastronomic obligations of Lincoln's Inn, my ambition to become a member of the Bar had in reality stalled, particularly given my decision that I would take the Bar examinations when I had 'more time available'. My career at the Bar needed to be kick-started. However, I was not turning my mind to that prospect. But, as always, Ash was, and fortunately he took the matter out of my hands. So, at yet another meeting in his room, Ash said, "I have been thinking it is time you started your pupillage at the Bar. As I mentioned to you some while ago, Hubert Monroe is the Head of a set of Revenue Chambers. Why don't you make an appointment to see him? This is his telephone number. I am sure he will do all he can for you."

I did as I was bidden and some two weeks later, having made an appointment to see Hubert Monroe, I made my way to 4 Pump Court. I went straight to the Clerks' Room (which I subsequently learned was the nerve centre of Chambers) and met the Senior Clerk, Alfred Griffin, a formidable man who seemed straight out of a Dickensian novel. Alfred took me down a short flight of steps and showed me into the presence of the great man. I was now in the holy of holies, the room of the Head of Chambers, the great and enormously respected Hubert Monroe. Until he spoke, I must admit I was absolutely terrified, being in such august and unfamiliar surroundings, and in the presence of a legend of the Revenue Bar. My terror evaporated as soon as Hubert Monroe started talking. It was immediately apparent that he was a charming, urbane man, delightful in every way, who was really interested in me and my career. Genuine interest, of that there was no doubt. Here was a man who had no side, was not in the least bit pompous, was completely down to earth and who wanted to chat, be informed and be informative. My interview could not have gone better and I found it most interesting and, at times, very humorous. The whole time he was talking to me, I kept on thinking that here was a great man who must have a million things on his mind and yet was prepared to spend all this time speaking to a mere student. But as I was to discover subsequently, Hubert loved being with students; he loved their youth, their vitality and their enthusiasm.

Towards the end of the interview, he indicated, to my great joy, that 4 Pump Court would take me on as a pupil. I never expected such a positive outcome from a first meeting. It was, to me, a quite incredible result, but thinking about it now, could there really have been any doubt that, prior to my interview with Hubert, Ash had promoted my cause as far as he possibly could? It must have been so, for Hubert to offer me a pupillage on the spot. I was walking on air. I had broken into the bastion of that completely unknown world to me of the Bar. 'Broken into', however, is hardly the right phrase. I had been accepted as a pupil because Ash had helped me to surmount a barrier in a way I could never have achieved by myself. In those days, invariably, aspiring barristers were taken on by a set of Chambers because it was anticipated they could introduce friends and acquaintances who would be in a position to bring work to members of Chambers. I obviously had no connections at the Bar and could not possibly bring any work to Chambers. But Hubert was prepared, quite simply, to accept me on the basis of my ability.

Hubert then said that, although Chambers would accept me as a pupil, I ought to go to general Chancery Chambers for a six months' pupillage to gain general experience before I specialised in Revenue Law. "My cousin, John Monroe, is in a set of general Chancery Chambers and I will have a word with him so that he will accept you as a pupil." So my two pupillages were arranged during one interview, my very first (and in the event only) interview for a pupillage in any set of Chambers.

As our conversation drew to a close, I not only thought how enjoyable the meeting with Hubert had been, but also that he had spent an entire hour with me. That interview was the start of a very warm friendship with a man who was to become one of my two great mentors at the Bar. As I left 4 Pump Court, it struck me how plush the Chambers were. They were held in high regard and, as one would expect, the décor matched that reputation. After my highly satisfactory interview I started to dream – what a set of Chambers in which to be a tenant! But once again I was rushing ahead of myself. After all, I hadn't even taken the Bar examinations and, to qualify, I also had to do my first six months' pupillage with John Monroe.

And so to John Monroe's Chambers on a wet, dismal November day. After the clean, bright, fresh, modern, well-decorated 4 Pump Court, seeing 13 Old Square, Lincoln's Inn, was a shock. It was so amazingly old-fashioned and dingy. And it got worse. The austere exterior led into a totally bare entrance area (I can't describe it in any other way), with a stark, stone staircase leading up from the entrance. As I went into this most unwelcoming building, I took the first door on the right, the entrance to the Chambers where John Monroe was a tenant. On entry I could see the Clerks' Room on my left, which housed only two people. The Clerk was universally called by his surname – Cox. He had probably forgotten his first name, and as I discovered subsequently, nobody in Chambers knew it either.

Cox sat on a high stool. I wish I could say he used a quill pen, for that would have completed the antiquated picture I described earlier. Sadly, he used a fountain pen. Opposite Cox sat Miss Leggit, about whom I remember little.

On that first November afternoon, when I went in to meet Cox, Miss Leggit was busily typing away on her Remington typewriter. And then a bizarre thing happened; before my very eyes Miss Leggit, as several dirty teacups were brought into the room, flipped over the top of her desk to reveal a sink. I then realised that the typewriter she had been using was screwed to the top of her desk so that the crockery could be washed in the sink that lurked beneath it. As Miss Leggit embarked on her domestic task, I realised the whole outmoded system was economically very efficient; a person who was both a typist and a washer-up, who used her desk for both purposes! In the meantime, Cox was busily entering the fees of a member of Chambers in longhand in a red leather-bound ledger.

Being somewhat nervous before my interview with John Monroe, I enquired as to the whereabouts of the lavatory. I should have guessed there was no such facility in the building. However, a good five-minute walk away in Chichester Rents, there was a loo but no hand-washing facilities, so one had to return to Chambers and descend below stairs to the basement, where there was a sink with a cold-water tap. To me at the time it seemed that the facilities could not have been much more primitive, and so the contrast with the luxury of 4 Pump Court was striking.

After the alarms and excursions set out above, I was ushered into John Monroe's room by Cox. Complete and utter chaos. Sets of papers, Instructions tied up with red tape, piles of books and dust everywhere. And behind this 'organised chaos' sat John Monroe, his face just peeping over a stack of books. John was one of the most gentle, kind and thoughtful people I have ever met. He was a superb lawyer, albeit exceptionally modest. He was also the country's leading expert on Stamp Duty, but his practice was very broad and extended beyond the realms of that subject. My interview with John went very well and he offered me a pupillage from January 1967, even though I had still not taken the Bar examinations.

I duly started at 13 Old Square and spent six very happy months as John's pupil. He was an excellent pupil-master and he took infinite care with my training and instruction. We got on so well that he even invited me to write a book with him entitled *Business Tax Planning*. I readily agreed and subsequently started writing yet another book, wondering how I was ever going to find the time to do so. This problem was solved, however, because of changes in Revenue Law. Those changes were so fundamental and comprehensive that the task of writing and rewriting parts of the book would have been overwhelming, so, very sadly, the project had to be abandoned.

Whilst I was at 13 Old Square, John and I had numerous discussions about the sets of papers that he had been requested to advise on. But one particular episode stands out in my mind. When John was in Conference with his clients, and of course I was present as his pupil, he would draw me into the discussion by asking me for my views on a particular point that had arisen. Even more unusual at that time, if a solicitor asked John a direct question, he would defer to me and indicate that I should provide the necessary advice, even before he responded. On one occasion, a very distinguished solicitor, Philip Morgenstern, instructed John to advise in Chambers. John drew me into the discussion in Conference and, as time passed, it became a three-way affair, with me participating fully. Indeed, on reflection, I was somewhat embarrassed because I was leading the legal advice that John had been instructed to provide. In any event, the Conference went very well, all the legal issues that Philip had raised were duly covered, and clearly he left John's room a very satisfied client.

Some two hours later, Cox came into John's room and said he had Mr Morgenstern on the telephone. John said immediately, "He must have a point on this morning's Conference. Please put him through to me."

Cox looked discomforted. He was clearly fumbling for words as he said, "Mr Monroe, he doesn't want to speak to you. He wants to speak to Mr Whiteman."

John and I were both taken aback. John recovered first. "Well, put him through on this phone and Mr Whiteman can speak to him here."

I was mystified by what was happening. Anyway, the call was put through and Philip said to me in his usual very quiet way, "Mr Whiteman, I was very impressed by your performance in Conference this morning, and I would like to instruct you professionally. I would like to send you this afternoon a set of Instructions for your advice."

I was flattered and embarrassed in equal measure. I was embarrassed for two reasons: first, because Philip was seeking my legal advice apparently in preference to John's, and secondly, more fundamentally, as I had not yet passed the Bar examinations, I was of course not a qualified barrister. I explained to Philip that, as I had not qualified, I could not accept his Instructions. I told him how much I appreciated his offer of Instructions but that very regrettably I was unable to accept it. Philip said flatteringly that he totally understood, although he was surprised, given the quality of the advice I had tendered in Conference. And then he added, "But don't worry, there'll be lots more sets of Instructions I will send you when you are qualified. Rest assured of that." And indeed there were, after I was in a professional position to accept them.

Having started my pupillage at 13 Old Square, I had little option but to grasp the nettle. I decided to take the Bar examinations in May 1967. Looking back on it, taking the Bar examinations in the 1960s was a somewhat ludicrous affair. To put it in obvious context, these were the examinations to gain admission to an illustrious profession. And yet at that time the examinations were of the most rudimentary nature. First, because there was no requirement to attend any lectures or seminars to complete the course for the examinations. Secondly, because there was no practical or advocacy training of any sort. In those days all one had to do was apply to Gibson and Weldon, who provided legal tutorial courses by post, for their booklets setting out their Summary Notes on the subjects that were part of the Bar examinations. The booklets were about 7 inches x 5 inches and approximately 30–40 pages long. The Notes had to be learnt parrot-fashion. If a candidate did that, he would pass the Bar examinations without question. Even in 1967 I thought that surely a more rigorous system could have been devised to test the ability of students to ensure they were fit to become barristers (of course, much later it was).

Before I sent off for the Summary Notes, in April 1967 I attended a reception at Lincoln's Inn for domestic and overseas students. There I met the famous and innovative Lord Denning for the first and only time. After the inevitable introductory question that a judge always asked a student at a reception in those days ("My boy, where do you come from?"), Lord Denning continued, "My boy, what are you doing?"

"I am teaching at the London School of Economics."

"But you are going to take the Bar examinations?"

"Yes, of course. I am taking them this May."

"Excellent. So when did you start working for them?"

"I haven't."

"You haven't?"

"No, I haven't. I am going to devote the whole of the Easter holiday, some three weeks, to studying for them."

"You mean you haven't started work on them yet?"

"No."

"You are treating the examinations of a highly respected professional body with contempt. I refuse to have anything more to do with you. I shall not speak to somebody who behaves as you do."

And with that he swept off, not only refusing to speak to me again that night, but, as he had indicated, ever thereafter.

As the Bar examinations loomed ever closer on the horizon, two events of significance happened, one bad, the other good. The first was that, when my Gibson and Weldon Notes arrived by post, the Notes on two of the subjects were missing. Very importantly, the missing Notes related to two subjects in the Bar examinations of which, being an academic, I had little or no knowledge, namely, civil and criminal procedure. Such subjects were simply not taught at Law School. Despite my complaints to Gibson and Weldon, they never arrived in time for my Bar examinations and so I had to make up my knowledge of these two arcane subjects as I went along.

The second event constituted an amazing stroke of luck. Two days before my Bar examinations, John Monroe received a set of papers for advice, of which he said delightedly, when he opened them, "These Instructions relate to a Tomlin Order." I did not have the faintest idea what a Tomlin Order was. But in his usual patient way John explained all the intricacies of such an Order. As a result, after John's analysis of the subject, I was an authority on Tomlin Orders. And two days later I took the Bar examinations and one whole question out of five was devoted to "What is a Tomlin Order?" With any luck I should have got full marks for my answer.

Despite my new-found expertise on Tomlin Orders, I was subsequently completely convinced I had failed the Bar examinations. There were six three-hour papers, and my knowledge of some of the legal and practical issues raised was such that many of my answers were skeletal. There were big gaps in my answer books. So with great apprehension I waited for the results of the Bar examinations to be published in July.

In those days one was never notified directly of the results of the Bar examinations; they were only published in *The Times.* On the day the results were announced in the paper, no one could wait for the first edition to be distributed to the news vendors. We all went to Fleet Street to pick up the paper as soon as it came off the press. There I purchased *The Times.* I turned to the appropriate page and saw the Bar Examination Pass List, a massive list of apparently some 2,000 candidates. I immediately began the search for my name. However, I was devastated as I looked at the list of Third Class passes. I had such a pessimistic view of my chances of success that I believed that, if I had passed, I would only just scrape through – a Third Class Honours. But my name wasn't there. I had failed. Disaster. The possibility of becoming a tenant at 4 Pump Court had evaporated totally. I felt terrible. Then something prompted me to look higher up the list of passes and there, to my astonishment, I read that I had not only passed the Bar examinations but had actually come top of the Lincoln's Inn list. I shall never understand how that happened, with my almost complete lack of knowledge of civil and criminal procedure (except, of course, for my outstanding expertise on the Tomlin Order). But top I was, and once again I was over the moon with the success achieved. Perhaps all those dreams of becoming a tenant of 4 Pump Court might become a reality.

My call to the Bar was scheduled for 20 July 1967 and of course I was looking forward to becoming a full practising member of Lincoln's Inn. To that end, to complete all the necessary formalities, I went once more to the Treasury Office to see Mr Pilkington. There he was, as usual, with a huge smile on his face. It was apparent that he was continuing to take a great interest in my career. "You are the top student at Lincoln's Inn, many congratulations! I am delighted. Because you are the top student, I can tell you, unofficially, that you will be awarded the Buchanan Prize. You will also be awarded the Kennedy Scholarship." I could hardly believe the news. From anticipating failure, I was now to be honoured by the Inn for getting the best results in the Bar examinations. It was one of those magical days in one's life, but obviously Mr Pilkington was bursting with even more good news. "As part of the Buchanan Prize," he continued with enormous pride and, I detected, excitement, "you will be seated next to Princess Margaret (who was our Treasurer for that year) for dinner and she will present you with the Buchanan Prize." Mr Pilkington may have been excited and delighted on my behalf at the honour the Inn had bestowed on me, but I was somewhat daunted at the prospect of sitting next to Her Royal Highness at dinner. Even I knew that she had a fearsome reputation and that one ill-considered word might result in my being consigned to oblivion. However, at least I thought there would be a number of other people seated around us, who would take the pressure off me as far as making conversation was concerned. How wrong can you be? But more of that later.

Before dinner, in the late afternoon, the Call Ceremony took place. The Call to the Bar very much followed the same format as a degree ceremony at university. The barristers to be called were seated in rows, and as their names were read out in turn, they proceeded to the lectern where their name was called by the Under Treasurer (the most senior member of staff of the Inn). Arriving some paces before the lectern, they then turned, walked a few steps forward, stopped and formally bowed to the Treasurer. The Treasurer then, having named the barrister, formally 'called' him or her to the Bar in the time-honoured way. Unlike many universities, however, they were not handed any certificate to mark the occasion. The formal 'call' having taken place, the barrister bowed, turned and returned to his seat.

The Call Ceremony had a very long history and, as far as was known, had not changed significantly, at least in modern times. Mr Pilkington had explained to me the precise order of events at the ceremony, and that this year it was to follow the traditional pattern. What else? To change it without precedent would be much frowned upon. But the Inn had reckoned without Princess Margaret. Evidently, when she was told the details of the ceremony, she insisted that, as each barrister came before her, she wished to shake hands with him or her, and her wish amounted to a command. When she asked to see the certificate she assumed each barrister would receive from her, she was told that this was not traditionally part of the ceremony. The Princess was astonished and stated that, as she was Treasurer, she would decide on all the details of the Call Ceremony she presided over. She insisted that each barrister would receive a formal and impressive certificate, recording their 'call', and she would sign it. In her opinion, which in reality became another command, each barrister should have a formal document to record such an important event in their life. No other procedure could be contemplated. Moreover, Princess Margaret stated that a draft of the certificate should be submitted for her prior approval.

On the night in question, when it came to my turn to be 'called', I was delighted to be 'called' by a Royal Treasurer, to receive my Certificate of Call from her hands, and finally to shake hands with her. As I did so, I looked at the Princess, her amazing sapphire blue eyes met mine and she gave me a delightful smile.

The Princess, by insisting on very significant additions to the Call

Ceremony, had made it a more impressive occasion and each barrister had received a formal certificate to record the most important event in their professional life.

At dinner I was seated on Princess Margaret's left as the prizewinner, and on her right sat the most 'Senior Student' – a polite way of saying the student who had taken the longest time to pass the Bar examinations. The Senior Student in 1967 had started studying for the Bar examinations in 1949, so he had taken eighteen years to qualify! Princess Margaret, who was not known for her open mind, appeared to take an instant dislike to him, perhaps because the only time he was allowed to address her, he called her "'er Royal 'ighness". This appeared to displease The Queen's sister and she completely ignored him for the rest of the dinner. Opposite Princess Margaret were two diners within conversation range. The first was Lord Snowdon (her husband), but whatever marital bliss may be, it was certainly not being exhibited that night. She appeared to treat him as though he had an infectious disease and ignored him throughout dinner. Two possible saviours down. So I was now reduced to pinning all my hopes on the other, Lord Justice Buckley. A delightful, charming, softly-spoken man who was Princess Margaret's cousin. At the start of the dinner he appeared not to be in disfavour, but at one stage, when the Princess was touching the gavel placed before her, he leant forward and said respectfully, "Ma'am, I don't think it is quite the time to use the gavel yet." That did it! Krakatoa erupted. The Princess exploded and I remember her exact words to this day, "Don't you dare tell me when I can and can't use the gavel! I will use the gavel as and when I choose to do so, and no one will tell me otherwise." She thereafter ignored him as well. Three down and only me left to make conversation with Her Royal Highness for the rest of dinner. At the beginning of the evening I had been apprehensive, but, with all the mayhem created around me and blood flowing everywhere, I was terrified at the prospect which now presented itself. But try I must, and of course, I did. Indeed, we really seemed to establish some kind of rapport, and she did have a reputation for enjoying the company of young men! The centrepiece of our conversation for most of the evening was Africa. We discussed the contrast between East Africans and West Africans, on which the Princess, unsurprisingly, had strong views. However, her most forthright opinions were reserved for the situation in Rhodesia and her wholehearted support of the white minority government's Unilateral Declaration of Independence. During the limited opportunities that were afforded to me to respond, I felt that I was walking on a carpet of eggshells. In the event, all the eggshells seemed to emerge unscathed and her aide informed me that he hadn't seen the Princess smile as much for a very long time. I believe my interpretation of our conversation was proved correct when I next met Princess Margaret some eighteen years later, when I became a Bencher of the Inn.

On that occasion, as I shall recount later, the Princess said she remembered we had met all those years before and how much she had enjoyed our conversation at that time. But much more of that later.

The dinner in 1967 concluded with the most emotional event for me – the presentation by Princess Margaret of the Buchanan Prize. The Princess carried out the very short ceremony so graciously and with real warmth, to the extent that I had to struggle to stop tears welling up. It was a truly unbelievable occasion for me to receive the prize for being the top student of the Inn, and to receive it from The Queen's sister.

Of course, this was one of the most momentous evenings that I have experienced. It was the day of my Call to the Bar, but in addition I had the honour of spending the evening in the company of the Princess who, however she may have behaved toward others, was delightful to me throughout the entire time we were together. From a distance, at various times during the dinner, I saw Mr Pilkington out of the corner of my eye, wreathed in smiles and obviously taking great pride in the whole occasion. I hope that people like Mr Pilkington (I never knew his first name), Paddy Clinch, Ash Wheatcroft and Hubert Monroe realised how important they were in forming and influencing the lives of others, and how much they were respected, revered and appreciated by those whom they assisted. In all cases they played a fundamental role in shaping my life and setting me on the path which I still follow today.

CHAPTER 11

NOW I'M REALLY IN(N)

*"Revenue Law is really most intricate and I sometimes despair
of ever having a comprehensive grasp of it."*
January 1955
MARGARET THATCHER
UK Prime Minister 1979–1990

I so wanted this day to happen. I have dreamed of it. And I am still in that dream as I walk slowly across the courtyard of Pump Court. So-called, totally unsurprisingly, as there was originally a pump in the middle of it. It was long ago removed, but a tree marks the spot where it once grew. I am walking slowly, deliberately slowly, as I want to savour every minute. I feel, almost as if I know, that this is going to be one of the great moments of my life. So I drink in the experience. I look to the left and right. It is such a beautiful courtyard. In my view, the most beautiful in the Temple. It is enclosed on four sides by buildings which have a stunning unity. This particular morning its beauty is enhanced by the summer sun, which, as it is early, casts long shadows as it caresses the three trees planted in a straight line across the courtyard. The beauty of the court is further increased by its two entrances. At the eastern side of the court there are the Cloisters, row after row of classical columns. At the western end a small archway leads to Essex Court, which somewhat sadly is now a car park. But here in Pump Court only pedestrians are allowed. So, in one of the busiest parts of London, here at its heart there is the most wonderful oasis of calm. It is only disturbed by the occasional bewigged barrister, accompanied by, one assumes, those instructing him, walking purposefully off to the Royal Courts of Justice. Usually walking at a very smart pace. I have no intention of imitating them. No fast walking for me today. I want to treasure and remember every second of my walk through this haven of peace. The experience will never occur again. My first day in my new Chambers. All the omens are so good. So why rush? I will probably be doing that for the rest of my professional life at the Bar. But not today.

This is such a sweet occasion. 4 Pump Court, where I will start my pupillage, is the finest set of Revenue Chambers at the Bar. And here I am, about to enter the portals of the place where I have so wanted to start, and obviously continue, my professional life. I pinch myself to prove that this is really happening to me.

I stop at the entrance to the building. I pause to look at the list of 'tenants' (that is, barristers) practising within. There are eight names on the list. Will my name ever be added to the illustrious roll-call of leaders of the Revenue Bar? It is a passing thought. There are so many pieces of the jigsaw that will have to fall into place before that happens. I put them out of my mind as I start to climb the highly-polished wooden stairs which lead to the first floor, where the Clerks' Room is located. I am very nervous. Maybe even a little frightened, even though, as mentioned in the previous chapter, I have been here before. I feel I am out of my depth. I am trying to achieve something which, on any realistic basis, is way beyond what I could ever have hoped to attain. But I am not going to let that show. I believe that I have to give the impression that this is my natural milieu, whatever I feel inside. I just hope that my performance will be convincing.

With all these thoughts in my mind, I continue to ascend the wooden staircase and arrive at the first floor. An arrow outside the Chambers informs all that the Clerks' Room is to the right, and that the Clerk is A R W Griffin. The legendary 'Alf Griffin', whom I had met briefly when I came to 4 Pump Court for my pupillage interview with Hubert Monroe the previous year. Alf was the <u>Senior</u> Clerk and in those days the Senior Clerk really ran Chambers, to such an extent that some Chambers were referred to by the name of the Clerk. Thus 4 Pump Court was known simply as 'Griffin's Chambers'. He was all-powerful, distributing Briefs (Instructions to barristers to appear in court on behalf of solicitors and their clients) and sets of papers (Instructions to advise in writing or in Conference) as he saw fit. Woe betide the barrister who fell out with his Senior Clerk. Over the years many had done so and, as a result, they were starved of work – my father-in-law was one such. But a 'blue-eyed boy' of the Clerk (assuming that he had the necessary ability) could be made for life by the Clerks' Room. And a successful barrister was very popular with the Senior Clerk, and not merely because he enhanced the reputation of the Chambers. Such a barrister would also put substantial sums of money into the Clerk's pocket by way of clerking fees. Before my time, barristers' fees were always quoted in guineas, that is, multiples of £1 and one shilling (i.e. five pence), an old-fashioned unit of currency. By tradition, the Senior Clerk's fee was one shilling in every guinea the barrister received. So the Senior Clerk received 5 per cent of every fee of every member of 'his' Chambers. When guineas fell into disuse, the Senior Clerk's fee somehow increased to 10 per cent of the receipts of every barrister for whom he acted. A Senior Clerk was not to be demeaned by being paid a salary. That was for employees, and earnings based on a percentage of fees emphasised that the Clerk was independent of, and not employed by, the barristers. And it also meant that the Clerk in a very successful set of Chambers, taking 10 per cent of all his barristers' fees, could even in the 1970s receive an annual income running into seven figures.

With great trepidation I knocked on the door of the Clerks' Room and entered. Alf was sitting in a high-backed chair. Although always spoken of at the Bar as 'Alf', nobody, not even Hubert Monroe, the Head of Chambers of 4 Pump Court, would have called him by that diminutive. We all addressed him as 'Alfred' in a somewhat reverential way. On the morning in question he was giving his orders to the Junior Clerks as to the tasks they should undertake that day. His tone was clear and that of a person who knew exactly what he was doing. Clear, precise, authoritative and firm, very firm. His entire demeanour was that of a most efficient man, who would brook no nonsense – either from 'his' assistants or from 'his' barristers. This was confirmed much later on when I had the temerity to propose to Alfred that I suggest the amount of the fees for the professional matters I had advised on. I was sensible enough to add the rider that it would, of course, be for Alfred to decide in the final event on the fee that should be charged, but my suggestion might be helpful to him in making his decision. No tenant in my Chambers, not even the Head of Chambers, had ever made such a suggestion before; fixing fees was exclusively regarded as part of the Clerk's function. Unsurprisingly on reflection, Alfred exploded with rage, his face going bright red as he spluttered, "I have never heard of any barrister fixing his own fees! It is the most ridiculous and insulting suggestion I have ever heard. What impudence, especially from a barrister of a few years' call!" And then he uttered words which showed how angry he was, words which I remember to this day, "Now get out of my sight and leave my Chambers now." He was furious. I decided that the best course of action was to retreat with dignity. So I left the Clerks' Room, having been ordered to do so. But even then I was a fairly determined individual, and as I took those fateful footsteps, I knew I would return. And I did. The following morning. The incident was never referred to again, either by Alf or me, but not to be cowed into submission, thereafter every week I gave him a list of the fees I 'suggested' for that week's work. I noted subsequently, with great satisfaction, that in nearly all cases he was charging the fees I had put on my weekly list. Nobody else in Chambers was prepared to follow my example, even though they knew Alfred had complied with my suggestion for fixing my fees. I shall have much more to say about Alfred later on in this chapter, when he features in a most bizarre yet comical incident in Chambers.

However, to return to my first morning in Chambers, everything that day was very formal and most polite. After the usual pleasantries Alfred said he would escort me to 'Mr Potter's room', he being the barrister in Chambers who was to be my pupil-master for the next six months, namely, D C ('Charles') Potter. Everybody of consequence in the tax world knew, or knew of, Charles Potter. His reputation preceded him. At that time he was 45 years of age. He had become an extremely successful member of the Revenue Bar and had co-authored with Hubert Monroe an outstanding and highly-regarded textbook on tax planning. It was the bible for all those who practised in that area of law.

As we entered his room in Chambers, Alfred introduced me to Charles Potter, a most distinguished-looking man. Charles Potter's first words were obviously intended to put me at my ease – "Welcome to Pump Court," he said with a big smile. I felt at home immediately. Charles Potter was tall, handsome, trim and very well-dressed. He was standing, with one hand in his pocket. He immediately gave me the impression that here was a very self-assured and charming man. From everything I had heard and knew, I believed that Charles was going to be an excellent pupil-master. He was an outstanding lawyer. His breadth of knowledge of Chancery Law, Trust Law, Company and Commercial Law, in addition to his encyclopaedic knowledge of Revenue Law, made him a most impressive member of the Bar. It also meant that he received Instructions on a very wide range of topics, which provided an excellent general grounding in Revenue Law for me. With his urbane, delightful and relaxed manner, it also meant that he had an excellent presence both in Consultation and in court. He was a gifted advocate, very well respected by other members of the Bar and, even more importantly, by the judges before whom he appeared.

My pupillage with Charles was a great success, and we got on extremely well from the very start. He not only discussed a set of papers for a Consultation with me beforehand, identifying the key points that required advice, but in addition afterwards he would always analyse the salient issues that had emerged. There was one matter which Charles was very keen to emphasise.

"The clients have come to us for advice. So, after discussing all the necessary points, make certain that your final view is very clear, and that the clients are not left in any doubt as to what you consider to be the course of action they should adopt. Whenever possible, always be clear, precise and constructive." Indeed Charles never adopted the archetypal approach so often attributed to lawyers of 'on the one hand, on the other hand'. Not for him the pusillanimous approach, the safe refuge of the ultra-cautious lawyer. He impressed me so much with the piece of advice I have quoted above that, whenever possible, I have always followed it.

It was a joy to be a pupil of Charles and generally to be in 4 PC. The set consisted of a genuinely friendly group of people, all of whom were unfailingly ready to assist and to be as helpful as they could be. It was, I would like to think, possibly a two-way street. By that time I had written the book on Capital Gains Tax with Ash Wheatcroft, and had started writing my magnum opus, *Whiteman and Wheatcroft on Income Tax*. As a result, many members of Chambers did ask for my thoughts on a particular tax issue when they had a difficult set of papers. Needless to say, I found that immensely flattering.

So matters were progressing very well at 4 PC. I had been welcomed into the Chambers, I liked my fellow barristers, the work was extremely interesting, and I was exceptionally lucky in having Charles as my pupil-master. What more could one ask for? A tenancy, being a permanent member of Chambers, of course. The question on every pupil's mind throughout their pupillage is, "Will they take me on?" And of course I was no different. In the early months I did not expect any indication of my prospects at 4 PC – it was far too soon. But the two-way flow of exchange of views was very encouraging. How I wanted to be a member of 4 PC! It was my dream. It was my ultimate aim in life, but there was a very black cloud on the horizon which was threatening to shatter everything I was hoping for. As I have related in the previous chapter, I was completely convinced I had failed the Bar examinations. I was awaiting with a sense of foreboding the results, which were to be published in July 1967. I remember so clearly, at that time, after I had started my second six-month pupillage at Pump Court, walking across the courtyard and thinking that I loved being there. Everything was going so well; there had to be a real possibility that I would be accepted as a tenant. Then the reality hit me. That was a wonderful aspiration, but given what had happened with the Bar examinations, there was little chance of that. However, as previously mentioned, I did pass the Bar examinations, and the black cloud that had hung over my prospects of success at the Bar and the possibility of a tenancy at 4 PC was lifted.

Even so, months passed by and there was no reference at all as to what would happen at the end of my pupillage. And then one day Charles said to me, "Would you like to be my guest for dinner at the Travellers' Club? The food is not particularly outstanding, but it is a very pleasant place to dine." I was, of course, absolutely thrilled and very excited by this invitation, which came out of the blue. No need to pause for thought, not when I was hoping to become a tenant at 4 PC. So my response was immediate, "I would love to." Quite apart from the fact that Charles was always good company, particularly in a social setting, an invitation to dinner surely must augur well for my future at 4 PC.

The designated evening duly arrived. I had never been to a London Club before, and although I did not expect it to be an exciting venue, it did seem to be a particularly dreary ambience for dinner. Brown wood everywhere. Members speaking in hushed tones and waiters creeping around in a somewhat subservient way. The waiter duly brought the menu (as I was a guest, mine showed no prices) and, even by the poor standards of cooking in the 1960s, the list of fare was very uninspiring. I cannot remember the main courses, but for a reason which will emerge later, I will never forget the list of starters. Indeed, that may well be regarded as far too grand a description of the three items that were available to commence the meal: tomato juice, that bizarre idea that existed in the 1960s that a glass of fruit juice could be a 'course'; Brown Windsor soup, a tasteless soup that mercifully has long ceased to be on any menu (indeed, what was it made of?); and caviar. I looked at this terribly boring menu, and as the first two starters could not have been less interesting, and as my brain was in the 'off' position, I ordered the caviar. What was I thinking of? It must have been that no thought passed through my mind, other than the one that caviar was the only thing worth eating. In retrospect, I ask myself if my lack of a sophisticated upbringing was showing through in this incident, or is that just a pathetic excuse for committing an appalling gaffe? Charles, of course, being the perfect gentleman he was, did not flinch (at least not outwardly) and duly ordered the caviar for his guest. On the other hand, Charles being also the modest man he was, ordered the tomato juice. The contrast could not have been greater. His selection of a starter should have sounded alarm bells in my mind, but sadly it did not, nor did it affect my appetite. In due course I tucked into the caviar, my first experience of this delectable treat, and thoroughly enjoyed it. Now there's a surprise! Indeed, I enjoyed the whole evening; as I have already mentioned, Charles was a delightful companion, a wonderful raconteur, and so the conversation flowed. Later on, as we parted company on the steps of the Club, I had a very warm glow. I had enjoyed the evening immensely and felt that surely such a convivial evening must have helped my chances of getting that highly sought-after prize, a tenancy at 4 PC. Later that night the reality of what had occurred hit me. As I sat up in bed in the middle of the night, I realised the enormity of the faux pas I had made. I had ordered something without thinking about the cost of it – how incredibly stupid and thoughtless! On reflection I was appalled by the way I had behaved. On an evening when I obviously wanted to make the best possible impression, I had committed a cardinal sin – at a very significant cost to my pupil-master and, by now, my dear friend. I woke up in wet sheets for weeks after that. Charles, being Charles, never referred to the incident. My behaviour that evening was not the ideal way to further my prospects of being offered a tenancy.

My agonising about the evening ended to an extent when, to my great surprise, after my foolish indiscretion, Charles invited me out to dinner again at the Travellers' Club. I was determined not to repeat the error of my previous ways, and to select the cheapest items on the menu. If I could have limited my order to a bread roll and a tomato juice, I would have done so. Anyway, I chose the simplest items on the menu, and hoped that I had redeemed myself.

October had come and gone. November likewise, and now in December the end of my pupillage was in sight. But still no word about my prospects of a tenancy. I could think of little else. And then the night that my pupillage was to come to an end, I was chatting to Charles about the Consultation he had just held. But still nothing was mentioned about my future at 4 PC. I felt that the time had come for me to take the bull by the horns and raise the issue. Nothing ventured, nothing gained. Fortunately, before I could say anything which might be construed as inappropriate, Charles said, "So it's back to academia for you next term. Are you looking forward to it?" I gathered up every ounce of courage I could muster and said, very diffidently, "Well, actually I was hoping to become a tenant here." It was, of course, a somewhat presumptuous statement to make, but in my defence I can say that nobody had told me that I would not be taken on as a tenant. The subject had simply never been mentioned. Charles was obviously surprised by my comment and taken aback by what I had said. "So you want to stay on as a tenant? Nobody told me that. I was under the distinct impression that you were doing a pupillage here to gain practical experience which would help you with your teaching at the LSE. I had no idea that you wanted to stay on and be a tenant here." So, unless I had spoken out, I could have left 4 PC without a tenancy simply because everyone there thought that I was merely doing a pupillage to gain practical experience for teaching. That night I learnt a valuable lesson for life – if there is no downside, make sure that everyone knows what your objectives are. Don't allow any room for misunderstandings.

"Now I see," said Charles, with emphasis. "I always thought you were a very practical person and that you were attracted by the Bar, but then I heard you were an academic who wanted some practical experience." The expression on his face said it all. He was clearly taken by surprise, and was trying to absorb this new information quickly. It was obvious he was thinking hard. And then he exclaimed, "Wait there!" I am sure his words were not meant to sound like a command to a dog, but they did. And with that he jumped to his feet, looking most elegant in his court attire, ran out of his room and along the corridor, coat tails flying, and dashed down the stairs from his second-floor room to the first, where Hubert, the Head of Chambers, had his room. Within what seemed like seconds, he came bounding back up the stairs to his room where, in accordance with his instructions, I had been waiting patiently like the dog who had received a command. As he came through the door of his room, he said, "You're in!" This was the second time in my life that those wonderful words had been said to me. When John Griffith used them at my interview for a place at the LSE, I was overjoyed. No less so this time, maybe even more so. Charles continued, "I have spoken to Hubert and he says you can start as a tenant immediately." So again I was overjoyed by receiving such sudden, unexpected and dramatic news. It may be almost impossible for a Bar student these days to accept that a pupil could become a tenant in a first-rate set of Chambers in the manner I have described, but this was the 1960s and matters proceeded in a very different way at the Bar at that time. Charles and Hubert had had what seemed to be a two-second discussion and that was that. No formal procedure whatsoever had been followed. There was no transparency of any kind relating to my admission to Chambers. This was as opaque as it could be. No written application for a tenancy; no formal interview; no consideration of any other candidates; no conferring with other members of Chambers to consider their views, let alone a Chambers meeting to discuss all of the above. Absolutely nothing of that kind; just a two-second discussion between two members of Chambers, with the others being informed in due course. That evening was one of the truly great nights of my life. So eventful, so dramatic, and a decision that would set me on a path that I have followed to this day.

There was an incident towards the end of my time at 4 PC that left everyone there laughing almost to the point of hysteria. But let me set the scene for the incident which caused so much mirth.

One room in Chambers, occupied by Stewart Bates QC, was rather separate from the rest. Its semi-isolation plays a part in this story. In his room Stewart had a long, unusually wide and very comfortable sofa. The staff in Chambers knew that Stewart never came in on a Saturday – that is also relevant to the story. But on one Saturday he decided to go to his room to carry out some research for a pending Consultation. On arriving at the door to his room, he found he could not obtain entry by using his key. The door had been locked against him from the inside. As he tried yet again to enter, the noise that he created seemed to cause alarm within. There was something of a commotion behind the door. Stewart heard voices. One was Alfred's, the other was a female voice. It was apparent to Stewart that the two were taken by surprise, and equally clearly that they were alarmed and horrified by the attempt of someone (obviously Stewart) to gain access. More excited, almost hysterical talking between Alfred and his companion, then complete silence ensued. Stewart realised what had been happening (and indeed thought that this might have been a regular Saturday afternoon tryst for the amorous participants). In order to leave everyone's honour intact, Stewart decided to leave. On the following Monday Stewart, being a very moral person and wishing to ensure that there was no repetition of such questionable behaviour, ordered the sofa to be removed from his room. He gave the order to Alfred (whose face was even redder than usual), without giving any reason for the despatch of his beloved sofa or elaborating in any way on the background to this sudden decision, but Alfred must have known why. Stewart was unable to keep the news of this incident to himself, and so he related it to another trusted member of Chambers, telling him not to repeat the story to anyone else. But barristers thrive on gossip and the Bar is a village. And nothing is more highly prized than gossip about a Senior Clerk, particularly when it is of a salacious nature. That Monday, laughter could be heard ringing around Chambers as one tenant told another what had taken place on the previous Saturday, and there was considerable speculation as to the identity of the other party to the assignation in Stewart's room. I know, but I have no intention of revealing the lady's name.

That day, and thereafter for a while, as Alfred walked past tenants in Chambers, any laughter would evaporate amidst many knowing nods and winks. There was also much sniggering behind hands held in front of faces. Alfred's reputation never recovered and an indication of that was that members of Chambers started to call him 'Alf' to his face. Interestingly, Alf, given his reduced status, never appeared to object to the use of this diminutive. No one ever referred to the incident in Alf's presence; it was a no-go area. However, it did amuse the members of Chambers for a long while. Being such a wonderful item of gossip, word of the incident spread and subsequently did the rounds of other Chambers. Needless to say, the persons who enjoyed the story most were Senior Clerks in other sets of Chambers, who so relished the retelling of such a spicy story.

I spent 9½ wonderful years at 4 PC and only left there in the happiest of circumstances, having taken a decision which 4 PC supported in every way. In those years I established a very busy Junior's practice, very often having three Conferences in a single afternoon. That thought is now almost unbelievable, particularly given that since July 2009 I have limited myself to one Consultation <u>a week</u>. I was also in court very frequently – a somewhat unusual experience for a young junior barrister in those days. I very often appeared with Charles, and with Michael Nolan QC (who later succeeded Hubert as Head of Chambers and became Lord Nolan), as their Junior, and that, of course, was always a most stimulating experience. Both were extremely accomplished advocates, and their preparation and presentation of their Briefs was always meticulous. For a young Junior like myself, it was entirely appropriate for me to write, as I did on the first page of my notes of every court hearing, "Listen and learn." And, indeed, I learnt an enormous amount from my appearances in court with the Silks of 4 PC.

I have said that I spent 9½ wonderful years at 4 PC. So why did I leave? It seemed to me at the time, and indeed even now on reflection, for the very best of reasons. In 1975 I had conceived the idea of an exciting venture based on an innovative concept. It was a dream, but I was determined to realise it, and I felt I was the right person to do so. However, I did accept that, to succeed, it would be essential to have the encouragement and support of a significant number of highly-placed individuals. I was so enthusiastic about my vision that I could only hope that my excitement in creating such a concept would capture their imaginations. And in the latter part of 1975 and throughout 1976 it did, and to an extent that I could never have realistically expected. And this despite the fact that what I was proposing was without precedent. The challenges along the way were numerous and significant, but I never for one moment considered abandoning what I was seeking to create. Indeed, as more and more people came on board, the venture created a momentum of its own. Support from highly-placed sources in itself incentivised others to join in what they saw to be an exciting but soundly-based enterprise. And so there was no way that I could disappoint those who had already shown their faith in me and what I was proposing. Nor did I wish to do so. There was only one way to go – forward – to realise my ambition to take the organisation of barristers' chambers into the twenty-first century.

CHAPTER 12

A PARTY HERALDS
A NEW DAWN

"My advice to you is to get married: if you find a good wife,
you'll be happy; if not, you'll become a philosopher."
SOCRATES

It was going to be difficult, perhaps very difficult. But it was certainly not impossible. If being told that something was impossible never dissuaded me from my objective, then thinking it was difficult certainly would not. But it had to be handled delicately and sensitively. Clearly they were attracted to each other and they were talking in a very animated way. Further delay would not help. She was a very attractive girl, laughing a lot, with a wonderful smile. She also had the most beguiling dimples in her cheeks when she laughed. However, the problem was that the two of them were sitting on a sofa which would only accommodate three at a pinch – at a distinct pinch. But then came a small breakthrough in implementing my strategy. The game was definitely worth the candle.

The breakthrough, although of minor significance, might be crucial to my entire strategy. Because it was then I realised that I knew the man on the sofa, Martin. At least it gave me an intro, and that was something I desperately needed. The quarry spotted, it was time to pounce, without, if possible, giving the impression of pouncing. I casually – or at least at the time I thought it was casual – made my way across the room. We were in the sitting room of the home of the parents of my friend, Michael Horowitz. The house was in Stanmore. The date was 29 December 1969. I had arrived a little late and the party was in full swing by the time I got there. Hence the sofa was already occupied by Martin and 'quarry'.

There was no option but to go up to them with a big smile, full of bonhomie, radiating friendliness in every direction. First objective, to dispose of Martin, but of course in the nicest possible way. Up I went. "Martin, how very nice to see you!" Bearing in mind how animated his conversation with 'quarry' was, I doubted whether he was silently reciprocating my sentiment.

"How are you?" Martin said very neutrally. "And this is …" looking in 'quarry's' direction. "I am sorry, I've forgotten your name." I thought, not a smart move, Martin. If you have any designs on this young lady, it is very bad news not to make the attempt to remember her name.

"Kate Ellenbogen," said 'quarry'. I made the usual pleasant comments while I introduced myself. Sure as hell, I wasn't going to forget her name. Listen and learn, Martin. "Do you mind if I join you?" I said. Did I detect a snarl on Martin's face? It was probably that he could see an opportunity slipping from his grasp because of this interloper. But worse was to come for him because I sat down on the sofa – between them! That was going to be the end of their cosy tête-à-tête – so much was obvious to Martin, I am sure. With the three of us sitting there (me in the middle), it was very cosy indeed, with Martin and Kate being pressed into the arms of the sofa. Cosy after a while became uncomfortable and, as Martin's tête-à-tête with Kate had somewhat abruptly been brought to a halt and was replaced by my convivial conversation with her, Martin decided that the time had come for him to 'circulate'. He left us with good grace and went off to 'mingle'. Objective achieved. I hoped not too single-mindedly so as to cause offence. But this was the prettiest girl that I had seen in a very long while, particularly with those enchanting dimples when she smiled, which she did often.

The impression I had made on Kate was clearly not an adverse one, and as a result we spent the whole evening together. Kate showed no sign of wanting to be elsewhere at the party and I really felt my luck was in. Maybe 1969 was going to go out with a bang. I had met a very attractive, lively and entertaining girl and the omens, as limited as they were, looked quite promising.

When the evening ended, we were still together and naturally I offered her a lift home. I was delighted when she accepted, and even more so when I discovered she lived in Maida Vale. The journey from Stanmore to Maida Vale is quite long and it would give me more precious time alone with this attractive girl. I have no recollection of the journey, except that the conversation, always interesting, always lively, always fun, never faltered. I was happy and sad when we arrived at Kate's flat in Maida Avenue – both for obvious reasons. Happy because I had met a girl who could only be described as sparkling, and sad because the evening was over. I had great expectations. I received a favourable response when I asked about going out together, and so we arranged that I would telephone her to see her soon. Things were looking good.

After two abortive attempts to fix a date, it was third time lucky and Kate agreed to meet me the following Saturday. I took her to a small intimate French restaurant just off St Martin's Lane. We had the most wonderful evening together, enjoying every minute of each other's company. And, as they say, "The rest is history."

From January 1970, we saw each other almost daily. I was always keen to arrange the next date each time we met and then looked forward to it with the greatest anticipation.

As the months passed and I saw Kate on a very regular basis, we realised we had an enormous amount in common. We both loved the opera, theatre, museums, art galleries and, indeed, everything artistic that London had to offer. Of all these interests, opera was our great passion. Our enjoyment of it, whether at the Royal Opera House, Glyndebourne, Verona, Torre del Lago or elsewhere, increased over the years. But there were so many other things we enjoyed together, particularly being in the countryside. We went on many holidays to Drumnadrochit, near Inverness, where Kate's uncles had a family home, Clunemore. And then there was a further passion we shared – a love of good food and in particular of dining in good (but usually inexpensive) restaurants.

It was also clear to family and friends that our relationship was becoming a very close one as the spring of 1970 gave way to summer. We even started to make plans for a summer holiday together in Sicily. We would drive there, and then enjoy all its wonderful treasures, and spend over three weeks in each other's company doing so. That was a real indication of how close our relationship was becoming. After our holiday everybody seemed to be expecting news of an engagement.

In the autumn of 1970 we did get engaged and our respective parents were thrilled. We subsequently married at St John's Wood Liberal Synagogue on 24 October 1971. There were four hundred guests at the reception, which was held, to my great joy, at Lincoln's Inn.

Above: My wedding to Kate, 24 October 1971

A wonderful honeymoon in the West Indies was seriously marred by a car accident in Grenada. Kate was thrown some 30 feet from the car and suffered back injuries, which left her with very unsightly scars. When people came to help us, I only remember one thing – Kate saying again and again, "You must find my husband's glasses – he will be lost without them." Not a word about her own injuries. As the reader will already know from Chapter 1, tragically this was not to be the last car accident in which we were involved. It foretold the future some thirty-eight years later.

CHAPTER 13

WE ARE A FAMILY WITH A DOG

"The importance of the family is vital to the health of our society
and it is vital to uphold it."
Engagements, 4 May 1989
MARGARET THATCHER

A family is never complete without a dog. Every family needs a dog. Or at least that was our opinion. Of all the breeds, our view was that the Jack Russell terrier is by far the best. So one of the first major decisions we made after we got married was to buy a Jack Russell puppy in 1972, which we called Haggis. It was the first of three dogs we have had: Haggis was in due course followed by Thistle (1986–2003) and Truffle (2003 onwards). Each of them has been an absolute joy to own, and unsurprisingly in recent years I have become very close to Truffle, also a Jack Russell, who is my mate and lifetime supporter.

At this time we were living in Clapham – to be precise, in a house on Clapham Common North Side, which was originally built in 1694. It was right on the Common and so had wonderful views. It was part of the house which originally stood at the entrance to The Chase Estate – it was the lodge. Hence the road in Clapham which still bears the name 'The Chase'.

We had decided in 1971 that we would purchase a house in London which had some green space nearby. There was never any doubt we would live in London – I was practising at the Bar from Lincoln's Inn and Kate was working for the BBC in Langham Place. So we decided on Clapham, which ticked all the boxes.

I remember our days in Clapham with the greatest affection. So many good things happened to us there. Our elder daughter, Victoria, was born at St Thomas' Hospital on 13 March 1975, with me in attendance. We brought her home to Clapham and were immensely proud of her.

Of those very early days I recall two experiences which took place in the Clapham kitchen, both of which foreshadowed what Victoria would be like when she grew up. The first related to food, which from the outset she took very seriously, and still does. At every birthday party, when Kate's delicious display of food was put on the table, Victoria considered the choices very carefully. She made her selection from the various delicacies after much deliberation, and then slowly and very carefully ate her way through them. But oh so seriously. It was as though she was considering the terms of a peace treaty, clause by clause. This was a very serious business and it showed on her worried little face. Such careful deliberation meant that she was always the last at the table, and long after the guests had gone off to play games, there was Victoria still sitting at the table in splendid isolation, munching away so very seriously. We have many photographs of her sitting at her various birthday parties, always alone, working her way through all thevarious 'goodies'. Her appreciation of good food continued to develop over the years and she has become a real gourmet, dining at some of London's best restaurants. The second memory of those Clapham days was one morning when Victoria was very young and I came down to the kitchen tosay goodbye to her before I went off to work. She was waiting for her breakfast in her high chair, but as yet it had not arrived. The tray on her high chair was empty except for a small dishcloth. I asked her for a kiss. Victoria was never a tactile baby or child and basically avoided kisses whenever she could. But on this occasion her avoidance options were very limited. She was stuck in her high chair and she couldn't even escape a kiss by saying she was eating. She wasn't. So I asked again, "May I have a kiss, please?" as I leaned forward towards her.

"No!"

"Why not?"

She looked around, bereft of ideas. She spotted the dishcloth on her tray, and an idea came to her almost immediately. She picked up the dishcloth and started moving it around the tray, as though she were cleaning it. She was clearly pleased now that she had an 'out'.

"Because I'm busy in my high chair!"

Game, set and match to Victoria! I was outclassed and I had to admit defeat because of her inventiveness. Needless to say, the phrase "I'm busy in my high chair!" became a family saying, which after all these years of repetition still makes me smile.

Kate and I decided to have a second child in 1977. No sooner had we conceived the idea than we conceived the baby. But then Caroline has never been one to wait for the grass to grow under her feet. In December 1977 she bounced into an unsuspecting world. Victoria had always been a somewhat serious child. By contrast, Caroline was always light-hearted, looking for fun and making very witty comments. She made so many comical remarks that I kept what Caroline in due course called her 'Funny Book', in which I recorded many of her witticisms. Indeed, when we burst out laughing at something she had said, she would turn to me and ask, "Daddy, will you write that in your Funny Book?" And I did.

One comment of Caroline's that was particularly appealing was when we were about to embark on a long car journey and we had told her it would take some four hours before we would arrive at our destination.

Despairingly, from the back of the car, came a cry of, "What am I going to do? It's going to be very boring."

An idea occurred to me. "Why don't you write a story? That will keep you busy. Why don't you write a nice children's story which begins, 'Once upon a time' and ends 'And they lived happily ever after'?"

No response from the back seat. Complete silence. She took out a pencil and a pad of paper. Still no response. I looked back. She was looking at a blank piece of paper and clearly thinking very hard about the story she was going to write, and maybe (the author's usual problem) how to start her magnum opus. Still no word from the soon-to-be-famous author. So I enquired, "Why aren't you writing anything? What's your problem?" More silence, and then, after this long pause, the reason that she was so troubled emerged.

"What comes after 'W' in 'Once'?"

We all collapsed into laughter. Caroline didn't understand why. But, of course, that did go into the Funny Book.

From the time Victoria was born, and certainly from the time she started at nursery school, it was clear she was very bright indeed. We were still living in Clapham, and Kate and I set our sights on James Allen's Girls' School (JAGS) in Dulwich as the school that had everything to offer as far as Victoria was concerned. We visited the school, went through the selection processes, and the result was that at the age of 3½ Victoria was awarded a scholarship to JAGS. We were, of course, absolutely delighted.

Victoria's education for the foreseeable future was now assured (in the event, she stayed there until she was 17). But Dulwich, although relatively near to Clapham, was a very difficult drive during the school rush hours. The idea of driving to Dulwich and back every day for so many years was a most unappealing prospect. We would, as so many parents had done before us, follow our child to her school, and live in Dulwich. However, apart from our occasional forays to see JAGS and deal with the admission procedures involved, we knew little or nothing about it, except, of course, the excellence of its schools.

The decision to move to Dulwich was easy to take – finding a suitable house there was a very different proposition. We decided on a 'full frontal assault' on the Dulwich property market. So in 1978 we had the temerity to walk up and down Dulwich Village, knocking on the doors of some of the most beautiful houses there and asking, "Are you thinking of selling your house?" I shudder as I now recall this episode – the cheek of it! However, Dulwich being Dulwich, all the householders who opened their doors were polite in the extreme. But the answer, however tactfully put, was the same, "No."

Then we came to a particularly delightful house. Kate and I loved it at first sight; it was not too large, beautifully proportioned, and an exquisite example of a Georgian residence. So we walked up to the front door. We rang the doorbell and after a short delay there appeared a quietly-spoken and charming man.

"We are very sorry for disturbing your Sunday afternoon, but we are hoping to purchase a house in Dulwich and we were wondering if you were thinking of selling yours."

"No. I haven't even considered it."

Our hearts sank; another rejection. But, on the other hand, knocking on doors of expensive, highly sought-after houses and expecting to receive a positive answer to our question was, as we recognised, a 'long shot'.

The owner hesitated, obviously thinking carefully, and said, "But…". And then there was a long pause. My spirits lifted as I wondered whether the silence indicated there might be a ray of hope as far as purchasing this house was concerned.

"But now you come to mention it, my only daughter is getting married next month and this house will be much too large for two people, so, although I have not thought about it before, yes … maybe we might be interested in selling, although, of course, I will have to discuss it with my wife."

Kate and I could hardly believe what the owner had said. After so many rejections that day, we might have struck gold. Never backward in coming forward, I thought we should press home any advantage there might be that afternoon.

"Well, in that case," I asked, "would it be too much to ask if we might look round the house? I hope that would not disturb your afternoon too much." On reflection, what amazing chutzpah! But David (as we subsequently discovered his name to be) was a gentleman, and he readily agreed.

Kate and I could not believe our luck. This, one of the most beautiful houses in Dulwich, might become ours one day. The exterior was stunning and the interior was equally beautiful. Kate and I smiled at each other as we walked round the house.

When the time came to leave, we told the owner, David, we would be putting in an offer for the property. As we made our way across the front garden, we were walking on air. Our bold strategy had seemed to work, at least so far. So in due course, without any complications, the house became ours. Our nerve in approaching the owner direct had paid off. I adored the property then and I adore it now, perhaps even more so. I have always regarded it as a privilege to live there and I have been so lucky to be able to enjoy it.

However, there is a final sad twist to the story of our purchase of this house that no one could anticipate. In October 1979, about a year after we had moved in, there was a knock at the door. I opened it and, to my great surprise, there was David. "Do you remember me?" he said. How could I possibly forget him – he was the person who made us so happy by agreeing to sell to us. I invited him in, but he declined. "Well, do you remember that I said on the afternoon we met that I would sell the house because it would be too large for only two people to live in? Well, very sadly, my daughter is getting divorced after just a year of marriage and wants to return to live with us. The house we purchased last year, when we sold to you, is too small for the three of us and I wondered if there was any chance that you might sell the house back to us."

I felt absolutely terrible. As David had behaved so well towards us, and as obviously his family was going through a traumatic situation, I really wished I had been able to help him. I was desperately trying to find words which would put my negative response to him as tactfully as possible. "David, if I could do anything to assist you I would. Your behaviour last year when we approached you was impeccable and I would like to respond in kind. But as a family of four, we have now settled here and Victoria is extremely happy at JAGS. We adore the house and so, with the greatest possible reluctance, I fear I have to say no. But if, for whatever reason, our circumstances change so that we decide to move, I promise that you will be the first to know."

He looked downcast and said, "I am not surprised at all. In fact, I couldn't and didn't expect any other answer. But I thought it was worth approaching you, just in case you might say yes. I am very sorry to have troubled you. Please go on enjoying living in this wonderful house. I wish you all the best." He turned and walked away. As he trudged across the front garden, he cut such a pathetic, dispirited figure.

But back to October 1978. We had decided to purchase the Dulwich house and our offer had been accepted. There was one, not exactly small, matter that had to be dealt with – the sale of the Clapham property. Yet here again there was another twist to the story. Our purchaser was Simon, an extremely pleasant, ebullient, hail-fellow-well-met character. In the same way we fell in love with our Dulwich home, he and his wife fell in love with the charm and character of our old home. This sale went through smoothly and provided the necessary funds to enable us to purchase in Dulwich.

Kate and I thought we had obtained a very good price for our sale and we believed that called for a special celebration. So off we went to one of our favourite restaurants. The first glass of celebratory champagne was slipping down very nicely when who should walk in but the purchasers of our old home. After saying, "Fancy seeing you here," Simon asked me, "What are you doing here?" I said, "Well, it is one of our very favourite watering holes and, to be honest, we are celebrating."

"Celebrating what, if I may be so bold?" Simon enquired.

"Now, this is a little tricky," I said. Somewhat embarrassed, but emboldened by the champagne, I continued, "Well you see, Simon, we think we sold our house to you at a very good price. No offence intended, but you did ask!"

"No offence taken!"

"May I ask you the same question, particularly as you are looking so happy?"

Simon responded, "For us it's not the least bit tricky, after what you've just said. You see, Peter, we think we purchased very cheaply." And with a real twinkle in his eye he said, "No offence intended!"

There was no need to reflect on either of our conclusions, or analyse them. There was only one thing to do. We all collapsed into fits of laughter. "This is marvellous. Everyone is happy," I said. "Let's drink to each other because we are all delighted with the outcome."

"Let's have dinner together to celebrate happy endings." And we did. We had a most enjoyable evening – Simon and his wife were great company.

As I said earlier, we left Clapham with the best possible memories of our life there. We arrived there as husband and wife, and left as a family of four with our adorable Haggis. From a family point of view, only good things happened while we lived there, nothing bad. Even now, when I am driving past our old home in Clapham, I can never resist the temptation to look at the house. And when I do, I always get a warm feeling inside as wonderful memories come flooding back.

CHAPTER 14

COWBOYS AND INDIANS

"Never pass up new experiences, Scarlett.
They enrich the mind."
Gone with the Wind
MARGARET MITCHELL

As my Pump Court days were drawing to a close, I received an invitation
from the Dean of the University of Florida to teach a course in International
Tax Law in January 1977. The Dean invited us to stay with him at his
home. I had always wanted to lecture in the United States and this was a
heaven-sent opportunity to visit the USA again and to teach in a stimulating
environment. I accepted the invitation with the greatest alacrity. Kate was
wholly enthusiastic about the idea. We could take Victoria – who by then
would be approaching 2 years of age – and show her the delights of Disney
World. It would be a wonderful opportunity for the family to have a great
time in the much warmer climes of Florida.

Except that they weren't. In January 1977 Florida had its first substantial
falls of snow for thirty years. And it was really deep. We had expected our
destination to be much warmer, so it was quite a surprise to see snow-
covered Florida as we landed at Jacksonville Airport. Never daunted, we
hired a car and set off in the snow for the Dean's house. Needless to say,
Victoria was extremely excited, first at seeing the snow and secondly
because we had told her that she was going to see Mickey Mouse and
Donald Duck at Disney World.

As we drove to the Dean's house, we saw a most beautiful carpet of snow
covering the countryside. The snow was everywhere. On the ground, on the
fields and on the houses – just like a Monet or Sisley painting. It even made
Jacksonville, not the prettiest of towns, look beautiful.

We had an extremely enjoyable time in Florida, despite the snow, and

Victoria adored Disney World which, because of the weather, was almost deserted. Dispiriting for the owners, but fantastic for us, as there were no queues for any of the attractions. There was one in particular that Victoria adored above all the others and which fascinated her. Indeed it entranced her – the Wild West Show. All the attendants outside the attraction were dressed as cowboys – ten-gallon hats, leather jackets, blue jeans and long cowboy boots with silver spurs. Victoria had seen cowboy films on television but had never understood they could be real people. At first, being fascinated by them, she kept a safe distance. But then she gathered up her courage, went over to them and gently touched their clothes – no doubt to make sure they were real. The attendants laughed and started to joke with her. Victoria dissolved into fits of giggles. Something she had seen on television had come alive and the actors were playing with her. The whole event to a lively 2-year-old was unbelievable and she found it hilarious. It made the most enormous impression on her; it was the highlight of her trip. Those 'Wild West' actors gave Victoria so much fun. As a result I became far more indulgent in my attitude towards 'Westerns'!

I recall two other incidents from our time in Florida, both of which may be regarded as amusing. The first at the very beginning of our stay at Jacksonville; the second almost at the end.

Our first stop on our trip was, as I have mentioned, the home of the Dean of the Faculty, with whom we were staying. When we arrived at his house, his wife opened the door, but the illustrious Dean was nowhere to be seen.

"Dick is in the television room," his wife explained. "He is watching the Muppets. He adores them and won't miss a single episode for any reason. He will skip or put back the time of meetings, conferences, dinner parties, anything that will prevent him from seeing the Muppets." This was, of course, long before the days of TV video recording. "He sits there like a child, gazing in wonder at their antics, and every so often he lets out howls of laughter." And he did, and we heard them. "He has given me the strictest of instructions, like any other night, he is not to be disturbed by the telephone or your arrival."

So this very famous lawyer, who was the most senior academic at the University of Florida, who guided the fortunes of the University, and who held in his hands the destiny of a very large number of people, was not to be disturbed because of his addiction to the Muppets. I thought this a very strange way to behave, but then, on the other hand, the Dean and his wife, as we discovered subsequently, were the most hospitable of people and did everything to make our visit enjoyable. And the Dean gave me the warmest of welcomes to the Law Faculty and subsequently introduced me to the students with comments that were so complimentary I was somewhat embarrassed.

I enjoyed teaching the students enormously. They were very bright, eager to learn, challenging and charming. What better combination could any teacher expect in a body of students? I reciprocated their enthusiasm and we accordingly had a very constructive relationship. The teaching method used at the University of Florida was the Socratic Method, which involved bringing the students fully into a dialogue with the lecturer on a question-and-answer basis. That method of teaching excited me enormously, particularly as it was almost unknown in the United Kingdom at that time.

Now to the second, somewhat bizarre, incident at the Law School that I alluded to earlier. As my course at Florida drew to a close, I was asked to see the Dean one afternoon. I duly arrived at his palatial academic abode. Yet again I was kept waiting a long while by the Dean. This time outside his office. After a long delay the door suddenly opened and out came a Native American (who at that time were still routinely referred to as Red Indians). His clothes were modern American – T-shirt and jeans – but his features were unmistakably those of a Native American. As he emerged, he was in deep thought and looking very troubled.

When I was ushered into the Dean's office, he apologised immediately. "Peter, I am so sorry to have kept you waiting, but I have had a meeting with a mature, I should say very mature, student. The problem is that this University, like every other public one in the US, is heavily dependent on Federal funding. Each year we have to fill in form after form to be sent to Washington, and some very important ones ask us about the composition of our student body. We have to be able to tick all the right boxes and, if we can't, our Federal support is reduced substantially, or even possibly withdrawn. Now here in Florida we have a significant Red Indian population and we have to state that at least one Red Indian student is enrolled here. If we don't, we suffer, as I have indicated, severe cuts in our Federal support. The student who has just left here is our only Red Indian student. He has been here for twelve years. After the first year he wanted to leave, but we couldn't let him go. That decision has cost us very dearly ever since. Each year we tempt him to stay at the Law School for another year by offering him ever-increasing financial assistance. So far he has accepted, but this year he feels he must go into the big wide world. But as he is our only Red Indian student and none are enrolled to start next year, it is vital that the Law Faculty keeps him. So I have been trying for over an hour, with more and more tempting financial offers, to persuade him to stay. He is tempted by them and I have left him to consider my latest offer. I had to use every means at my disposal – which is only money, really. He is going to think about it. That is why I kept you waiting; I am sorry about that."

I couldn't blame the Dean for taking so much time to use his powers of persuasion for his desired purpose. I could only think that it did seem very bizarre that Federal support should depend on one student's decision as to whether he should stay on – and then for the wrong reason.

The Dean continued, "But the real reason I have invited you here is that you have made a great impression on both the students and the other members of the teaching staff. We would love to have you teach here on a permanent basis. So on behalf of the Law Faculty I would like to offer you the post of Professor of Law on a permanent full-time basis for the future." I had only been teaching at the University for a very short time and so I found this offer of a full-time post immensely flattering. However, as much as I enjoyed teaching at the Law School in Jacksonville, Kate and I both knew that our future, professional and otherwise, was in London. So in due course I graciously declined the Law School's very gratifying offer.

Returning to the meeting with the Dean, I left his office bemused and very surprised by what I had heard. It was all new to me. As I left Jacksonville soon afterwards, I never did discover whether the Native American stayed on. But that, of course, is not really relevant to my story. It was the first time I had come across such a stringently enforced example of positive discrimination.

I shall always remember my days at Jacksonville with the greatest affection, all three of us having had a wonderful time. For me, standing in front of a group of first-rate students thirsting for knowledge, throwing questions at me and vice versa, was a most enjoyable and stimulating experience. I had never enjoyed teaching in England as much as that.

As we drove off to the airport, the snow still covered everything in sight. It had been a wonderful experience, despite, maybe in some way because of, the snow. So in a very cold climate Florida left me with a very warm feeling. The more so because, after our return to London, I received a framed certificate from the University of Florida, thanking me for my outstanding contribution to the teaching of Law at the Law Faculty, and appointing me a Professor of Law at the University for life. I believed it to be a most wonderful, kind gesture from my new colleagues, all of whom had signed the certificate. My love affair with the United States, always strong as I record later, had become even more intense as a result of my visit to Florida.

CHAPTER 15

MY ONE-STOP SHOP OPENS

"I know the price of success: dedication, hard work and
an unremitting devotion to the things you want to see happen."
FRANK LLOYD WRIGHT (1867–1959)

"When I went to the Bar as a very young man,
(Said I to myself – said I),
I'll work on a new and original plan,
(Said I to myself – said I)"
Iolanthe I
W S GILBERT AND A SULLIVAN

Would it succeed? The decision had been made. I knew what I wanted to do. It would be exciting, exceedingly challenging and so very worthwhile. It had never been done before, but it was so obvious that it was the way my profession should develop. Must develop. There was a distinct possibility that my plan might fail because so many factors were outside my control. However, even if I failed, I would have the satisfaction that I had tried. The game was very much worth the candle. I realised that I could only achieve my objective if there were judges and barristers who shared my innovative ambition and who were prepared to support me. The barristers would have to entrust me with their already successful careers. I knew I would be asking a great deal from others, but I could only hope that my excitement at creating a new concept would capture their imagination. I had to hope that they would share my vision of the future and be prepared to take some not inconsiderable risks along the way to see it fulfilled.

I realised that this aspiration could only come about if I was prepared to undertake a wholly new venture. And being me, of course, I was more than prepared to do so. Prepared? It was far more than that. I relished the prospect of being the standard-bearer of an exciting new development at the Bar. One without precedent. Simply put, I wanted to take the Bar forward in a totally different direction. A new initiative was called for and I was the one who should undertake it.

My idea was simple enough and it related to the way specialist Chambers at the Bar operated. At the time it was accepted that specialists at the Bar practised from a set of Chambers where all its members advised on one and the same area of law. So there were, for example, sets of Revenue Chambers, Company Chambers, Commercial Chambers, specialist Chancery sets and so on. My idea, as I say, was simple. Why not bring together various specialists from different but allied areas of the Bar, who became members of the same set, which could accordingly provide specialist advice on a one-stop-shopping basis? So if, for example, a set of Instructions required advice on both Revenue Law and Company Law, the solicitor could go to one set of Chambers and the Clerk could arrange everything under one roof. That would provide a better and more efficient service for solicitors, accountants and their clients.

Of course, also integral to my thinking was that the Chambers I would create would have as tenants the most able practitioners in their particular fields of specialisation. So the aim was a tip-top set of Chambers, very efficiently run, with the most distinguished practitioners of the day bringing their specialist practices to one location. That was the revolutionary concept. That was the dream, and I was determined to realise it. I knew that it would require a considerable amount of effort, planning, foresight and persuasion. Persuasion would be necessary to encourage leading members of the Bar to leave established sets of Chambers to join me in a new untried venture, based on an innovative concept. I could only hope that my excitement at the prospect of introducing such a novel idea to the Bar would be infectious and that others would share my view of the future. It was a daunting undertaking for a relatively young member of the Bar, but I was determined to succeed. I recited my lifetime mantra again, "Anything's possible."

To succeed, my strategy would have to be well constructed, and appear to be so to those I approached. I came to the conclusion, after much reflection, that there would have to be three essential aspects to my plan and that they would have to fall into place in the right order.

The first was that the bold concept I had in mind would only be taken seriously by barristers if they knew I had the support of senior members of the Judiciary. After all, they were being asked to put their careers at risk and would obviously want to be reassured that 'the powers that be' were in favour of the creation of this new set. So I decided the first step was to approach and seek the support of judges who were not only senior, but also well respected by the profession at large. Quite apart from anything else, their views would be a good sounding board for me.

After careful consideration, I decided on the judges who might be entirely appropriate and hopefully sympathetic to my concept. They were very senior judges indeed: Lord Oliver, Lord Scarman, Lord Templeman, Lord Justice Parker and Sir John Arnold. I duly made appointments to see them in their respective rooms at the House of Lords or Royal Courts of Justice. I was warmly welcomed by all of them and they were very supportive, indeed enthusiastic, about what I had in mind. They all promised to do whatever they could to help. I was extremely encouraged by their positive approach. Nor did their offers of support turn out to be hollow words easily spoken in the course of a relaxed conversation. Their support in one respect, as I mention later, turned out to be critical to the foundation of the new set. My first step in taking my plan forward had been more successful than I could ever have dreamed. So now, when I approached any barristers to join me, I could truthfully state that I had the support of five eminent judges. I was now ready to move on to stage two: approaching other members of the Bar to join me in the venture.

I had in mind to approach four highly respected Juniors at the Bar. All were extremely experienced, very successful and clearly destined to take 'Silk' (become a Queen's Counsel) and indeed probably in due course be elevated to the Bench. Moreover, and vitally, they were all charming, delightful people who, if they accepted my invitation, would work well together as colleagues in the new set. They were all very progressive in their attitude to changes at the Bar. They all fitted my template for perfect members of the set, but would they accept my invitation to join me in my new venture? I have said they were all very successful; they all had tenancies in very well respected sets – why should they join me and take a risk with their careers, which they clearly would be doing? I realised it was all down to my powers of persuasion, now so fortunately endorsed by solid judicial support.

So, shortly afterwards, I contacted each of my select band of prospective colleagues. These approaches had to be handled extremely carefully and carried out surreptitiously so that their position in their existing Chambers was not compromised. The only way to proceed was to send handwritten letters, inviting them to come to my Chambers for a personal chat. After all, I could not go to see them! Tongues would start to wag. So I had to engage in real cloak-and-dagger activities. Of course, I had to face the possibility that they would decline my invitation. But, having come so far, and with my new-found enthusiastic judicial support, I had no reason to do anything other than pursue my chosen path with the utmost vigour. But, of course, carefully, secretively and graciously. This, I knew, was going to be a real test of my ability to convince people to make a fundamental change in their professional lives. A particularly tough test for me at that time (the summer of 1975), as I was only 32 and a barrister of only seven years' standing.

In due course I was delighted that all the barristers I had written to accepted my invitation to come and meet me. I was apprehensive before I met each one of them because I knew I had to marshal in the most persuasive way the reasons why they should join me. Somewhat to my amazement, three of them said when I first met them that they were most interested and would feel privileged to join such a forward-looking, progressive set based on such an imaginative idea. The fourth took a little longer to decide, but when he did agree to do so later, he seemed to be equally enthusiastic. With the support of all four, I now had a sufficient number of barristers to make the establishment of the new set viable.

At the time I reflected with pride on the astounding progress I had made in attracting four practitioners who were among the most distinguished of their generation. That they were so highly regarded and successful was confirmed by subsequent events. In due course one became a member of the House of Lords Judicial Committee (now the Supreme Court) and two were elevated to the Court of Appeal. The fourth has become one of the most distinguished and outstanding members of the Revenue Bar. Those subsequent appointments and developments I felt entirely justified my selection of the four in 1975 – and also, very gratifyingly, endorsed my choice of colleagues in the first place.

Overall, the respective practices of the four fulfilled the whole raison d'être of the set – to bring together specialists from different areas of the Bar under one roof. Thus the new Chambers would be perfectly placed to provide specialist advice on Company Law, Commercial Law, Chancery Law and Revenue Law. My vision for the future was becoming a reality.

The second stage of my planning for the new set having fallen into place, I then turned to the practicalities of establishing what was to be 'my' Chambers. At the top of the list were, of course, accommodation and clerking. As far as accommodation was concerned, I had been told on the grapevine that the fourth floor of Queen Elizabeth Building (QEB) was to change from residential accommodation for judges to professional use for a set of Chambers. I lost no time in making it known to Middle Temple (where QEB was located) that I was very interested in becoming the professional tenant of the fourth floor, and in due course I made a formal application in that regard. Everything connected with the new Chambers had been going so well that I was totally crestfallen when I was told my application had been rejected. Never daunted, I decided to play my trump card. If 'my' judges were so supportive of my plans, possibly they could provide me with some assistance in my application for accommodation at QEB.

Of all the judges, Lord Oliver had been particularly outstanding in granting me interview after interview whenever I wanted to seek his guidance about the new Chambers. By now I had seen him many times and his very wise counsel on each occasion had been invaluable in deciding how I should move my plans forward. So he was the obvious choice to advise me on how the accommodation problem might be resolved. I was desperate to obtain the accommodation at QEB because I was very keen that the new set should convey the impression of a modern, progressive and dynamic enterprise. There was only one possible place that fulfilled the vital criteria that I had in mind – QEB. Could Lord Oliver help me to achieve my objective?

Soon after I entered Lord Oliver's room in the Law Corridor of the House of Lords, I realised that I should never have worried. After I had explained the situation, Lord Oliver said simply, "Leave it with me. I shall have words in the appropriate quarter." It was said so clearly, so definitively, that there was obviously no need for me to pursue the matter directly with Middle Temple.

I was very happy to leave the whole issue of accommodation in the capable hands of such a very helpful judge. But I was in for a very big surprise. There followed a conversation which took me back to my discussions in Room E305 with Ash Wheatcroft.

"Peter," Lord Oliver started, "I am very glad you came to see me today, as there is another important matter I have wanted to talk to you about for some time." Now I was a little apprehensive. I need not have been.

"It is very important to us" (I liked the reference to "us") "that this new set is a great success. It will show the rest of the Bar the direction that the profession should take, led by a group of progressive, dynamic and very able practitioners. And the best way, we think, that purpose could be achieved is by the set being led by a Silk. It would show that the powers that be in the legal world wholeheartedly approve of the venture – it would give the set a judicial seal of approval, the imprimatur of the legal establishment. And so, if you took Silk around the time the set began life, that would have the maximum impact on the legal world as showing that we were very firm supporters of the concept. What I am saying is that you should apply for Silk now. The timing is perfect. Applications for Silk close in December (1976) and the result of your application will be known in April, about the time you hope to open the doors of your new Chambers. So the timing could not be better. As for referees, of course I would support you, and I know Leslie (Lord Scarman), John (Sir John Arnold) and Roger (Lord Justice Parker) would all support you as well." So once again my judicial supporters were going to play an invaluable role. I was totally taken by surprise by what I regarded as a complete vote of confidence in me (not just my Chambers) by four such distinguished judges. Once again I could hardly take in this amazing news, although of course it only related to an Application for Silk, and whether it succeeded or not was another matter. However, as I walked back to my then Chambers (4 Pump Court) through Embankment Gardens, I thought that surely, with four judges acting as referees, my chances of success must be reasonably good. I should mention in passing that at that time the norm was to have two referees for an Application for Silk, and possibly one would be a judge. Continuing my walk through the Gardens, I looked to my right to see the Thames shimmering in the autumn sun. I felt life was good. It was being very kind to me. I was so very, very happy about the way everything was proceeding.

For some time I had been chairing fairly frequent meetings of the members of the nascent Chambers. There was an enormous amount to discuss if we were to get the set up and running in the near future. At times the logistics of the operation seemed daunting. But, meeting by meeting, we got through the agenda and made considerable progress.

Matters relating to our existing Chambers required the most careful consideration if we were, as far as possible, to maintain good relations with them. We needed their continuing cooperation to make the transition as smooth as it could be in the circumstances. Although not strictly necessary, we decided to give our respective Chambers an extended period of notice that we were leaving, namely, three months. We also agreed that we would all do this on the same day and at the same time.

So when the day came, at H hour on D-Day, we all told our respective Heads of Chambers of our plans to establish a new set in three months' time. When I told Michael Nolan, my then Head of Chambers, that I was establishing a new set on the basis of bringing together a number of specialists with different areas of expertise, he said, very encouragingly, that he thought it was a "splendid idea". He wished me luck with the new venture and, indeed, went further and said that, if there was any way in which he could assist, he would be more than happy to do so.

Although I had decided that I would not attempt to poach anyone from 4 PC, one day a Senior Clerk, Edna Wittey, approached me, saying, "I understand you are setting up new Chambers. I have always admired you and, if you would have me, I would like to come with you." I jumped at the opportunity of having this very experienced person as my Clerk, particularly as she had a comprehensive knowledge of my practice. This would provide an excellent basis for continuity. I informed Michael Nolan of Edna's approach and he graciously agreed that she could join the new set and, if it would help, she could leave immediately.

The rooms on the fourth floor of QEB were some of the most modern in the Temple. The building was completed in 1952 (hence its name). It had wide, spacious corridors and large light rooms. Nonetheless, it needed considerable work to turn it from residential accommodation into premises fit for professional use. So, in the months before the Chambers opened, I visited QEB every working day to oversee the building and decorating work that had been specified by me. It was time-consuming but absolutely essential.

However, not everything went smoothly on the day we informed our respective Heads of Chambers of our intended departure. One Head of Chambers, George Rink QC, was furious and threatened to make a formal complaint to the Bar Council about my conduct, claiming that it was "ungentlemanly behaviour". I asked myself repeatedly how the action of a group of barristers, combining to form a new set of Chambers with judicial approval, could be regarded as "ungentlemanly behaviour". I regarded this allegation as totally unwarranted. Be that as it may, George Rink did report me to the Bar Council and did make a formal complaint about my conduct. At the initial hearing the Queen's Counsel designated to adjudicate on the complaint threw it out after a very short 'trial'. He then said:

"The hearing is now over and what I am going to say forms no part of it. But I have to say, what a silly old woman! What a stupid complaint to make." The hearing may have been over very quickly, but beforehand it had caused me some real concern, although my conscience was completely clear.

As the New Year started (1977), I became increasingly anxious about the outcome of my Application for Silk. It was my first Application for Silk and the received wisdom at the Bar at that time was that a first application rarely succeeded. The point of a first application was to put one's name on the ladder so that, by the time of the second, third or, more likely, fourth application, a track record had been established and the coveted letters 'QC' were then hopefully conferred on the applicant.

At that time the names of the new successful candidates for Silk were always published in *The Times* on Maundy Thursday. With the uncertainty about whether my application had succeeded, ensuring that QEB opened on the designated date, and resolving the professional and other problems that arose with Middle Temple, my time in those early months of 1977 was fully occupied. I had decided to take on the full burden of all these tasks myself and, although they were very demanding, I did so enthusiastically. The set was, by agreement of all the prospective tenants, to be known as 'The Chambers of Peter Whiteman QC'. So if I was to enjoy the kudos of having an eponymous set, it was only reasonable that I should shoulder the responsibility of ensuring that everything that needed to be done before the Chambers opened had been achieved.

The agreed date for the opening of the new Chambers, 26 March 1977, duly arrived. However, the view of the supporting judges that this was a very welcome development at the Bar was not shared by all lawyers. One partner in a leading firm of solicitors was heard to remark that a set of Chambers consisting of specialists from different areas of the Bar was not appropriate, as it undermined the very basis upon which firms of solicitors were established. He stated that he would never instruct anyone in the new set and, to my knowledge, given his prejudice, he never did.

There was no special ceremony to mark the opening of Chambers. We opted for a low-key celebration consisting of wine and canapés shared with a few selected legal friends. For me, it was of course a case of one down and one to go. It was still nine days before I would know whether my Application for Silk had succeeded. This was a nerve-racking time for me. Each day seemed an eternity, and concentrating on a set of papers placed before me was a real challenge.

D-Day was 6 April 1977. That was the day the letter from the Lord Chancellor's Department should arrive, informing me of my fate. I could hardly wait, but I was fully prepared for my application to be unsuccessful. I was so excited and apprehensive that I arrived in Chambers early – at about 8.15 am. Nobody else was there. The post had already been delivered to the Clerks' Room. It was never necessary to open the letter to see whether the application had succeeded. The size, colour and weight of the envelope told the whole story. A small brown envelope of little weight meant failure. All it would say was, "The Lord Chancellor regrets …". A large white, bulky envelope, on the other hand, indicated success, the weight being attributable to all the information the applicant needed to have about the forthcoming New Silks Ceremony. I rifled through the pile of post and there it was – the most beautiful envelope I have ever seen. Large, white and bulky! I could hardly believe it; I was overcome with happiness. My legs were shaking. I took the envelope into my room in Chambers; I could barely contain my emotion. My hands were shaking too as I opened the precious envelope. Yes, I had succeeded. I read the rest of the letter and the further information provided for new Silks. I read it all, but on that first reading I didn't absorb a word. The only thought in my mind was that I had succeeded. I would be a Silk! I would now be 'Peter Whiteman QC'. It was just incredible how far

Above: Taking Silk – on the way to the House of Lords

the boy from Walthamstow had progressed, and it reinforced my mantra that anything is possible. What a momentous ten days! There has never been such a fantastic ten days in my professional life, and how could there ever be again?

I sat in my room and what I had achieved started to sink in. I regarded myself as extremely fortunate to have been elevated to the rank of Queen's Counsel after only nine years' practice at the English Bar. In fact, because it was such an exceptional application, I had checked at the time with the Lord Chancellor's Department whether a barrister of less than ten years' standing could be appointed a Silk. The answer was in the affirmative, but save in highly exceptional cases, such as distinguished overseas barristers coming to England to practise, it had not occurred, if at all, for a very considerable time. But still I had gone ahead with my application. As far as I am aware, no other barrister practising at the English Bar for less than ten years had ever been appointed Queen's Counsel. Also, I was only 34 and, according to the *Guinness Book of Records*, I was the second youngest Queen's Counsel ever. Only Lord Evershed was younger; he was appointed at the age of 33. I was then, and still am now, very proud of those two achievements. When I next went to see Lord Oliver, he congratulated me on my appointment as a Queen's Counsel and added very significantly, "It is a tremendous boost to the new Chambers and a mark of recognition of the new set by the legal establishment."

Among the many letters of congratulation I received, the one that stands out from all the others said, "How courageous it was to open a new set of Chambers and take Silk within the space of ten days!" The writer was being tactful; for "courageous", probably one should have read 'foolhardy'. Courageous or foolhardy, my initiative, enthusiasm and determination to do something unprecedented at the Bar had become a reality with a new set led by a Silk. Other people clearly had faith in me and now I had to justify that faith by working even harder and applying myself as diligently as I could to being a good Head of Chambers.

My overall aim was to ensure that the new Chambers and all its tenants should succeed. That was paramount. After all, the other tenants of the new Chambers had also shown great faith in me by agreeing to leave their previous sets and join me in the new venture. They had taken a significant risk with their professional careers and I owed it to them to do my utmost to make QEB a resounding success. Looking back on it now, some forty years later, I am amazed by the decisions I took then. And even more so that others were prepared to stand alongside me. I shudder to think now of the risk I was taking with our professional careers. What it is to be young and so full of enthusiasm, excitement and ambition! I say that because it was then, and is even now, highly unusual for a member of the Bar to take the step of establishing his own Chambers. But to do so at the age of 34 was, to my knowledge, again without precedent. A risky step to take at any age at the Bar, it was at that time unheard of and I was so gratified by the flood of congratulations that came in.

After 7 April 1977 we had many celebrations at home for family and friends, and more letters of congratulation arrived each day. But the next big event was the New Silks Ceremony at the House of Lords on 19 April. A very formal ceremony, but clearly a once-in-a-lifetime experience and accordingly to be savoured as such. Although the day the announcement appeared in *The Times* was momentous, this day was the really big one. First I dressed in the formal attire of a Queen's Counsel at my new Chambers and then I was driven to the House of Lords. There the newly-appointed Silks were to be presented in order of seniority to the Lord Chancellor to receive their Letters Patent – the court document stating that it conferred upon the recipient the appointment as 'One of Her Majesty's Counsel learned in the Law'. The Letters Patent were signed by Her Majesty The Queen. Having assembled at the Peers' Entrance of the House of Lords, the new Silks processed to the Moses Room. There each new Silk stood up and made a Declaration that he would "well and truly serve Her Majesty Queen Elizabeth II and all whom I may lawfully be called upon to serve in the office of one of Her Majesty's Counsel learned in the Law according to the best of my skill and understanding". After I had read the Declaration, I resumed my seat.

The Letters Patent were then presented by the Lord Chancellor, Lord Elwyn-Jones, to each new Silk in turn. I knew the Lord Chancellor well, as I had appeared as his Junior in a number of cases. He was a most wonderful man with a tremendous sense of humour. I liked him enormously and we were great friends. When I stepped forward to receive my Letters Patent, there was Elwyn, positively beaming. As I stood there, he uttered words I will never forget: "Peter, I am so glad the honour has fallen to me to make you a Silk. I am absolutely delighted and you have my warmest congratulations. I wish you every success." Those were his actual words and I was, of course, extremely touched by them.

That concluded the first part of the day's proceedings. Soon afterwards, clutching my Letters Patent in their bright red pouch, I was driven back to Chambers to have a small lunch party with my family and friends.

The second part of the day's proceedings was to go to the Royal Courts of Justice to be 'introduced' as a new Silk to the Lord Chief Justice and the Heads of the Divisions of the High Court. Being 'introduced' was a somewhat bizarre ceremony and, on reflection, bordered on the farcical. I say 'farcical'

Above: In my room in Chambers at Queen Elizabeth Building

because throughout the whole proceedings the new Silk said nothing. By 'nothing', I mean absolutely nothing. Not a single word. But it was a tradition over many centuries and that was sufficient justification. That tradition took the following form. The new Queen's Counsel went into court, dressed for the first time in his Silk's attire, proceeded beyond the Bar of the Court – that is the division between where Queen's Counsel and Junior Counsel sit – and bowed to the judge. The barrister then sat down for the first time ever in what is familiarly known as 'The Front Row'.

The judge then intoned the formulaic words, saying in my case, "Mr Whiteman, do you move?" At which point I duly rose, bowed to the judge, bowed to the left, to the right and finally to the rear, then walked along the row of seats and left the court. I then went in turn to a number of other courts and engaged in the same ritual, some because I was obliged to do so, and others because I wanted, in open court, to thank the judges who had been so supportive in setting up the new Chambers. Without their help it was most unlikely there would have been a new set of Chambers, certainly not at QEB.

With that, the formalities of the day were at an end and the curtain came down on the most momentous period of my professional life. It had been an immensely significant and fulfilling time. The comment in that letter of congratulations that I was "courageous" rang in my ears. I still wondered whether that was a euphemism for 'foolhardy'. Time would tell.

CHAPTER 16

MY AMERICAN DREAM

"I like the dreams of the future better than the history of the past."
THOMAS JEFFERSON – US President 1801-1809

*"America lives in the heart of every man everywhere who wishes
to work out his destiny as he chooses."*
Speech 1905
WOODROW WILSON – US President 1913–1921

Throughout my life, I have always taken the greatest interest in the United States. I have always been fascinated by the history and geography of the USA and by the entire political process of the country (something in which I was to participate at the highest level in due course and which I enjoyed enormously – but more about that later).

As a lawyer and a person with an abiding passion for history, I believe that the establishment of the United States and the creation of its Constitution, embodying amongst other things the separation of powers between the Executive, the Legislature and the Judiciary, to be fascinating. My great interest in all things American will certainly last for my entire lifetime, fostered by the large number of American friends I have.

The US will always be the most exciting place for me, and I particularly love New York, where there is a 'buzz' that doesn't exist anywhere else in the world. That 'buzz' is really the feeling that it is all happening there and that nothing is impossible in the 'Big Apple'. Of course, there are many other aspects of the American way of life which are not so endearing and indeed many which are very worrying. But, warts and all, I have had a love affair with the USA and the American people since forever, and I know that will never change. I have often asked myself, why so?

Perhaps my fascination with the USA started with *The Saturday Evening*

Post which, as mentioned earlier, my father regularly purchased during my childhood. I was an avid reader of it for many years. The content portrayed a wholly different world from the one I inhabited in Walthamstow, East London. To me, the *Post* was a revelation which informed me about a far-off world that seemed glamorous, exciting and always interesting. And then there were those wonderful Norman Rockwell covers, which were incredibly inspiring – he was a man of enormous talent. The *Post* was delivered to our house in the afternoon and I eagerly awaited the 'thud' as it landed on the doormat. I would snaffle it immediately (my father was not usually home that early) and take it off to my bedroom, where I would be lost to the world for hours, if not days. I suppose, on reflection, that, as a 10-year-old, I was dreaming the 'American Dream', such a far cry from the run-down, bombed-out surroundings I saw every day on my way to and from school. Looking back, it was also quite amazing that my father, a London taxi driver, should have been so enlightened and interested that he knew about this American publication, which he read from cover to cover. Perhaps a diet of Hollywood films also played a part in my abiding interest in the 'American Dream'. But the real catalyst was probably, once again, the teaching of Paddy Clinch at LCHS. For my history A level I had to take an elective subject and I chose, or rather Paddy chose for me, 'American History 1776–1865'. I ask myself rhetorically, is there any period in the history of any other country that is equally fascinating and profoundly impressive? In particular, the period from 1776 to, say, the 1820s produced so many men of huge stature, not only Presidents of the United States, but many others who played such a vital part in the early development of the country. To list the statesmen I have in mind would be invidious, but amongst them I became particularly interested in Benjamin Franklin and Alexander Hamilton. Paddy taught American History in his usual way; he was totally inspiring. Despite my readings of the *Post*, I had no real idea of how the country we now know as the United States of America came into being. I simply assumed, not very brightly, that the huge continental land mass that is now the USA had always been such. So to learn at the feet of my mentor about the creation of the Constitution, the Louisiana Purchase, the Mexican Wars and so on, was to me completely riveting. And that, of course, was before one came to the compelling subject of the American Civil War. By that time I was totally 'hooked' on American History, and I still am.

My real interest in the American political process was heightened by the Kennedy era. At that time, I purchased *Time* magazine regularly and read it avidly. I was fascinated by the whole structure of the government of the United States and the people who were at the heart of power. The political process and the structure of government were and are so very different from the UK and it seemed, and still seems, to me a much more open process and indeed society.

Despite my passionate interest in the USA, it was not until 1973 that I was to set foot on American soil. An American oil company I advised instructed me on a North Sea oil and gas problem that necessitated my visiting their headquarters in New Orleans. I had extremely high expectations of my stay there and I was not disappointed. I had the most enjoyable time visiting, as it then was, such an exciting and attractive city.

I return to the early 1970s to trace the story of how the USA came to play such a big part in my life. In 1971 I was invited to a dinner party in Blackheath, where I met Charles ('Chuck') Lubar, an American attorney specialising in US Tax Law. He subsequently became, and remains, a very close friend. A year later Chuck introduced me to John van Merkensteijn, another US attorney specialising in US Tax Law. He also soon became a lifetime friend. The final link in the chain I am describing, which led to my 'American Dream' becoming a reality, occurred in 1978. I had invited John to dinner at our house in Clapham and he was accompanied on this occasion by a close friend of his, Bill McKee. I had no idea what this evening would lead to. Bill was a Professor of Tax Law at the University of Virginia (UVA) and the author of an encyclopaedic work on the US Taxation of Partnerships, which was the standard work on the subject. During the course of the evening Bill extolled all the wonders of teaching, particularly teaching Tax Law, and even more so, teaching Tax Law at UVA. He asked me about my career history in Revenue Law and I mentioned I had been a lecturer at the LSE. This struck a chord with Bill, who then became particularly animated.

"Peter, you must come to UVA and do some teaching there. You would love it, and I'm sure the students would love you too!"

I said immediately, "Why not? It sounds a great idea. I would love to get back to the United States and see Virginia, a State I have never visited. But best of all, it would be great to do some teaching at UVA, which I know has a great tax programme."

"OK," said Bill, "I will put it in train as soon as I get back to the University at Charlottesville. I know exactly what we can do. Every year we invite a distinguished foreign lawyer to give a series of lectures over the course of a week. We leave the topics to the speaker, but obviously the more it is geared to an American audience, the better. I am afraid the University doesn't pay very much, and the amount we do pay is really meant to cover expenses and no more."

It was a lovely idea to visit Virginia and teach at UVA, but on the basis of experience in similar contexts, I never really expected to hear any more about teaching there. To that extent, I grossly underestimated Bill and his intentions.

A week later a telex arrived in Chambers. Bill was as good as his word, stating that UVA had authorised him to write to me along the lines he had mentioned at our dinner party. The fee was only $2,000, but that was never the point as far as I was concerned. This would be an entirely new experience and, although it was only teaching for a week, it might open up a new chapter in my life. It certainly did!

So in October 1978 Kate and I arrived in Virginia, full of excitement. I duly delivered my lectures and, as far as I could tell, they seemed to be well received. There was only one thing that puzzled me. It was not that Bill McKee attended every one of my lectures (that was to be expected, as he was the person who had invited me to UVA), but that the Dean of the Faculty of Law, Emerson Spies, and many other members of the Faculty, also attended every day. Neither courtesy nor obligation required that. Possibly a more perceptive person would have realised what was happening. Kate and I had a most enjoyable time in Virginia and we arrived home with fond memories of both a stimulating and enjoyable working holiday.

A month later, when I received a telex from Dean Spies, the mystery of the unusually good academic attendance at my lectures was solved. The Dean and the other members of the Faculty who came to hear me speak were 'sizing me up' for a full-time Chair of Law at UVA. They wanted to hear how good I was and whether, overall, I would fit in at the Law School. Fortunately I must have acquitted myself pretty well because the telex contained an invitation

Above: The Columbus Group having fun in Charleston, South Carolina

to teach in the Faculty of Law on a full-time basis. The offer was of a full Professorship (not a Visiting Professorship) of Tax Law, to start at such time as was mutually convenient. The telex set out all the terms of the offer in great detail. I was not only surprised but extremely gratified by the formal offer that UVA had made.

And that is where I thought the matter would rest: an offer that was most pleasing, but I would not be in a position to give it a positive response. I thought that Kate would not agree to go to Virginia for an extended period and leave the lovely home we had just purchased. Without speaking to her, in my own mind I had ruled out the possibility of accepting the offer. How wrong I was! To my great surprise, when I got home from Chambers and showed Kate the telex, she was very enthusiastic about going to the United States. We both realised that such a fundamental change in our life would require a considerable amount of planning, particularly in relation to the girls' schooling. But in principle we had both decided that this was a wonderful offer that I should not refuse.

So, in 1980, eighteen months after the chance encounter with a friend of a friend, there began the exciting episode in our lives which I always think of as the 'Virginian Adventure'.

However, I cannot leave the events of the late 1970s without mentioning a further development which cemented my links with the USA and established some of the very closest friendships I have had in my life. I have related in this chapter the friendships I established with Chuck Lubar, John van Merkensteijn and Bill McKee. These friendships were so close, and our respect for each other's knowledge and professional expertise was such, that we decided to form our own legal 'club', which would meet once a year to discuss international tax problems. We decided that there were two other outstanding lawyers who would add further lustre to our select group, namely, Bill Gifford of the Cornell Law School, a partner in a leading New York law firm, Davis Polk; and Perry Lerner, a partner in an eminent Los Angeles law firm, O'Melveny and Myers. In the event, they both accepted our invitation to join our group and we unanimously agreed to call it 'The Columbus Group' because we intended to hold our annual meeting in the autumn over Columbus Weekend. Once again I was immensely flattered that these five brilliant lawyers invited only one Englishman to join their select band. The group met annually from 1979 onwards. It was a tremendous success and all its members benefitted hugely from our in-depth discussions. However, the most important aspect to me was the wonderful friendships that were created and flourished, and which still exist to the present day.

CHAPTER 17

THE VIRGINIAN ADVENTURE

"Adventures are to the adventurous"
Coningsby (Book III, Chapter I)
BENJAMIN DISRAELI

"There is a tide in the affairs of men.
Which, taken at the flood, leads on to fortune …
And we must take the current when it serves,
Or lose our ventures."
Julius Caesar (Act IV, sc. iii)
WILLIAM SHAKESPEARE

I am lost in thought as I gaze out of the window, not focussing on the ground below because I have so much to think about. I am filled with so many emotions, but the most important one is excitement. Excitement at the prospect of what lies ahead. I am staring at the ground, which is a runway at Heathrow Terminal 4. I am in a window seat, 7A, on BA flight 185 bound for Washington DC. When the plane takes off, *I* shall be taking off for the greatest adventure of my life. It is a beautiful sunny day, a perfect day to start such an adventure. I could not be happier. And as the plane soars ever upwards, I shall be at one with it because today I feel that, as far as my future is concerned, the sky is indeed the limit.

So, sitting in my seat, my overriding thought is that this is the start of a new, wonderfully exciting adventure which could lead to – well, so many things. The range of possibilities is limitless. To begin with, I am going to take up my appointment as a Professor of Law at the University of Virginia, one of the foremost Law Faculties in the United States, almost on a par with Harvard and Yale. It has made enormous progress in recent years and now has

Above: Darby's Folly, Virginia, USA, 1980

the reputation of a thriving Faculty which is on the way up. In other words, a stimulating place to be. I shall be a member of the Tax Faculty, which has six full-time Professors of Law, the largest such Faculty in the United States. And I shall be invested with the grand title of Professor of International Tax Law. That may be the beginning, but certainly not the end, of what lies ahead for me. Bill McKee has told me that I can practise law from the offices of the law firm to which he is attached. In my dreaming mode, I can see myself sitting in a deep leather armchair in a plush law office on Wall Street in the 'Big Apple'. I know full well that I am building castles (or more accurately offices) in the air, but why not? Today, anything seems possible. I even harbour the notion that we may settle in the United States and not return permanently to England. After all, having been twice before to Charlottesville, we have found our new family home just outside the town, a clapboard house called Darby's Folly. A glorious white house, built before the American Civil War. The bullet marks in the wood of the house bear testimony to the fact that skirmishes raged around it during that terrible conflict. Now, however, it will be a wonderfully comfortable and friendly home. We have also been very busy planning other essentials to make Charlottesville the centre of our world. We have found places for both Victoria and Caroline at two very good local schools. We have taken care of everything that can be done in advance and it augurs well for a fabulous future. Hence my feeling of anticipation of what lies ahead for us. This is our 'Virginian Adventure' and it is about to begin. I can't wait to be there and start enjoying a State renowned for its beauty, and teaching law in a wholly different environment. There is noise outside. The engines of the plane are roaring. We taxi and then lift off. I am taking off for pastures very new.

I savour all these thoughts as the plane flies across the Atlantic on a journey which, in contrast with what I foresee for my future, is uneventful.

On arrival at Dulles Airport in DC, I hire a car and drive to Charlottesville along Route 29, a highway with which Kate and I are to become very familiar over the coming months and years. Arriving in Charlottesville some two hours later, I make directly for the home of Bill McKee. After my overnight stay at his home, and not wanting to lose any time in becoming a part of the Law School, I drive the next day to the campus with Bill. When we arrive, he takes me straight to the office of the Dean, Emerson Spies. No introductions are necessary as, of course, I met him when I lectured at UVA in October 1978.

But right at the start of my interview, I was in for the most enormous shock. Something which had not occurred to me in all the preparations I had made for my teaching at UVA was lightly tossed out in conversation by the Dean. In an instant, my mood changed from excitement to considerable apprehension. What was I to do about this startling piece of news which had suddenly, metaphorically speaking, dropped into my lap? My concern was heightened by the immediate realisation that there was no way back. No way back to London, that is. We were here to stay, whatever the Dean had in mind for me. We were locked in. The shock came in the form of a question from the Dean.

"Are you looking forward to teaching US Tax Law, Peter?" I gulped and spluttered out a very American expression, "Excuse me?" I was petrified at the thought that I would not, as I had assumed throughout, be teaching United Kingdom Tax Law, but US Tax Law. My previous assumption had seemed to be confirmed by the fact that the Law Faculty had conferred upon me the title of Professor of International Tax Law. But the thought of teaching only US Tax Law caused me great consternation. I had no in-depth knowledge of the US Tax Code, all my training, experience and knowledge being in UK Tax Law. Moreover, when I had visited UVA Law School in 1978, I had taught UK Tax Law, a further reason why it did not cross my mind that I would be doing otherwise when I became a full-time Professor. Nobody, not even Bill, had indicated anything to the contrary. However, the Dean clearly had an entirely different idea. But with no training in or knowledge of US Tax Law, how could I teach such a complex subject and, even worse, at an American Law School? Impossible. I was horrified. Inwardly I was thinking that this was a non-starter. Yet I had to comply with the Dean's wishes somehow, as I was committed to teaching at the Law School, living in Charlottesville and, indeed, making our home there. There was no way out. I was so worried by the prospect of teaching a subject of which I knew nothing that I was literally lost for words. Silence descended. So the Dean repeated: "Are you looking forward to teaching US Tax Law here?"

Somehow I managed to remain calm, hiding the hideous churning going on inside my stomach. "But I thought I was going to teach UK Tax Law."

"Well, I am not sure why you should have thought that," the Dean said a little curtly. "This is an American Law School," he said with heavy emphasis. Indeed, that was a fair point. Something had got lost in translation and seeking to discuss the issue with the Dean would get me nowhere. There was only one thing to do. Concede the point and concede it graciously. So I did. I composed myself. I allowed a broad smile to spread across my face. I hoped I looked the picture of contentment and confidence. "Oh, I am sure it will be enormous fun and very stimulating." Not necessarily having complete faith in what I then said, I continued, "All I have done, in fact, is to teach and practise UK Tax Law, and teaching a different tax system in another country should be exciting and intellectually very challenging."

"Anyway," said Emerson, "it's great to have you here. Bill will take you round the Faculty and make all the necessary introductions and tell you everything you need to know." And then I realised that with those words Emerson believed that the 'Welcome to Whiteman' interview was over. Bill did as he was bidden, but it took me a while to become completely familiar with my new surroundings.

Bill gave me a tour of the Faculty buildings and we eventually arrived at the office which had been allocated to me. It was quite pleasant, if a little functionally furnished. However, it had a lovely view over the campus, towards the Blue Ridge Mountains in the distance. It was stunning, a somewhat different view from that which I had in the Temple. After some more conversation, with Bill as humorous as ever, he departed to carry out his Faculty duties. I sat in my chair and surveyed the view, contemplating the morning's events. I had experienced a severe shock with the realisation that I would be teaching US Tax Law. I would have to learn an extremely complicated subject and teach it at an American university. Initially, the thought was appalling. But now, sitting in my peaceful room with its lovely view, I came to the conclusion that I must talk myself into an optimistic frame of mind. I invoked my mantra once again – "anything is possible". So I convinced myself, although it took a little while sitting quietly in my room, that learning and teaching US Tax Law was not impossible for me. Indeed, as a last resort, if I needed assistance, I could always consult my new Law Faculty colleagues. No, the task ahead, I convinced myself, was not totally impossible. The sun was definitely coming out from behind the clouds. Think positive. It will all be just fine. For the moment I was enjoying staying with the McKees and looking forward to the time two weeks later when Kate and the girls would join me in Charlottesville.

When they did arrive, we soon became seduced by our new lifestyle. I was enjoying teaching US Tax Law because it was so challenging. After fifteen years of being immersed in UK Tax Law, I was delighted to find it so refreshing to learn (and teach) a totally new subject. On a different plane, being reunited with my family – albeit in very different surroundings – was wonderful. I felt as though I was welcoming them myself to the United States of America. The girls, who were then aged 5 and 3, fell in love with Darby's Folly. They (and Kate) adored living in the countryside and particularly being able to enjoy limitless riding. At the very start Kate and I made a number of resolutions as to how we would organise our life while we were in Virginia. We had moved to America for a life-changing experience and so our first decision was that we would really involve ourselves with the American way of life and everything that went with it. We were going to enjoy the 'American Dream' to the full, so we made two further decisions. Firstly, we would travel

Above: The family on the porch of Darby's Folly, Virginia, USA, 1980

extensively round the States and cover as much of the country as we could. In the event, we went to the four corners of the US mainland and visited some thirty-six States of the Union. Secondly, the best method of maximising our experience of the American way of life was to broaden our horizons by meeting Americans of all races, religions and political views. With so many stimulating things to see and enjoy, we decided that we would not spend our time circulating at dinner parties in the British expatriate community. As cosy and reassuring as that might be, that was not the reason why we had come to Virginia. The principle we had adopted at the beginning of our 'adventure' we adhered to throughout our stay.

Soon we became ensconced in our new home and settled into our new life in Charlottesville very quickly. On school days, for example (Law School for me, day schools for the girls), we had a set routine. I set off for the Law School at 7.30 am, taking the girls to their respective schools on the way. In the car, as I so vividly remember, we played the game of counting the fire hydrants, police cars, school buses, etc. It was great fun. The girls enjoyed it enormously and loved the excitement of all their new, unfamiliar surroundings. The car was usually ringing with laughter. On the journey I could look forward to a stimulating day at the Law School with colleagues and students alike. Usually I would be able to fit in a run with Bill through the glorious Virginian countryside – sometimes in summer in temperatures as high as 100°F. And of course at some point in the day I would have a class with the students. Then, around four o'clock (everybody had left the Law School by then), the morning process would be reversed. I would set off for home, collecting the girls from their schools on the way. In summer very often there was a variation to this itinerary. We would meet Kate at the local Country Club, to enjoy its amenities and particularly its swimming pools. Otherwise, I would drive directly home with the girls on board.

When I did go straight home from the Law School, I soon felt that the car could drive itself back to Darby's Folly. All I had to do on a fifteen-minute journey was make one left turn, followed by a second. As I took that second left turn, I never ceased to be amazed by the spectacular view of the Blue Ridge Mountains in the distance. In the fall, when the leaves on the trees were turning, producing a fantastic array of colours, the sight ahead of me was, to use that American word, 'awesome'. I often thought of the contrast between that journey and driving home to Dulwich through the urban jungle of south-east London. In Virginia, on my journey home, there would usually be no traffic at all and, indeed, there was not even a single traffic light. Our lifestyle was becoming very seductive, not least because Kate could indulge her passion for riding on her newly-acquired horse, Fred. The longer our stay continued, the more I enjoyed our Virginian experience. The Law School was becoming more and more attractive to me; I was exceptionally fond of it and of the academic staff and students there. When I contrasted this with the pressure of my working life in London, I could not resist the conclusion that this was an idyllic lifestyle. My 'American Dream' had become a reality.

What was the reality? It was wonderful. The purpose of going to Virginia was to teach law. That was totally fulfilled. The anxiety I felt when Emerson told me I was to teach US Tax Law soon evaporated. The answer, I concluded, was in the words of the old adage, 'Keep one chapter ahead of the students.' So that's what I did. And believe it or not, except for one blip, it worked brilliantly. The blip was when I was teaching Chapter 6 from the textbook *US Tax Cases and Materials*. That chapter, like most of the others, dealt with issues of substantive law. However, one student asked me a question on procedure slightly related to the issues raised in Chapter 6. Now that was a problem, as all procedural issues were dealt with in Chapter 26 and I had no idea whatsoever how the student's question should be answered. So I was driven to the last refuge of the lecturer who is completely lost and said, "We'll come to that a little later, when we can consider that issue in its proper context." (Or more realistically, "when I've read the chapter.") To be honest, did I fool any of my super-bright students? Almost certainly not, but at the time I thought I had squeaked by.

I so enjoyed teaching that I threw myself into making my classes as much of a success as I could. I also made them fun wherever that was appropriate. I even dressed up on occasions to amuse my students, one such being when I donned the formal attire of a Queen's Counsel. The *Virginia Law Weekly* of 10 April 1981 recorded the event as follows:

"Professor Peter G Whiteman, Queen's Counsel, swept into Room 119 (of UVA Law School) fully attired as a proper English barrister: flowing black silk robe, white Ascot collar trimmed in lace, and an elegantly curled full-bottomed wig. In his hands, several papers were rolled and secured with red tape. Whiteman began his speech as a plea to His Lordship the Judge on behalf of Mr Archibald Bloggins-Snooks. Mr Bloggins-Snooks was accused of seeking to obtain a pecuniary advantage by means of a 'trick'. He had travelled to America to 'an institution alleged to be a university, to teach, of all things, American Tax Law'."

The students fell about with laughter. They loved it, and other similar humorous episodes I concocted, but it was still a flattering surprise when I was voted 'Most Popular Professor of the Year'. However, I did not mislead myself into thinking that 'Most Popular' necessarily meant 'Best'. However, this episode and others similar were a reflection of how much I threw myself into the task that was surprisingly thrust upon me on that first morning when I arrived in the Dean's office.

So during my time at Charlottesville there was much fun to be had in the Law School. Outside the Law School it was as much, if not more, fun. We were invited to many dinners and parties by my colleagues and students. The parties given by students were particularly good fun, so our life was a rich one in many respects. Indeed, when we left Virginia, we gave a large leaving party at Darby's Folly for all my students, to thank them for their hospitality and generosity to us.

My university teaching in the USA also blossomed in other ways. After I had been teaching at UVA a little while, a steady stream of invitations started to come in from other US Law Schools. I found this particularly gratifying, as the Law Schools in question were all highly prestigious ones, such as the University of California at Berkeley, Cornell, New York University and so on. I accepted all such invitations and thoroughly enjoyed going to other Law Schools and meeting other distinguished Professors of Law. I built up a great network of academic connections in the United States, which I have maintained to this day and value highly.

The reality of my 'American Dream' flourished in other ways too. Following Bill's suggestion, I decided to practise law, so I applied to become an 'Attorney and Counsellor at Law of the State of New York'. I followed and complied with all the necessary formalities, which were quite onerous, but the result was that I became a New York Attorney and was thereafter qualified as a lawyer in my two favourite jurisdictions. The only drawback to becoming a New York Attorney was that I had to travel to the State capital, Albany, to be sworn in. Travelling to Albany, although a little tedious, was not itself a problem. The problem was the Declaration I had to make at the formal swearing-in ceremony. The Declaration included swearing an oath of allegiance to the United States of America and a formal undertaking to uphold its Constitution. As a citizen of the United Kingdom, it did not seem entirely appropriate for me to swear such an oath. However, having come this far (both literally and metaphorically), I felt I was being pedantic in the extreme if I allowed a detail of no real practical consequence to stand in my way. So, at the critical time, I overcame any qualms I might have had, raised my right hand and made the necessary Declaration. I didn't even cross my fingers when I did so. My status as a lawyer in America was further enhanced when I was subsequently admitted as a Solicitor of the Supreme Court of the United States.

Of all the memories I have of UVA Law School, the most flattering concerned the offer Dean Spies made to me after I had been teaching for some two years. He called me into his office and said the Faculty regarded my appointment at UVA to have been a complete success. Apparently my colleagues respected me as a lawyer and also found me to be a very welcome addition to the Faculty. He continued, "So much so that the Faculty has authorised me to offer you a permanent full-time post of Professor of Law at UVA. Will you accept?"

I said I was immensely honoured by the offer and, of course, I would consider it most carefully with Kate, as it would mean residing permanently in the States. A huge decision. Kate and I discussed the offer of a Chair at UVA at great length, but in the end we decided that, however much we had enjoyed living in Virginia, our hearts and our home were still in England. So very reluctantly, and I hope graciously, I conveyed our conclusion to Emerson. But the story has a most delightful ending. Emerson was determined that I should continue teaching at UVA and he was not to be thwarted in that ambition. So at the meeting when I informed him of our decision, he immediately invited me to retain my Chair of Law and teach a course for one semester (term) a year in US Tax Law (no surprise and no problem in that connection this time!). Emerson said that, if I accepted, I could live in London and fly to the US to carry out my teaching commitments whenever it was convenient for me to do so. This was a most flexible and generous offer. I was extremely grateful and told Emerson so immediately. I readily accepted the Faculty's invitation, which clearly pleased him. For my part, I was delighted that I would retain such a wonderful connection with the University I had grown to love.

In the event, when we left Charlottesville after two years in residence, I continued to visit UVA for a number of years, teaching a semester's course each year. So, pleasingly, there was no abrupt end to the 'Virginian Adventure'.

Taking everything I have related in this chapter into account, it is obvious that the 'Virginian Adventure' was hugely enjoyable and enriched our lives. Even now, when I think of Virginia, it gives me a very warm glow. One of the best decisions Kate and I made was to move there and change our way of life dramatically. We were able to do this without prejudicing the girls' education, as they were so young. It presented a huge challenge to both of us, but we rose to it. As a result, the stay in Virginia represented a major chapter in our family life and the possibility that it might lead to greater things was thrilling.

When I arrived in Charlottesville, I believed my professional opportunities were limitless, and to have that belief in America was particularly appropriate – America was the 'land of dreams', the 'land of opportunity', and I had plenty of both. In the event, my optimism on arrival at UVA was justified. My teaching at the Law School was crowned in 1982 with the flattering offer of a permanent Chair of International Tax Law at the School. I had acquired a thorough knowledge of US Tax Law, which encouraged me to become an Attorney and Counsellor of Law of the State of New York. So, in addition to my expertise as a Queen's Counsel in England, I was now qualified to practise law in that State. Invitations to give lectures at other US Law Schools had considerably expanded my network of US contacts. My original hopes might have seemed over-optimistic, but in the event I felt I had achieved so much that I could now truly claim to be an international tax lawyer. So many doors were now open to me. I had reached for the stars with my 'Virginian Adventure' and I had touched them. I felt my life would never be the same. And it wasn't. The next big episode in my professional life proved just that.

CHAPTER 18

"YOUR COUNTRY NEEDS YOU"

1914 Military Recruitment Poster

Home again. We returned to Dulwich Village to resume our life there; Kate took up her cookery writing again and Victoria and Caroline returned to their school. However, Virginia, or more precisely UVA, would continue to play a part in my life for many years to come.

Professionally, my most important objective was to re-establish my practice at the Bar. I was a little apprehensive about whether I would succeed in doing so, as I had been away for some time. In the event, I need not have been concerned because my practice got off to a flying start on my return.

The day after we arrived back in London, I went into Chambers and was delighted to be told that my colleagues and staff had arranged a 'Welcome Back' lunch for me. It was great to return to the Temple, but even more so to be greeted so warmly by everyone in Chambers. However, halfway through our celebratory lunch, a clerk came in, somewhat apologetically, to say that a firm of solicitors would be sending a set of Instructions for me to advise on as soon as possible. They wanted to have a quick word with me on the telephone right away to explain the background to the case. I excused myself from the lunch, sadly never to return. This 'call to arms' set the pattern for the future – I was 'back in business'. So despite my concerns I very quickly established my practice again. It was as though I had never been away. Indeed, my professional practice became even more hectic than it was before I left for Virginia. Very soon there was a considerable amount of work coming into Chambers for me, and one new development was that I was frequently travelling overseas to advise clients in their own jurisdictions.

In the beginning, flying to all parts of the globe to honour professional and academic commitments was stimulating, exciting and very flattering.

Flattering because clients were prepared to fly me around the world to advise on international tax matters of the most sophisticated kind. I felt I was at the cutting edge of research, planning and developments in the international tax world. To belong to a comparatively small coterie of acclaimed tax lawyers around the globe was a great privilege. Moreover, it was an extremely exciting way of life. On and off planes, staying at first-rate hotels, advising multinational corporations in their prestigious global headquarters, was both thrilling and enjoyable. I was totally seduced by the life I was living. Effectively it gave me one 'high' after another, the zenith being the most fascinating experience. It occurred while I was teaching at UVA. A German client of mine who was visiting the USA learned that I was in Charlottesville. When he phoned me at UVA, he said he needed my advice urgently because the matter in question involved him personally. It was obvious that he was dependent upon my advice in order to be able to plan his next steps.

"Can I come down to UVA to see you?" he asked. This presented me with a self-induced difficulty. I felt it would be inappropriate for me to advise a private client while discharging my professional duties on University premises. I explained my dilemma to my client.

"OK," he said. "When do you return to London?"

"Tomorrow."

"Then I will fly back to London tomorrow and see you in Chambers the day after."

"I am sorry, and I certainly don't want to appear to be difficult, but that won't be possible either, as my week in London is solidly booked with Consultations."

"OK, this is what we're going to do. I will travel to London with you tomorrow and then return immediately to the States. I will buy two tickets on the BA Concorde flying out of Washington tomorrow, which will give you plenty of time in London on your return to prepare for your Consultations. But critically for me, you could give me your advice during the flight, 70,000 feet above the Atlantic, when I will have your undivided attention. Now what about that? After all, three hours of your time should be enough to develop a strategy for my international tax problems." I agreed with the greatest alacrity, as I always thoroughly enjoyed flying Concorde. It was always a stunning experience, particularly when I was allowed by the Captain to sit in the 'fourth seat' in the cockpit.

When we completed our call, I put my phone down thinking, "Wow!" How my career had progressed when a client would alter his schedule to the extent that he was prepared to travel to London with me and return immediately to the States, solely to get three hours of my time. Moreover, he was offering to purchase a Concorde ticket for me, which even in 1984 cost about £5,000, and take my advice in-flight. It was to be the first time that I would hold an airborne Consultation, and the client was very happy, indeed grateful, that I was prepared to do so. I found it truly amazing – no wonder I thought, "Wow!"

But then, after a while, the excitement of my 'jet-setting' career started to pall. What once gave me a 'buzz' started to become just another way of organising my professional life. So what had previously been exhilarating had become exhausting. Moreover, my international practice was making ever greater inroads into my professional time in London.

However, I still continued to work at the same frenetic pace on my treadmill (as it had become), being seduced by the thought that clients worldwide sought my professional advice. As so often happens, the extent to which I had allowed my practice to take over my life was put into context by a child's question. On one occasion, an organisation which I advised on an honorary basis had professionally instructed me to advise at a meeting in California with the Governor. It meant leaving London on Wednesday and returning two days later, on Friday. As the BA steward on the outbound flight said to me, "I return on Friday as well, but then it's my job. What's your excuse?" Clearly he thought I was mad.

On the day I arrived in California, I had a meeting at five o'clock in the afternoon (local time) with a multinational corporation, a meeting preparatory to seeing the Governor the next day. I arrived at the hotel feeling very tired, so I decided to have a rest that afternoon. I fell asleep as soon as I hit the bed. When I woke up, I did not know what time of day it was. My watch showed the time as four o'clock. I couldn't think properly. Was that Californian time or London time? Was it four o'clock in the afternoon, four o'clock in the morning that day, or the following morning? I simply didn't know. I was completely disorientated. And still exhausted after my nine-hour flight. I discovered the time from Reception and in the event I arrived promptly for my meeting. However, that didn't prevent the whole day from being a very disconcerting experience.

The following week, I was due to fly Concorde to New York on Monday, returning to London the following day. Wednesday was a different destination. I was scheduled to go to Hong Kong to present a case to the Court of Appeal there. Looking back, it was a ludicrous way to arrange my life. However, it took a question from my 5-year-old, Caroline, over breakfast on the Monday morning in question, to bring me to my senses.

"Daddy, are you going to Hong Kong today?" she asked.

"No, I am going there on Wednesday. Today I am off to New York." Just articulating my answer to Caroline's question, with its lunatic scheduling response, showed how much matters had got completely out of control. That answer, together with my discombobulating experience in California the previous week, seemed to be sending me a very clear signal: I should change my life and particularly curtail the frantic rushing from one Consultation or court in one country to another in a different part of the world. So there and then, in front of my daughter, I made the resolution that I would never allow myself to get into such a situation again. However superficially seductive, however flattering, however financially rewarding, I vowed I would change my lifestyle forever. And I did. I never again attempted the like of my California-New York-Hong Kong dash around the world.

However, even having made that commitment, it was clear that the 1980s were still going to be a very hectic time for me, and not just at the Bar. The previous decade had been so exciting and full of achievements that, as a result, I had established a framework for my future professional life including, but not limited to, the Bar. Now I had to make that framework really work – make it a practical reality on a day-to-day basis – and where necessary, fill the gaps in it. There were three vital elements to this modus vivendi. First, the Bar. As I have mentioned, I had to re-establish my career as a barrister and, although the first signs were really encouraging, I was determined not to take anything for granted. Secondly, my books on Income Tax and Capital Gains Tax. New editions of both had to be prepared, particularly to take account of the tax reforms of the incoming Conservative Government. As always, that demanded painstaking work and meticulous attention to detail. I had to ensure that, as the leading practitioners' textbooks on the subjects, they were completely comprehensive, totally accurate and right up to date, incorporating the latest developments in the tax world. Again, a very time-consuming, albeit very satisfying, occupation. Finally, my Chair of International Tax Law at UVA was a commitment I took very seriously. It therefore meant that I had to return to Charlottesville frequently to teach my semester's course there. But teaching in Virginia did bring me unalloyed pleasure.

All the activities I was undertaking in the early 1980s (and thereafter) I found exciting, stimulating and intellectually rewarding. I believed at the time that I was fortunate to have so many strings to my professional bow. I could not expect anything more from my working life. I did not know that soon my expectations would be exceeded by two more exciting developments in my legal career. The first I relate in this chapter; the second – my elevation to the Bench as a Recorder of the Crown Courts – I will describe later.

In those heady days, one way or another, I was always able to squeeze in everything that I was committed to doing. Nevertheless, I did believe that, with three such demanding elements in my professional life, there was no scope for anything else. Or so I thought. What I couldn't anticipate was that, from a totally unexpected source, something was going to explode into my life. And that 'something' was going to be so exciting and so challenging, it would open up a whole new legal world to me. A world of which I had no knowledge or experience, and as far as I was aware, neither did any other barrister. Nor, when it was presented to me, could I fail to appreciate that, as it fitted in so well with my other professional activities, it would produce the most pleasing intellectual symmetry.

The manner in which this 'something' exploded into my world also struck a real chord with me, as it picked up the most significant recurring theme of my life. Namely, that at every stage of my career distinguished people had seen in me skills, talents or other attributes that they thought it worthwhile to cultivate and bring to fruition. On this occasion the 'something' came in the form of an invitation to undertake a task that appealed to me on many different levels. It may have come from an unexpected source, it may have been at a time when I was exceptionally busy, but there was no way I could refuse such a fascinating opportunity. I never intended to, from the first moment it was put to me. And how did this invitation, which opened up so many new avenues to me, come about? It happened at a formal dinner in the City of London and it took the form of a 'tap' on the shoulder, metaphorically speaking. I shall set the scene.

The setting: Guildhall, with its sumptuous interior. The occasion: a formal dinner given by the Lord Mayor of London for distinguished guests. The long dining tables were laid exquisitely; glass and silver sparkling everywhere.

Before dinner I look at the table plan. I make a mental note of those who will be seated near me, including Mr (subsequently Sir) Michael Grylls MP. Dinner is announced. We take our seats. A distinguished silver-haired gentleman takes his place opposite me. He has a pleasant demeanour and is smiling warmly at his dinner companions. Including me. I recognise him from his media appearances and, of course, I know from the table plan that it is Michael Grylls. I can see he is very eager to engage in conversation with his fellow diners but, apparently, particularly with me.

After the usual pleasantries, Michael says:

"I have heard a lot about you and I was delighted when I saw on the table plan you were sitting opposite me. I am right in thinking you are the Whiteman of *Whiteman on Income Tax* and also an international tax lawyer?" This is all very pleasant and indeed most flattering, but I am curious to know where this conversation is going. Curious is the right word because there is no reason to be apprehensive, not after Michael's delightful words and the broad smile he still has on his face. I respond eagerly, in the hope of discovering sooner rather than later what Michael has in mind, for obviously he wants to discuss something of importance.

"Yes, you are right on both counts, if it is not too immodest to say so."

"Not at all. I have looked forward to meeting you for some time and I hoped an opportunity like this might arise where we could discuss matters of common interest."

From being curious, I am now on tenterhooks as to what Michael is going to say next. At this stage Michael is focussing his attention so much on me, it is as if there were no other diners at the table. He obviously doesn't intend to be discourteous, but as I look at his eyes and 'read his lips', it is clear that he is a man on a mission. A 'mission' that plainly involves me. I think to myself that there is everything to be gained by remaining silent and letting Michael finish what he has to say. As I have done so many times in my social life, most notably with Margaret Thatcher (as you will read in Chapter 26), I adopt the approach of Polonius: "Give every man thine ear but few thy voice." So I sit there amidst the general hubbub, sphinx-like, waiting for Michael to unburden himself.

The waiters commence serving our meal in their usual smart, very well-drilled fashion. Guildhall is buzzing with the many conversations taking place in these elegant surroundings. But all of this, however delightful, is just background to me, as my mind is preoccupied with thoughts of what Michael is going to say. I do not have to wait much longer.

"Well, Peter, I will tell you why I wanted to meet you. I am the Parliamentary Adviser to the Unitary Tax Campaign and I represent it in Parliament and on all other appropriate occasions. In fact, the UTC is in some senses an offshoot of the Tax Committee of the Confederation of British Industry." It is apparent that Michael is acting on behalf of an organisation that has an excellent pedigree. That much I know, as I have researched the history of the UTC previously. Simply put, it was an international tax organisation which represented nearly all of the largest United Kingdom multinationals (MNCs) operating in the USA. It was therefore a real force to be reckoned with.

The UTC was formed by UK MNCs to oppose the introduction and the use generally of Unitary Taxation worldwide, but particularly in individual States of the USA. I apologise in advance for the explanation which follows of the consequences of Unitary Taxation. I appreciate it is very detailed and difficult to absorb for the non-specialist. However, I explain it in the hope that it is helpful to some readers and will enable them to realise how exceptionally important the tax consequences of Unitary Taxation were. Of course, having given a statutory health warning, those who only want a high-level view of the issues involved may well decide to skip the following analysis.

Shorn as far as possible of technicalities, Worldwide Unitary Taxation (WWUT) is a form of taxation where a State ('a Unitary State') imposes tax on a quantified proportion of the global profits of an international group. Thus, such a State refuses to accept for tax purposes what an MNC declares as its profits made in that State, but instead insists on taxing in that State a quantified proportion of the worldwide profits of that MNC which that State regards as attributable to its activities there. Almost inevitably, Unitary

Taxation produces a higher, possibly much higher, taxable profit in an individual State than normal international tax principles.

A further important consideration is that the costs of complying with the information demands which WWUT gives rise to are considerable. Hence, for both the above reasons (increased taxation and higher compliance costs), MNCs vigorously oppose Unitary Taxation. In the United States, California was the most important protagonist of WWUT, although over time some twenty States in the USA introduced or attempted to introduce it. (For those who, despite the statutory health warning, found the above analysis fascinating, I have provided a more detailed technical analysis in the postscript to this chapter.)

During the course of my international tax practice I had become very aware of the Unitary Tax issue and all the matters I have related above. They were at the forefront of my mind as soon as Michael referred to his involvement with the UTC. As I was keenly interested in the whole topic, Michael had my full attention in relation to the points he had made. However, I was puzzled as to how the introduction of Unitary Taxation into our discussion was of relevance to me. Michael explained why.

"Well, Peter, you see, the point is this. The UTC has a very wide membership and has powerful backing, and that is not only from the largest British MNCs. There are others, equally powerful, who cannot be seen to oppose Unitary Taxation but who are providing invaluable support behind the curtain. They have to act behind the scenes, otherwise international relations between the UK and the USA would be prejudiced. After all, to oppose Unitary Taxation is to attack vested interests in the United States." This comment was not lost on me, as I knew the UK Government, and particularly HM Treasury, was opposed to Unitary Taxation, as it was contrary to the internationally accepted principles of taxing MNCs. It had previously become clear to me that Unitary Taxation was an issue between the two governments. So when Michael referred to "others…providing invaluable support", it was not unreasonable to read, for "others", the UK Government.

Michael continued, "The Unitary Tax issue has been one that has created a real difference of opinion between the United Kingdom and United States. It has been simmering for a number of years, but now it has developed into a full-blown dispute between the two countries. The problem is not really at the Federal level but at the individual State level, with those States which have introduced Unitary Tax. The Federal Government has, however, been drawn into the dispute, as the individual States expect Washington to support them against foreign MNCs. Of course, anything which affects relations between the US Government and Her Majesty's Government (HMG) is taken very seriously here, and Unitary Taxation has been doing precisely that. So this thorny issue cannot just be ignored. It is of vital importance to MNCs operating in the USA, and the UTC and 'others' supporting them are determined to see a satisfactory outcome to the issue."

I was fascinated and intrigued by Michael's comments in equal measure. I was fascinated that there should be such a very significant difference of opinion on an international tax matter between the two countries. I was intrigued because I could not see what role I could play in such a dispute on behalf of the UTC. Michael was about to enlighten me.

"The reason I am so delighted to see you here tonight is that the UTC needs advice from an international tax lawyer of your reputation and experience on the delicate issue that has arisen. Your general guidance would be of inestimable value to the UTC and the 'others' supporting them. To have an international tax lawyer giving us advice on how to promote the case against Unitary Taxation, and in particular on how we should handle the delicate tax negotiations on the issue between the two countries, would help us enormously. Indeed, the issue is even more delicate than I have indicated because the powers that be want to introduce retaliatory tax legislation against the States in the USA that have adopted Unitary Taxation. This opens up a whole can of worms, as the UK Government cannot be seen to be taking any unfriendly action against the individual States in the USA. That is where you would have a vital role to play, that is, in drafting the legislation in the most appropriate and sensitive way. However, I cannot say anything more about it tonight on an occasion like this."

Indeed, I was surprised he had said as much as he had at a public dinner. All his attention had been focussed on me, to the extent of ignoring his other dinner companions. I was still in Polonius mode as Michael reached his peroration.

"So, Peter, all I am asking you tonight is if you would consider what I have mentioned and be prepared to talk to me in the future in a more private setting. As you can see, a whole series of detailed and delicate issues arise which affect British industry, and the UTC and others would be so grateful if you would help. If the whole matter is to reach a satisfactory conclusion, we really do need someone like you to assist us. It really is a case of 'Your Country Needs You'!"

I had found this an exhilarating conversation and I was extremely flattered by what Michael had said about me and the role I could play in such a high-powered and sensitive dispute. I found it somewhat difficult to believe that this conversation had actually taken place, one which had come as a total surprise to me. But taken place it had, and Michael was looking for an answer.

I responded, "I would be delighted to assist you in any way I can. The matters you have mentioned interest me on so many levels: international Tax Law, a dispute between the two countries over a tax issue, the possibility of being able to assist in its resolution, and finally, participating in drafting retaliatory tax legislation. Absolutely fascinating. So of course I would be pleased to discuss the whole issue with you in a more appropriate setting."

"That's all I needed to know. I will be in touch."

Clearly Michael believed he had taken the matter which was so important to him as far as he could, so he then turned to converse with one of his other dining companions. I followed his example, but for the rest of the evening I found it difficult to concentrate on anything other than the extremely exciting prospect Michael had held out to me – advising the powers that be in industry and government on an international tax matter which involved my two particular areas of expertise: US and UK tax. Think about it as I might, all I could do was wait for Michael's call.

In the event, the next development in this saga was a telephone call from Ian Spence, then Head of the Policy Division of the Inland Revenue. I knew Ian very well, as he was a near neighbour of mine in Dulwich and I had met him many times, not only socially but also professionally. I had enormous respect for him. He was an extremely intelligent man and had a most enviable reputation for his knowledge and experience of tax matters. (As a footnote, when I told Ian many years later that I was writing my autobiography, he was extremely enthusiastic about the project and offered to help me write the section on Unitary Taxation, an offer which I was delighted to accept. Very sadly, before it was completed, he died.)

Ian's call was short and to the point. He informed me that a meeting on Unitary Taxation was to be held in the Board Room of the Inland Revenue at Somerset House and that representatives of HM Treasury, the UTC and the CBI would be invited to attend. He would also be present, together with other very senior members of the Inland Revenue. The purpose of the meeting was for all the vitally interested parties to formulate the future British approach to Unitary Taxation. He then said that he had been authorised to invite me to attend the meeting. Of course, I accepted with the greatest enthusiasm, for all the reasons I have mentioned above.

The meeting duly took place and there was a comprehensive discussion of all the important issues relating to Unitary Taxation, including retaliatory legislation. For me, on a personal note, the high point of the meeting was at the end when, sitting at the very long oval table in the Board Room of the Inland Revenue, I was formally invited to draft that retaliatory legislation which would be included in the next Finance Bill. I was thrilled, excited and very enthusiastic about being entrusted with such an important project with such wide-ranging ramifications on both sides of the Atlantic. Throughout my life, as the reader will by this stage be well aware, I have always sought new challenges to test me, and by any standard this would be the challenge to top all previous ones. But more important than that, I was overwhelmed by what was being proposed; namely, that an independent lawyer was being asked to draft part of the annual Finance Bill. As far as I was aware, that was totally unprecedented. The drafting of the Finance Bill was, and was always regarded as, the exclusive preserve of government officials. It was drafted by the government's official draftsman, the Parliamentary Draftsman's Office. I had never heard of a lawyer in private practice being requested to draft part of the Finance Bill because that was the domain of government officials, who were responsible for the necessary wording to ensure that it implemented precisely the government's policy and proposals. I found the prospect of drafting legislation somewhat daunting, particularly as any form of retaliatory legislation was likely to be very complex. It would probably constitute a new sub-code of legislation in its own right. However, if I was apprehensive about the task I was being invited to undertake, I was determined not to show it. In any event, I felt confident (I hoped justifiably) that I was up to the challenge and that it would be a wholly enjoyable learning experience. It was!

As I walked back to the Temple, I reflected at length on what had taken place. The fact that the government had selected me to advise on such a very delicate international matter, and draft the required retaliatory legislation, was both flattering and surprising. Be that as it may, I realised that what I had to focus on was the substance of the proposal that had been put to me. The more I thought about it, the more enthusiastic I became. I would be participating in an attempt to solve an international tax problem (itself fascinating to me), affecting the two tax jurisdictions in which I was most interested. It was clear that I would be working with the UTC, CBI and government officials, and that also represented a new and exciting opportunity.

That experience started soon afterwards when I was invited, with a small group of UTC and CBI leading lights, to a formal interview at the offices of HM Treasury in Whitehall. The meeting had been called by John Moore, the Financial Secretary to the Treasury, who was then a rising star in the government. The purpose of the meeting was to discuss Unitary Taxation and, in particular, for me to explain the nature of the proposed retaliatory legislation, how it would work in practice, and how effective it could be. In essence, it was for me to demonstrate that such retaliatory legislation constituted a viable proposition. I was not fazed by the burden that was being placed on my shoulders. I would prepare meticulously for the meeting, trying to anticipate as far as possible the questions the Minister might ask. That done, my only emotion beforehand was one of excitement. After all, the discussion was about a subject that fascinated me, and it was with a politician who had such charisma and talent that he was being talked about as a future Prime Minister. The day of the conference arrived and I presented myself early – horribly early – at John Moore's office in the Treasury. So early, in fact (forty-five minutes before the appointed time of 9.30 am), that I was there sitting on a sofa outside his office even before he arrived for the day. When he came in and saw me, his jaw dropped – he looked horrified. Maybe because he had a reputation for starting work very early and to an extent I had blown his cover! He certainly looked flustered for quite a while, scurrying backwards and forwards in a way that seemed to indicate that he had been caught off guard and unprepared.

When the other attendees arrived, the meeting started in a very positive atmosphere, the Minister being wholly supportive of the UTC's proposals.

As we were being introduced, John Moore's first words to me gave a great boost to my confidence: "So you're the person responsible for drafting the framework for the legislation." These and other comments showed that clearly the government was onside. What had been implicit in the Revenue's approach at the meeting at Somerset House was now being made explicit by John Moore on behalf of the government.

All the questions the Minister subsequently asked me I dealt with comfortably. Vitally, the Minister indicated that the government would provide the Ways and Means Resolution in the House of Commons to enable the retaliatory legislation to be discussed. Without it, no such consideration was possible. So my initial surmise when Michael spoke to me at Guildhall that "others … providing invaluable support" meant HMG was shown to be correct. For me the meeting had been both exciting and productive. I had answered all the questions asked of me and now I had explicit government backing for drafting the retaliatory legislation. It was full steam ahead with the most exciting professional venture I had ever embarked upon. 'Full steam ahead' was what I envisaged, but it was to turn out to be a very different experience when I started to move my pen across the sheet of A4 paper. As we shall see, there were numerous problems that I had to face and overcome, some of them highly sensitive and political.

POSTSCRIPT
MORE DETAILED EXPLANATION OF UNITARY TAXATION
WWUT could have had a very serious effect on British MNCs in the following way. Under the principles of international Tax Law, a United Kingdom headquartered group which established a branch or subsidiary in a foreign jurisdiction would account for the profits of that branch or subsidiary as a separate entity. In principle, the Revenue authorities in that foreign jurisdiction would impose taxation on the profits of that separate (local) entity, making such adjustments (usually relating to transactions with other members of the group) as it was entitled to make under the local Tax Law. Such separate entity accounting was, and is, the internationally accepted method of taxing local branches and subsidiaries of foreign groups of companies. In contrast, Unitary Taxation is a method of taxing corporate groups which firstly requires the combined reporting of all the financial results of subsidiaries and branches within such a group, and then allocates the profit (or loss) of that entire group by formulary apportionment

to all its subsidiaries and branches. So a parent company and its various enterprises are treated as if they are a single entity and the profits of the group are apportioned amongst its group members.

Such formulary apportionment has been used for many decades domestically in the United States. The problem arose when individual States ('the Unitary States') sought to apply Unitary Taxation to foreign headquartered groups of companies which had subsidiaries or branches in their jurisdiction (WWUT). Tax in each Unitary State would thus be based on the unitary combination of all the profits or losses of all related entities and then assessed on the part thereof apportioned to that Unitary State. The related entities included in the unitary combination could extend to all the worldwide entities where the group in question had a taxable presence.

As more and more States introduced or threatened to introduce WWUT in the 1970s and 1980s, the more vigorous the opposition of British MNCs became. Hence the creation of the UTC to oppose the introduction of WWUT anywhere in the world.

The British MNCs used many arguments to oppose Unitary Taxation, three important ones (there were several others) being that WWUT led to double taxation of profits, that it did not reflect the economic profit or loss of each entity, and that compliance costs were extremely high. Simply put, as set out earlier in this chapter, WWUT would have significantly increased British MNCs' State taxes in the Unitary States and their compliance costs. Hence the vigorous opposition to WWUT in this country.

CHAPTER 19

TAXING TIMES ON CAPITOL HILL

"... ask not what your country can do for you –
ask what you can do for your country."
Inaugural Address 1961
JOHN F KENNEDY – US President 1961–1963

However much the task of drafting the retaliatory legislation for the government excited me, that excitement was soon to be dwarfed by something even more thrilling that came out of nowhere. Later on I realised it must have been under consideration for some time, and only when it became a real prospect was it revealed to me with great aplomb by those who had made it possible. HMG (almost certainly acting through the Financial Secretary to the Treasury, John Moore), the UTC and the CBI had promoted the novel idea of despatching a delegation of top-rank individuals to visit the United States. Its role would be to meet all the key players on the Unitary Tax issue, both in Washington and in California, to discuss the whole topic and seek to persuade them of the justice of the British case and that WWUT should be repealed. No easy task, but these three promoters of the visit had pulled out all the stops and it had been agreed with their US counterparts that the delegation would have meetings with, amongst others, the United States Secretary of the Treasury (Donald T Regan) to hear the Federal take on the issue, and the Governor of the most powerful State of the Union which had adopted WWUT, Jerry Brown of California. When I was informed of the delegation's visit to the US, with its wide-ranging brief and top-drawer composition, I was delighted that, at last, the UK would have the opportunity to present its case face to face to sceptics and opponents to seek to win them over. My delight turned to euphoria when I was invited to become a member of this high-powered delegation and specifically to act as its legal adviser throughout. After all, the meetings in London with like-minded experts and captains of industry, however important, were nowhere near as significant as the golden opportunity to present our case 'live' to highly influential American 'doubters'.

I found the entire project most exciting, particularly as it had been arranged that we would go to Capitol Hill (not only to see Donald Regan, but also to meet various US Senators) and also visit Sacramento to see Jerry Brown and several powerful State Senators there.

After many preliminary meetings in London to discuss the strategy and details of the delegation's approach at the meetings in the US, we arrive in Washington DC. Now I am in my hotel bedroom and from my high perch I see the city's avenues lined with cherry trees in full bloom and iridescent in the sunlight. A breathtaking sight – maybe the most iconic in this grand capital city.

These are the 'Ronald Reagan Years' and today I shall meet an outstanding talent of his administration, often referred to as his 'right-hand man', Donald Regan. Certainly the President places the greatest trust in him, and his ability and tenacity are respected throughout the Administration and Congress.

But first things first. The delegation is to assemble on the steps of the Capitol at 9.30 am and then we will make our way along the corridors of power to meet a number of Senators and outline the case against the use of International Unitary Taxation. Some, we know, will be sympathetic to our cause, others opposed on account of the tax producing, as it does, significant revenue for the Unitary States from the often distrusted multinational corporations.

So we set off for our series of meetings, accompanied by our 'handlers', the political and legal Washington advisers to the delegation. They know Capitol Hill like the backs of their hands – no doubt because they 'work' it on a very regular basis. They are pumping us full of information before we meet each Senator. Every time they seem to deliver at great speed a never-ending briefing on the man in question. We receive a short lecture on the character and history of the next Senator we are to meet – how long he has held office, whether he is well respected (or not), whether he is likely to be 'hard-nosed', possibly belligerent, and what we can expect to obtain from the meeting. Most important of all, we are told we must not alienate in any way a (powerful) Senator who is likely to support our cause. We are also told that any reference to such and such is to be avoided at all costs, that it is vital to show some knowledge of the Senator's home State, that we must not appear to be the archetypal arrogant 'Brit', and so on. My head is in a whirl – so much information to absorb in such a short time. Thus prepared, we meet the elected representatives of the American people; some are charming, courteous, welcoming, prepared to listen attentively to the case we are making. Some even ask 'softball' questions, making the meeting 'a walk in the park'. Others are somewhat brusque with us. They have faces creased with the years of political bargaining and intrigue and convey the feeling that they are not really interested in Unitary Taxation at all. But even they listen carefully to our case.

The series of meetings on Capitol Hill comes to an end and the members of the delegation are generally pleased with what has been achieved. The British case on WWUT has, we believe, been presented comprehensively and forcefully. In particular, we have made them aware for the first time that the United Kingdom Parliament is contemplating retaliatory tax legislation against US companies. This made a number of the Senators sit up, particularly as it has the potential to harm relations between our two countries. The delegation feels that the meetings this morning have, by themselves, justified our visit to the US.

Next stop, our meeting with the US Secretary of the Treasury, Donald Regan. Before the meeting I have done my homework and researched his life history. Obviously he has the President's ear, but it is more than that; he is a colossus in the Administration. Indeed, there are those who say that it is the President who is Regan's puppet and not the other way round. They support their view by citing the famous "Speed it up" anecdote. On one occasion, when Ronald Reagan was delivering an important speech at some length, Donald Regan leant forward and said, not in a stage whisper, "Speed it up!" This to the President of the United States. And what's more, the President complied with the impertinent command. Such an instruction by Donald Regan was hardly the sign of a puppet dancing to his master's tune.

That such an important and powerful man in the Administration has agreed to meet our delegation is a clear indication that WWUT is being seriously considered at the highest levels in the US Government. But now, walking towards the US Treasury Building, I am becoming anxious. It is a daunting prospect that the burden will fall on me to address the US Treasury Secretary on the intricacies of the UK Government's position on WWUT. If he can say to the President of the United States, "Speed it up!" I am concerned that, if he is annoyed and impatient about the course the meeting is taking, he might well tell the delegation just that, in no uncertain terms. He is known to be a straight-talking, no-nonsense politician, who can be very blunt – indeed offensive – to those he considers to be wasting his time. So blunt that, if the occasion demanded, he would contemptuously dismiss the offending visitor with the saying he is famous for in Washington, "And the horse you rode in on!" Anyone who worked in government knew what the phrase was intended to convey and realised Regan was angry and their time with him was up. Apparently he had heard the phrase uttered by a Texan friend losing at poker, who actually had said to someone who angered him, "F★★★ you and the horse you rode in on!" Regan adopted the latter part of the phrase only, but his meaning could not have been clearer to someone who was on the receiving end of his diatribe.

I believe that the whole delegation, myself included, is in for a testing time. The Treasury Secretary is bound to be an expert on Unitary Taxation, given his reputation for mastery of every subject within his domain, and we are going to be put to the sword if we are found wanting.

We are shown along the corridors of the impressive Treasury Building and are eventually led into the anteroom to the Treasury Secretary's Office. We sit, somewhat apprehensively, in very comfortable deep armchairs, waiting to be ushered into 'the presence'. And then something happens that I could never have anticipated; it is a complete surprise. Suddenly, an aide emerges from behind a huge panelled door and proclaims in stentorian tones, "Would Professor Whiteman be kind enough to come this way and see a senior Treasury official prior to the meeting with Mr Secretary Regan. Only Professor Whiteman for the moment." I am very puzzled and, as I look to the other members of the delegation, they appear equally bemused. A couple raise their eyebrows and another shrugs his shoulders. What on earth is happening and why have I been selected to meet the senior Treasury official? I rise, follow the aide, and suddenly all is revealed as the door is opened, giving a view of the 'official's' room. It is huge, with an enormous desk behind which sits, in solitary splendour, my dear friend and UVA mentor, Professor Bill McKee. Of course, I knew Bill had left UVA after the President had appointed him Tax Legislative Counsel (a very senior position in the Department of the Treasury), but it had never crossed my mind that I would see him today. I am overwhelmed and delighted in equal measure to see him again and in such august surroundings. We have not seen each other for a year or more, so there is much to talk about and, as always with Bill, much to laugh at. However, then comes a most fascinating piece of information about the run-up to the official meeting scheduled for 2.30 pm. Bill explains all and, in doing so, shatters my illusions about the awesome, impressive man sitting next door, whom we are going to see very soon. Bill has an expression on his face which indicates he is about to let the cat out of the bag as to how, in reality, his boss actually operates, and this is quite obviously something he would rarely reveal. Bill says, "Let me tell you something that may surprise you. The Secretary is next door, closeted with his key advisers, and in particular those who are experts on Unitary Tax. I can tell you that, when the experts arrived at 1.45 today, the Secretary knew nothing about Unitary Tax. Nothing whatsoever. Zilch. Since 1.45 they have been pouring everything he needs to know about the issue into his ears so that he can appear to be fully briefed and up to speed when you meet him. They are feeding him the information at breakneck speed. It's always like this. And by 2.30 he will be totally prepared. He always is."

I am amazed. Forty-five minutes to master all the intricacies of Unitary Taxation, then meet a formal delegation of experts from another country and have complete mastery of the topic! If he can do that, then all I have heard about this impressive, shrewd and highly intelligent man will be justified. Bill has given me the inside track about the meeting and I can't wait to see how this man takes control of a subject, when he has had only forty-five minutes to master it.

It is time for me to take my leave of Bill – one of the most fascinating conversations I have ever had. I return to sit with the other members of the delegation. I can't wait to see what happens when we are all ushered into the Secretary's presence. Only I know the background to the educational process which is now being conducted next door, and I realise that this is sensitive information, not to be passed on.

We are shown into the Secretary's Office promptly at 2.30 pm. An even larger room than Bill's, cavernous and impressive as befits the rank of its occupant. Regan's appearance is everything I anticipated. Here is a man of great stature; he has a most impressive appearance and bearing (he was, after all, a Lieutenant Colonel in the Marines). He is an imposing man, and that is entirely in keeping with all I have read about him. He has real gravitas and the aura of power that surrounds all astute statesmen.

The meeting starts with the necessary introductions and it is immediately apparent that the previous forty-five minutes have been well spent and the Treasury Secretary is now completely on top of the subject we are here to discuss. Those forty-five minutes have given him, through his newly acquired knowledge of the subject, the ability to completely control the meeting now taking place. It is an amazing performance – a real tour de force. No one would believe that, in such a short space of time, he has absorbed everything he has been told to such an extent that he appears to have immersed himself in this highly technical subject over a long period. He does not 'fluff' a single question and speaks with authority on everything that arises. I am the only member of the delegation who can truly appreciate the staggering ability, intelligence and clarity of thought possessed by this man to be able to pick up the ball and run with it at virtually no notice. His officials, however, have let him down on one important point. They have failed to advise him of the prospect of the retaliatory legislation that the UK is planning. As this is my 'baby', I am able to give the Treasury Secretary a bird's eye view of what HMG is proposing to enact.

Eventually we leave Secretary Regan, the delegation to a man being very impressed by his performance. I am even more so because of the background information Bill has given me. But whatever Regan's performance, the real purpose of the meeting was to ascertain the Administration's view – that is, the Federal view – of the future, if any, of WWUT in the United States. There we are mightily encouraged, as we have been left in no doubt that the Administration would do all it could to accommodate the views of the United Kingdom Government on the issue. Certainly it appears that the Federal Government would not actively support the Unitary Tax States, and would seek to defuse the whole issue, which is clearly creating tension between the two countries. A tension which will increase if the United Kingdom introduces retaliatory legislation. In the event, the delegation's conclusion as to the Treasury Secretary's view is proved correct by subsequent events (which I describe in Chapter 20). Overall then, mission clearly accomplished.

The Federal view was one thing. The collective view of the Unitary Tax States was, of course, something fundamentally different. A constructive response in Washington was not totally surprising. However, no such reception could be expected in California, where the delegation is heading next.

And so it proved to be. In a very large hall in Sacramento we are met by a massive Californian delegation. Our reception is not unpleasant but could best be described as coolly polite. Both sides to the meeting know exactly where the battle lines have been drawn and neither side is expected to rapidly change its standpoint. There is far too much at stake. For the United Kingdom delegation, the excessive burden, tax and administrative, resulting from Unitary Taxation has to come to an end. For the Californian delegation, any such change will result, of necessity, in a large loss of revenue flowing into the State's coffers. Neither party can expect a dramatic change of stance from the other. The best that can be anticipated is a 'full and frank' exchange of views so that each side fully understands the position of the other. And so it is to be, with one very important exception. At the meeting, the United Kingdom delegation casts into the melting pot something which has a profound effect on the Californian delegation, namely, the prospect of the UK's retaliatory legislation. The Californian delegation has not grasped the effect of the UK proposal and, taking it on board at the meeting, they are clearly very concerned about its impact.

For that reason alone it is worth having the Sacramento meeting so that the Californian team realises that the UK has upped the stakes. Indeed, in reality, the meeting signals the beginning of the end for WWUT.

All that remains, of course, is to fulfil the vital task that has been assigned to me by HMG, namely, to draft the retaliatory legislation so that it can be inserted neatly into the UK Tax Code. It is a great challenge for me, but it is a prospect I relish and one which will give me the greatest satisfaction. I have just experienced a world which is totally new to me, and I am about to experience another. What more could I possibly ask of life?

CHAPTER 20

THE AYES HAVE IT

"To be made honest by an act of parliament"
The Devil is an Ass
BEN JONSON

I regarded the UK delegation's visit to Washington as a great success. From my personal point of view, I had found it not only informative but also very productive. I felt the key players in relation to WWUT in Washington had a much better understanding of, and were more sympathetic to, the case the UK was putting forward against WWUT. The meeting in Sacramento was also important in showing the Californian delegation that the UK was in earnest about the abolition of WWUT, and the reference to the impending retaliatory legislation had significantly altered the scales in favour of action to accommodate the UK position. In the event, my conclusions proved to be correct, and the reverberations of our meetings in the USA, and the case we submitted to the appropriate authorities there, went all the way up the ladder to the President himself.

However, I had to descend from the cloud I was flying on after my return to London and get down to the reality of the situation. That reality was, as requested initially by the UTC, and then by HMG itself, to actually draft the legislation effecting retaliation against the Unitary States.

So, to begin at the beginning, I literally had to start with a clean sheet of paper and commence the task of drafting the legislation in question (this was, of course, long before the computer drafting age had arrived). It was a more difficult task than I had imagined, and this basically for two reasons.

First, the legislation had to hit precisely the intended target (companies resident in Unitary States), but no more than that. This required very detailed consideration of the substance of the legislation, which raised some complicated issues. Secondly, as the Parliamentary Draftsman's Office has its own unique structure, style and phraseology for drafting tax legislation, it was essential that the provisions I crafted adopted exactly the same approach in every respect so that 'my' provisions meshed in with the existing tax code. There had to be no stylistic inconsistencies. As no other lawyer in private practice had ever drafted tax legislation, and as I could not liaise with the Parliamentary Draftsman's Office because that would run counter to the government's desire not to be involved in the promotion of this legislation, there was no one I could turn to for guidance as to how I should approach my task. I was 'flying solo'. It was certainly going to be very challenging. In the event, in my desire to draft something that was meticulously correct in every respect, I produced seventeen drafts of the legislation. Only then was I completely satisfied with my handiwork. My final draft represented a new sub-code of UK Tax Law, running to some eight pages of the Statute Book.

Throughout this time there was, behind the curtain, much discussion in various quarters of the way forward. The retaliatory legislation drafted, the next step was to consider how it was to become law. For that, an amendment to the Finance Bill had to be put down in the House of Commons by a Member of Parliament. It was agreed that the UTC would arrange for an MP to propose the new legislation and that I, as the author of it, would brief the selected MP on its purpose, structure and impact on the intended targets. I anticipated that MP would be Michael Grylls, but when the time came, the UTC selected another one of its advisers, Neil Hamilton. Accordingly, my secretary arranged a meeting with him at the House of Commons to discuss the proposed legislation on the day it was to be debated in the House. This was to be my first, but not my last, encounter with Neil Hamilton, who features in Chapter 25 in a very different context. As the reader will see, the contrast between those two experiences could not have been greater.

When I was shown into Neil Hamilton's office, my first impression was of a man who was highly focussed and totally self-confident. He appeared to be a most intelligent individual, who could master any legal situation. My view of Neil Hamilton soon proved to be correct (but that was in 1985!). My brief was to explain the nature and history of Unitary Taxation, the purpose of the legislation, and what its effect would be on the targeted United States companies. In other words, Neil Hamilton had to absorb a considerable amount of very detailed and complex material in a short space of time. He had to digest and master it to such an extent that some six hours later he could address the House with complete authority when he proposed the legislation. He did this with great aplomb. It was clear that he had absorbed all the information I had given him at our meeting, and he spoke in the House as if he had been an expert on the subject of Unitary Taxation for many years. As a result, the retaliatory legislation was passed without any opposition, both the Conservative Government and the Labour Opposition supporting it wholeheartedly. The retaliatory tax legislation became Section 54 of the Finance Act 1985 and, as a direct response to the enactment of that law, President Reagan took the initiative of announcing his support for US legislation to prohibit WWUT and this duly became law. In the UTC we were absolutely delighted with this development and regarded it as showing that our mission had been crowned with total success.

My job was completed. My years of advising the interested parties and drafting the legislation were now over. I had done everything that had been asked of me. I had had one of the most exciting, challenging and stimulating times of my life. In the course of those three years I had met many interesting people along the way – at the beginning the very senior government officials and later many extremely impressive captains of industry. I continued to advise them and the UTC on a regular basis until 1996. My involvement with the UTC and CBI was a most rewarding experience. At the outset I had resolved that it was an honour to represent both organisations and that any services I provided would be on an honorary basis. And indeed they were throughout.

Perhaps the memory I treasure most from this entire experience is that my contribution to the formulation of the retaliatory legislation was acknowledged in Parliament and recorded in Hansard. Michael Grylls MP, in commending the retaliatory legislation to the House of Commons when it was in full session, said:

"I pay tribute to Professor Peter Whiteman QC, a highly skilled lawyer who helped us to draft the new clause. If the new clause is accepted, the House will owe him a great debt." Mr Grylls, Finance Bill HC Deb 9 July 1985.

It should be noted that the retaliatory legislation achieved its objective and nearly all the States in the US that had adopted it abandoned it quickly after 1985. By 1988 only one State, Alaska, had Unitary Taxation. It was very gratifying to contemplate that all the advice I had provided and all the drafting

I had done had been brought to a most successful conclusion. So much so that in 1996 the Unitary Tax Campaign was wound up, having, according to Peter Welch, its Chairman, fulfilled all its objectives. I was touched to be presented at a formal dinner in my honour with a silver ice bucket engraved as follows:

"Professor Peter Whiteman QC
In appreciation of your tireless efforts.
Unitary Tax Campaign"

CHAPTER 21

ANOTHER NIGHT WITH THE PRINCESS

"Why does it always rain in South London?"
October 1985
HRH PRINCESS MARGARET

"The brightest man at the Bar"
Tatler, July/August 1988
BARONESS HELENA KENNEDY QC

In the months following the UTC's success in securing the inclusion of the retaliatory legislation in the Finance Act 1985, I reflected on the fact that it had been a notable achievement for a private body to sponsor and steer an unprecedented provision through Parliament so that it became part of UK Tax Law. It had been very exciting and rewarding intellectually for me to be involved in the drafting, discussions, meetings, negotiations and strategic planning that were necessary to ensure the UTC achieved its parliamentary objectives. I had been both fascinated and inspired by the entire parliamentary process. That was now over. As a result, my professional life might have felt a bit flat. It didn't, partly because over the years I had acquired a whole series of fascinating clients from the world of show business. My practice had become a glitzy one, attracting some of the biggest names, such as Sir Elton John, Rod Stewart, Adam Ant, Emerson Lake and Palmer, Olivia Newton-John, Sir Roger Moore, Sir Colin Davis, Daniel Barenboim, Alan Whicker and Albert Finney. Having such a high-profile practice not only gave me enormous pleasure and satisfaction, but also it fed on itself with one star frequently leading to another. Of course, the most exciting aspect was when such clients came to see me in Consultation. I enjoyed meeting them enormously and it certainly created a stir in Chambers when 'James Bond' was seen heading for my room! On such occasions there was a real buzz in the Clerks' Room and there were many requests for autographs.

I was, of course, also very busy advising my other clients, whose affairs would not be as interesting to members of the public generally, but which were of great interest and importance to me. And in the remaining years of that decade there were three significant, though unrelated, events which are also worthy of recall.

First, in the same year, 1985, I was elected a Bencher of Lincoln's Inn, that is, a member of the governing body of that Honourable Society. There can be few greater professional accolades than being chosen by one's peers for elevation to such an exalted status. My election came as a complete surprise to me, as I had neither applied, nor sought in any other way, to become a Bencher. So I took particular pleasure in my elevation, the more so since, at the age of 43, I was to become the youngest Bencher by some margin. So here again another highly significant advance in my career path came about, not because of any initiative on my part, but because others (in this case, my peers) had identified me as deserving of this honour.

Having been elected a Bencher, I was to be introduced formally to the Royal Bencher, HRH Princess Margaret, when she next visited the Inn on an official occasion. As I recounted in Chapter 10, I had met the Princess in 1967 when I was called to the Bar and was seated next to her at dinner as part of the Buchanan Prize for being top Lincoln's Inn student in the Bar examinations.

When Princess Margaret subsequently came to Lincoln's Inn sometime after my elevation, I was presented to her as a new Bencher. She immediately offered her congratulations, speaking to me with a cigarette in a long black holder in one hand and a tumbler of whisky in the other. After further pleasantries, in order to make conversation, I said, "I am sure you will not remember it, but in fact I have had the honour of meeting you before, in 1967, when I was called to the Bar and I was seated next to you at dinner." I noticed straight away that the Princess looked offended. She interrupted me before I could say anything more.

"Why do you say that?" she said indignantly. "I remember it very well indeed. That day I had been to a funeral in Surrey and had been driven back through South London in heavy rain." And then she asked me, looking aggrieved, "Why does it always rain in South London?" The critical way in which she expressed herself seemed to imply that I was solely responsible for the weather conditions south of the Thames. Having built up a head of steam and looking quite intimidating, she continued, "That day had been a thoroughly miserable one for me and I remember my evening at Lincoln's Inn which I spent with you as being the only enjoyable part of it. It cheered me up enormously and I particularly remember our stimulating conversation during dinner."

I was greatly flattered by what Princess Margaret said and was amazed that she apparently remembered meeting me some eighteen years previously. Could she really recall a conversation that had taken place so long ago, bearing in mind the number of people she had met in the intervening years? But then why should she say it if it wasn't true? To this day I am still somewhat intrigued by the comments of the Princess, although of course I was delighted to hear them. Her kind comments and the delightful evening that followed the renewal of our acquaintance are memories I shall always treasure.

The second event most certainly worth relating from the late 1980s began with a telephone call from *The Times* in 1987. The Obituaries Editor phoned to say I had been selected to write the obituary of Professor Wheatcroft, who had died the previous day. As this was the man who had had such an enormous and beneficial impact on my life, I felt it an honour to be chosen to pay tribute to such a distinguished gentleman. I told the Obituaries Editor I would regard it as a privilege to write the obituary. However, as I wanted to ensure that I did justice to the memory of Ash, I would need a little time to do the research necessary to ensure I covered all the significant aspects of his life. He accepted my comment entirely but said he would need my copy by mid-afternoon at the latest that day. To meet that deadline I said I would be grateful if he would send me the draft obituary of Ash that *The Times* had on the stocks. (The reader will bear in mind that this was long before the digital age, and long before anyone of significance could be 'Googled'.) His answer: "It is a popular misconception that we have draft obituaries ready for publication, subject to updating. Obviously we do for real VIPs like The Queen, The Queen Mother, the President of the United States and so on. We have to have them ready for publication at a moment's notice. But as for the rest, we simply do not have the resources to have hundreds of obituaries on the stocks. Sorry, but you're on your own."

So I put all my other commitments to one side and started to research Ash's life. In short order I did all the necessary preparatory work and by mid-afternoon, as requested, I phoned in my 'copy' to *The Times*. I was transferred to a typesetter, who literally set the type for the obituary as I dictated it over the phone. My heart-warming task was complete. It was a moment to savour. It had been a privilege to write the obituary of a man I respected so much. But more than that, it was the protégé paying tribute to his mentor. The relationship had now come full circle.

The last of the three events I am describing here relates to an article in *Tatler* magazine which, as far as I was concerned, came out of nowhere. In the issue for July/August 1988, in an article by Baroness Helena Kennedy entitled *Wigs Might Fly*, I was referred to in complimentary terms as follows:

"It is normally after about twenty years' practice that a barrister will consider applying [for Silk]. Some very high-flyers like Peter Whiteman – 'the brightest man at the Bar' – took Silk at 34 after only nine years' practice."

It was a stunning tribute to receive and it gave me great pleasure to be so described. As with many of the significant events in my life, it came as a complete surprise. I felt I was leading a charmed life.

Overall, the 1980s had been the most wonderful decade for me professionally. It had been very exciting and constructive and full of diversity. My experience with the UTC and government ministers and departments had been fascinating and I felt that possibly I had 'put back' something into the system from which I had benefitted so much. Michael Grylls had said, no doubt with tongue in cheek, "Your Country Needs You." I could only but hope that I had justified the faith that had been placed in me. As I was to discover later, others certainly believed I had. The acknowledgement in the House of Commons of my professional skill in drafting the legislation and the presentation of the silver ice bucket certainly seemed to bear testimony to that belief.

CHAPTER 22

DEPUTY HIGH COURT JUDGE PETER WHITEMAN QC

*"Lawyers are the only persons in whom ignorance
of the Law is not punished."*
JEREMY BENTHAM (1748–1832)

An important new chapter in my life is about to unfold. There is a tap on my shoulder. Once again I am dining in New Hall, Lincoln's Inn. In the twenty years that had passed since I joined Lincoln's Inn, I had never had a 'tap' on the shoulder at dinner, or indeed on any other occasion. I had heard, of course, of the expression 'being tapped on the shoulder'. Was this one such 'tap', with all the significance that attaches to that word in legal (and indeed other) circles? I looked up. Who was the 'tapper'? Although I did not know him well, I immediately recognised Lord Steyn. On the occasions I had met him in the past, I had found him to be utterly charming and a most delightful person to talk to. His first words that evening took me a little by surprise, albeit in the most pleasant and flattering way.

"We have been thinking about you, Peter." My immediate thoughts were, first, who are "we"? In the event I never did discover who "we" were. Secondly, what had they been thinking about?

"We think you should apply to become a Recorder" – that is, a part-time judge who 'sits' twenty days or more a year, very often presiding over criminal trials.

Then I realised, this was a real 'tap on the shoulder'. My first thought, however, was how could a member of the Revenue Bar, dealing in practice exclusively with Tax Law and with no experience of Criminal Law, sit as a judge presiding over a criminal trial?

Lord Steyn continued, "We think that you are ideal material to 'sit' as a Recorder." Still being a little surprised at the suggestion, I stuttered, "But I practise at the Revenue Bar and I know nothing about Criminal Law. My knowledge of Criminal Law stopped when I finished my second-year course in the subject at the LSE. That was in 1963 and since then I have had no acquaintance with Criminal Law professionally at all."

"That's irrelevant. It's all a matter of common sense." Those words still ring in my ears some thirty years later. I thought, how can that be right? "It's all a matter of common sense." Surely at least some knowledge of the current Criminal Law would be necessary?

Following the tap on the shoulder at Lincoln's Inn, I thought very carefully about whether I should apply to become a Recorder. I was, as I have mentioned, somewhat apprehensive about the prospect of presiding over criminal trials. Moreover, the commitment to sit for at least twenty days a year, together with the preparation in the days prior to going to court and the necessity to ensure at all times that I was aware of recent developments in Criminal Law, would restrict the time available to pursue my practice at the Bar. In the end, however, the deciding consideration for me was very straightforward – not the judicial salary, which was low, but the fact that I felt I should 'put back' something more into the system. For over fifteen years I had enjoyed all the rewards of being a member of the Bar. Of course that included the financial rewards of practising as a barrister. However, what I really had in mind was that for over fifteen years I had had the privilege of spending my working life in the most delightful way, not only enjoying the company of my colleagues in Chambers, at the Inn and elsewhere, but also of being constantly stimulated by the challenging nature of my practice. It was a wonderful way to spend my working days and I felt it was 'payback time'. And the English legal system did indeed rely to a great extent on part-time judges, as it still does. Their willingness to sit means that the system functions properly and efficiently. I felt I had a duty to discharge, so I decided to respond positively to Lord Steyn's tap on the shoulder. Moreover, having consulted a number of barrister friends, I decided definitely to sit in criminal cases only. If I was going to become a part-time judge, I wanted a complete change from my professional practice. I wanted my time sitting as a judge to refresh me for my return to practising Revenue Law, and vice versa. The greater the contrast between the cases I dealt with in practice and those I heard in court, the more likely it was that

I would enjoy both more. And indeed that proved to be true over the years that followed.

But first I had to be instructed by the Lord Chancellor's Department as to what was expected of me so that I was fit to don the mantle of a judge, albeit part-time, and sit in judgement on my fellow man or woman. The instruction at that time was extremely limited, maybe because it was "all a matter of common sense". It consisted, first, of a weekend course given by judges who heard criminal cases, followed by a visit to a prison (in my case, Wormwood Scrubs). And that was the limit of formal instruction. After that I was deemed 'fit for purpose'. Admittedly, I was not to be let loose on the public before I had 'sat' with an experienced judge who would, and did, act as my judicial pupil-master. In my case, I had advised in practice with the late Gerald Butler QC before he was appointed a Circuit Judge. By the time I arrived on the judicial scene, he was the Presiding Judge at Southwark Crown Court. I had always had the greatest respect for him when he was at the Bar and he was a man who was full of enthusiasm and good humour. He was a very stimulating and enjoyable colleague. As he was by then presiding over the second most important criminal court in London and had a wealth of judicial experience behind him, he was the ideal choice to be my mentor in the criminal courts. I could not have had a better lawyer to assist me in the transition from revenue silk to criminal court judge. Gerald was a kind, thoughtful, encouraging and above all informative judicial pupil-master. I benefitted enormously from sitting with him, particularly from his careful explanation of the points arising in the trial he was about to preside over, from his analysis of the trial after it had ended, and at all stages in-between.

One day, after I had commenced my judicial pupillage with Gerald, he was otherwise engaged and said that for that day I should sit with the Deputy Presiding Judge, His Honour Judge Mota Singh (subsequently His Honour Judge Sir Mota Singh QC). I had already come across this judge at Southwark a number of times and I found that he lived up to his excellent reputation. Compassionate, thoughtful, thorough and very calm. He was, and is, a most delightful man. Indeed, in 2009 he was knighted.

I really looked forward to my day 'sitting' with Mota Singh. I knew it would be most instructive in every way, but particularly as to how a judge should conduct himself so that, in the time-honoured phrase, justice would not only be done but be seen to be done. One unusual aspect of Mota Singh's appearance in court was that he did not wear a wig but the traditional white Sikh turban, which covered almost his entire forehead.

The day came when I was to accompany Mota Singh in court. He preceded me as we went through the judges' entrance to the court and mounted the steps to the judges' dais. He was, as always, wearing his white turban, spotlessly clean and wrapped immaculately round his head. Seeing him thus attired reminded me of an anecdote which has so often been related at the Criminal Bar.

One day Mota Singh was presiding over a trial in his court. The defendant was an Irish tramp by the name of Patrick Fitzgerald, who, because he always pushed his pathetic collection of belongings in a little cart, was known as 'Wheelbarrow' Fitzgerald. In the case in question, it was alleged that he had assaulted another tramp for interfering with his wheelbarrow and had inflicted serious injuries on him. He was charged and found guilty of causing grievous bodily harm, an offence which usually carries a custodial sentence. However, this was a trial before Mota Singh and, having heard all the evidence, and Counsel's submissions, he delivered a very long speech to 'Wheelbarrow', indicating the very serious nature of the crime he had committed. 'Wheelbarrow' looked petrified and was obviously terrified as to the length of the sentence he might receive. But then Mota Singh continued:

"However, in all the circumstances, and particularly because of the matters brought to my attention by your Counsel, I have come to the conclusion that the correct sentence would be to place you on probation for twelve months."

'Wheelbarrow' was of course mightily relieved and indeed overjoyed by the fact that he was going to avoid a custodial sentence. He was literally lost for words for a time, but he eventually pulled himself together and said, "Thank you, thank you, My Lord. You are a very kind person. God will bless you and look after you." And then there was a pause while 'Wheelbarrow' gathered his further thoughts together and, trying to please this kind judge as much as he possibly could in return for his lenient sentence, said in his broad Irish accent:

"And I hope your head gets better soon."

The whole court collapsed into fits of laughter and Mota Singh even allowed a wry smile to cross his face. The compassionate attitude of the judge could not have been more appreciated by 'Wheelbarrow' and he had just wanted to say something kind to the judge to indicate the depth of his gratitude.

It was one thing to sit next to Gerald Butler or Mota Singh in court and see them preside over a trial with complete authority; it was quite another for me to sit on the Bench in splendid isolation. I remember very well the first morning I did so. Mounting the steps to my chair on the Bench, I was apprehensive but at the same time aware that the impression I should give in court was one of complete authority and being entirely in control of the proceedings. I had to appear calm, relaxed and totally authoritative, whereas I actually felt somewhat nervous. I felt alone, so very alone, sitting in that judicial chair. The feeling of isolation and responsibility was overwhelming. I said to myself: listen, concentrate, and look as though you have been doing this job for years. Internally I felt I was completely out of my depth, but somehow I survived that first morning without anything untoward occurring or indeed in any way giving the impression that I was new to the job. And that set the pattern for the following days, weeks, months and indeed years to come.

I had decided at the outset to adopt one guiding principle in the light of my judicial inexperience and my extremely limited knowledge of Criminal Law and procedure. The principle was quite simple: when presiding over a trial, I should let the proceedings develop, and not intervene unless it was clear that I must do so. After all, nearly all the Counsel appearing at such an important court centre were both knowledgeable and experienced. Thus, for example, if such Counsel did not make a point or allude to a particular feature of the trial, there would invariably be a good reason for them to adopt such a course of action. It was not for me to intervene, make what I thought was an obvious point, only to discover that, for whatever reason, my intervention led to the trial being aborted. (However, I note in passing that of course there are certain occasions when, as a matter of established procedure, a judge must intervene, irrespective of the approach adopted by Counsel.)

Very early in my career the adoption of my guiding principle proved to be absolutely right in a trial I will always remember for two very different reasons. The first was, as I have indicated, that an intervention I was tempted to make in court would have had the most disastrous consequences. The trial related to the robbery of a shop on Clapham High Street, alleged to have been committed by the three defendants. There was CCTV footage of the robbery taking place and I was convinced that one of the people appearing in it was one of the defendants standing in the dock. This was to me clear beyond any doubt, and yet Counsel for the prosecution made no reference to the CCTV footage confirming the participation of the defendant in the robbery. I was very puzzled. I was minded to intervene to ensure such vital identification evidence was brought to the attention of the jury. And then I thought of my guiding principle – let the proceedings unfold and do not intervene unless it is absolutely necessary to do so. After all, Prosecuting Counsel would no doubt have pored over the CCTV footage many times and it was not credible that I, on a first viewing, would have spotted something the prosecution had missed in their detailed preparation for the trial. So I abided by my principle and kept silent. Later on I was very pleased that I did. During the course of the trial it emerged that the person in the CCTV footage who I was convinced was one of the defendants had in fact been tried previously and convicted of his part in the robbery and was already serving a long sentence in prison. If I had intervened with my erroneous identification of one of the defendants, I would not only have looked very foolish, but it would also have meant that the trial might have had to be aborted and a new trial ordered. A considerable waste of time of everyone involved in the trial and a complete waste of taxpayers' money.

The second reason why the Clapham robbery case is indelibly inscribed on my mind is for a wholly different and worrying reason. The key evidence for the prosecution was given by two police officers, who stated that they had seen the three defendants running out of the shop immediately after the alarm had been given by the shopkeeper. The officers in question were in a police car some 200 yards away, in a side road on the other (south) side of Clapham High Street. The car was stationary at the time because the traffic in the High Street was at a standstill. The evidence of the police officers came to this: in their seated position in the police car, they could see over the top of the cars and other vehicles which were stationary in the High Street to the north side of Clapham High Street. They also stated that, at a distance of some 200 yards, they could positively identify the three men fleeing from the shop as the defendants in the dock. Under cross-examination the officers were adamant that they could see the defendants' faces so as to identify them. Defence Counsel never challenged the ability of the police officers to identify the defendants when they were such a considerable distance away from the shop and on the other side of the street. In the event, the three defendants were acquitted. Whether the jury acquitted them because they did not accept the identification evidence of the police officers, or for some other reason, one will never know. The secrecy of the deliberations of the jury is, of course, inviolate.

Be that as it may, purely by coincidence, a few weeks later Kate and I had been invited to dinner by friends who lived in Clapham. The details of the Clapham robbery case were still very fresh in my mind. As we were driving there, I turned to Kate and said, "Do you know what I would like to do? I want to drive to the very spot where the police officers said they were in their stationary car and look down Clapham High Street and see whether they could have observed the three defendants so as to positively identify them."

So that is precisely what we did. I looked in the direction of the shop. Unlike the night in question, the traffic was flowing freely in the High Street, so our view was much better than the police officers' would have been. Kate and I agreed that there was no way the police officers could have seen the faces of the men coming out of the shop sufficiently clearly to make a positive identification. It was not a close call: the police officers might have seen the outline of the three men emerging from the shop, but there was no way they could have seen the faces of the men so as to be able to identify them at that time or thereafter. Kate and I were both shocked. The police officers had given evidence on oath and it was abundantly clear that they had not told the truth.

A second trial I presided over soon afterwards was to give me similar cause for concern. This was the Euston Station grievous bodily harm ('GBH') case. Again the critical evidence was provided by two police officers, and I shall refer to them as an Inspector and a Sergeant, although these were not their actual ranks. The case for the prosecution was straightforward: the Police Inspector and Sergeant saw, on a CCTV monitor, a car parked outside the station which they believed was illegally plying for hire. The Inspector ran down the steps to the road below and then along the slope which emerged into Eversholt Street. The Inspector's evidence was that, when he turned right at the top of the slope into Eversholt Street, the car in question was started up and deliberately driven at him, making him jump out of the way. He lost his balance and fell onto the road. He was bruised but otherwise suffered no injury. The driver of the car was charged with attempted GBH which, if he had been convicted, would have resulted in a significant custodial sentence of some years. The Inspector gave evidence before me. Dressed in his uniform, he cut an impressive figure. When he was giving his evidence for the prosecution, I formed the view, provisionally, that he was telling the truth. However, I thought to myself (not for the last time in my judicial career), "Remember the Clapham robbery case." That my thought was totally justified plainly emerged when it came to the cross-examination of the Inspector. When he was asked by Defence Counsel about the prevailing conditions at the time of the incident, the Inspector stated that it was a clear evening, it was not raining and it was daylight (the incident having occurred in June). The Inspector's view was that the visibility of the driver that night must have been very good and was not obscured in any way. The next witness for the prosecution was the Sergeant. He had run up the slope, following the Inspector. He saw him turn right at Eversholt Street and then observed him falling backwards. So far so good for the prosecution. But then warning bells started to ring in my head when Counsel for the defence asked a number of searching questions.

"Did you see the car being driven at the Inspector?"

"No."

"Did you see the Inspector stumble?"

"Yes."

"Either before, at, or immediately after the time the Inspector stumbled, did you see the car at all?"

"No."

"So your evidence comes to this: you followed the Inspector up the slope, you saw him turn right as he reached Eversholt Street, and you saw him stumble, but you didn't see the car in the immediate vicinity of the Inspector as he fell?"

"That's correct," confirmed the Sergeant.

It seemed to me that the Sergeant was distancing himself from the evidence that the Inspector had given. Worse was to follow for the prosecution, as Defence Counsel adduced evidence, first, that the driver was not plying for hire – he had been booked to pick up a customer who also gave evidence to that effect; secondly, contrary to the Inspector's evidence, it was raining on the evening in question and the defence produced a meteorological report to that effect; finally, the driver (aged 43) had no previous convictions for driving or indeed any other offences.

The jury took very little time to acquit the defendant and, in my opinion, rightly so. I reflected on several aspects of the trial. First, what initially sounded the alarm bells ringing for the prosecution's case was the Sergeant's apparent desire to distance himself from the Inspector's evidence. Secondly, the nagging feeling I had that the prosecution might have been brought in a fit of pique at the injured pride of an Inspector stumbling to the ground in front of his Sergeant and members of the public. Finally, the defence team (unlike Defence Counsel in the Clapham robbery case) had done their homework in producing the meteorological office report. But the overriding thought in my mind was that once more this was a case where the only evidence to support the prosecution was provided by police officers. That thought reminded me of the words of a judge at Southwark Crown Court: "You will never get a Southwark jury to convict on police evidence only; they are too worldly wise to do this."

He was certainly right, in my experience. In no case I presided over at Southwark was a conviction obtained on police evidence only. The view of the senior judge was proved correct time and again. For example, in a prosecution for attempted GBH, where a vagrant was alleged to have attempted to injure policemen with a broken glass bottle, seven police officers (but no independent witnesses) gave wholly consistent evidence for the prosecution. Counsel for the defence placed heavy emphasis on the fact that there were no independent witnesses, despite the fact that the incident took place outside Charing Cross Station at a busy time, when numerous members of the public must have witnessed it. Unsurprisingly, with a Southwark jury, the defendant was acquitted.

As time went by, of course I became somewhat more relaxed about sitting as a judge at Southwark, but I was still determined to leave nothing to chance. So, for example, I always wrote out my summing-up beforehand and (to cover the possibility of a guilty verdict) considered the appropriate sentence, having researched all the relevant authorities. That attention to detail did, in the event, seem to pay dividends. For example, as far as I am aware, there was never any successful appeal against a summing-up that I delivered. Similarly, I can only recall one successful appeal against a sentence I had passed. The Court of Appeal decided that a sentence of six years for robbery that I had imposed was excessive and that it should be reduced to five and a half years. Apparently the Court of Appeal was of the opinion that such fine-tuning of my sentence was necessary.

Over the years I came to realise that, by and large, the jury system worked very well and has much to commend it. In the vast majority of cases the conclusion of the jury seemed to be eminently sensible, and they were usually very quick to spot a defendant or witness who was not telling the truth. They were not overly impressed by a police uniform. But although I concluded that the jury system worked well, there were instances where I was left open-mouthed by the verdict the jury reached. Three cases in particular stand out in my mind: the Justin de Blank case, the heroin in the fridge case, and finally, the most bizarre of all, the Peckham Common knife case.

The Justin de Blank case related to the company which owned a chain of very upmarket small shops selling bread, patisserie and similar products. The trial concerned the Chelsea shop where, at the relevant time, there were two employees, the manageress and a shop assistant. The charge on the indictment was one of theft brought against the shop assistant. It was alleged that he had stolen money from the till. The prosecution's case was very straightforward. The manageress had long suspected that cash was being taken from the till in the shop on a regular basis, so one afternoon she decided to take action. As the shop was essentially a bakery, the afternoons were a very slack time, with few customers entering the premises. So late afternoon was the perfect time to implement her simple plan. At about four o'clock one day, she checked the till in the absence of the employee, counted all the money in it, and therefore knew precisely what was there. She went to see her assistant and told him she was going out for a meeting and would return in an hour or so. She duly left the shop in the sole charge of the employee, returning just before it closed. The last part of her plan was, on her return, to cash up the till and find out precisely how much was there. When she did cash up that second time, there was a shortfall. The difference between the amounts in the till when she left the shop and when she returned was £75. The police were called and the assistant was arrested and duly charged with theft.

It was very difficult to resist the conclusion that it was the assistant who was responsible for the theft. Indeed, any such doubts in my mind were swiftly removed by Counsel for the prosecution, who carried out a searching and very effective cross-examination of the employee.

"Is it true that you were in the shop without interruption between the times the manageress left and returned?"

"Yes."

"Were there any other employees working in the shop during that time?"

"No."

"Did any customers come into the shop during that time?"

"No."

"So is it correct to say that, between the time the manageress left the shop and the time she returned, you were the only person there?"

"Yes."

"So you were the only person who had access to the till during that time?"

"Yes."

"So you had access to the till, the only person to have access to it, and you stole £75 from it?"

"No."

"Well, you were the only person on the premises when the money was taken from the till, so, if you didn't take it, how did the money disappear from the till? Can you give the court any explanation for the disappearance of the money other than that you stole it?"

Silence. More silence. Answer came there none. The defendant said nothing, looked at the ground, shuffled around in the witness box, and finally, so it seemed, looked to the heavens for inspiration. However, there was no intervention, divine or otherwise, to break the deafening silence.

In the twenty-five years or so that I sat as a Recorder, this was the only occasion when a defendant gave no answer whatsoever to such a critical question. Defendants in similar situations would often give far-fetched, ludicrous or totally unbelievable answers, but they did provide an answer, however grotesque it might be.

The failure of the defendant to provide any answer to the question from Counsel for the prosecution seemed to me to effectively mean the end of the trial, although one can never really predict the verdict of a jury. However, here it did seem to me that only one verdict was possible, or to be more precise, only one verdict that would be consistent with the evidence adduced before the court. As the trial drew to a close, I received a little surprise. The Clerk of the Court gave me a list of the defendant's previous convictions, a list that a jury is not allowed to see or know about during the course of the trial. The exclusion of previous convictions is based on the thinking that such a list is wholly irrelevant to the question as to whether <u>this</u> defendant is guilty of <u>this</u> offence. However, the judge in such circumstances may be shown a list of previous convictions of the defendant, although, of course, he or she is not allowed (apart from clearly established exceptions in well-defined circumstances), prior to the jury's verdict being made known, to refer to it in any way in the presence of the jury. (None of the exceptions applied here.) I studied the list of the defendant's 'previous'. It went on for page after page, and nearly all of his convictions were for offences similar to the one now before the court.

The list of the defendant's 'previous' was in my mind when I came to compose my summing-up. However, as I have mentioned, I could not refer to it. Despite my own view of the evidence in the case and my overall view of the defendant's guilt or otherwise (something which is, of course, entirely a matter for the jury to decide), in my summing-up I sought to present a totally fair and unbiased view of the case before the jury. I summed up, as I always sought to do, 'right down the middle', never seeking to influence the jury with my own views as to how they should decide the case before them.

The jury went out to consider their verdict and returned fairly soon afterwards to deliver it 'according to the law'. Their swift return did not surprise me – I had thought as I sent them out that this was a trial where extensive deliberation was not necessary.

"How do you find the defendant? Guilty or not guilty?"

"Not guilty," said the jury foreman in a firm and resolute way.

I was astounded by what I heard. I could not understand how, on the basis of all the evidence and the devastating cross-examination, the jury could reach such a verdict, and so quickly, indicating there was no doubt in their minds at all.

However, the jury's verdict is the jury's verdict, and that is the end of the trial, except that this time, before I discharged the jury, I did one thing that I also did occasionally thereafter. From the file of judge's papers lying on the desk before me I took out the list of the defendant's previous convictions and read part of it to them. There were some very surprised faces on the members of the jury, but I thought it right that they should be able to reflect on what the defendant had been convicted of in the past. It might make them wonder whether they had, in fact, delivered the correct verdict.

I was very annoyed with the jury's inexplicable verdict and at lunchtime that day I told another senior Southwark Court judge what had happened at the trial. I asked him whether he felt frustrated when a jury reached a verdict which was, in his opinion, clearly contrary to the evidence adduced. His answer: "Not now. I used to be, but it is pointless to allow your emotions to become aroused in a trial or at the jury's verdict. The only situation where I do become very annoyed with a verdict which is clearly inconsistent with the evidence is when the prosecution is a very significant one involving, say, a drug-smuggling gang responsible for supplying very substantial quantities of heroin or cocaine to the public, and the prosecution has been extremely time-consuming and at enormous cost to the taxpayer. Otherwise, no. I just move on to the next trial."

As time went by and I acquired more experience, I realised that the approach of this senior judge was absolutely right. But the Justin de Blank case has always stayed in my mind as one of the most striking, if not the most striking case, where I was at a loss to understand how the jury could possibly have reached the verdict they did.

Next we come to the heroin in the fridge case. A police raid on the defendant's flat yielded the discovery of a large quantity of heroin in a magnetised container stuck on the underside of the freezer compartment in a fridge. The defendant had lived in the flat for some two years with his girlfriend and it was admitted that the fridge had been there throughout his occupation. He claimed that he did not know about the heroin; he had not put it there, nor had his girlfriend, and he did not even know of its existence before the police discovered it. The defendant said it had nothing to do with him. Although here again, having perused his list of 'previous', I saw that he had been convicted on numerous occasions of drug-related offences, some of them very serious. Of course, the jury would not be informed of that during the trial. So the obvious question was, if the defendant had not put the heroin in the fridge, who had? I thought nobody was likely to admit that the heroin was theirs, with the possibility of a lengthy custodial sentence to follow. But, not for the last time, I hadn't considered all the possibilities. There was one person who was prepared to admit that he had put the heroin in the fridge. It was the defendant's brother-in-law who, so it was claimed but never actually proved, lived in the flat in question before the defendant moved in.

So why was the brother-in-law prepared to accept responsibility for such a serious crime, with the dire consequences that might follow? The answer was very simple. The brother-in-law had just started a twelve-year sentence for carrying out an organised armed robbery, where a number of people were seriously injured, and he was currently enjoying Her Majesty's hospitality in Belmarsh Prison. Indeed, he was brought to court in manacles. He had nothing to lose by admitting that he had placed the heroin in the fridge – he was already in prison and likely to remain there for a very long time – so the prospects of any action being taken against him for this offence seemed to me to be virtually nil. But there still remained the question of whether the jury would accept the evidence of the brother-in-law. After all, it was hardly credible that he would have moved out of the flat and left an extremely valuable quantity of drugs there for more than two years and not tried to recover them. Also, it was most relevant that this evidence came from a convicted felon serving a very long sentence for an extremely serious offence. Even so, the jury returned a verdict of 'not guilty'. As the defendant left the dock 'without a stain on his character', I looked at him and could not resist the thought that he was a very lucky man. However, over the years there were, so I thought, a series of such lucky men.

One was the central figure in the Peckham Common knife case. The evidence for the prosecution was straightforward. Three police officers saw a young black man (a material fact in the case) running across Peckham Common with a long knife in his hand. The police officers called out to him to stop, but the defendant continued to run. He then ran round the back of a large tree and so was out of sight of the police for a few moments. He then emerged from behind the tree, walking slowly. When the police officers called on him for a second time to stop, he did so. But crucially, when the police officers reached the defendant, he was no longer carrying a knife. The police believed that the defendant had dropped the knife while he was out of their sight behind the tree. A search of the ground behind the tree immediately confirmed their suspicions. A knife with a long blade was recovered. The defendant was arrested and charged with carrying an offensive weapon.

The defendant did not dispute the fact that he had handled the knife. Presumably he thought it was pointless to say he had never touched it, when he knew his fingerprints would be all over it. So how was he to explain that he had handled an offensive weapon in a wholly innocent way? Well, his evidence was as follows. He had been walking across Peckham Common. He had not been running, as the police officers had alleged. As he walked behind a tree, he saw a knife lying on the ground. He said that, being a responsible citizen (although his list of 'previous' might indicate otherwise), he decided he would pick up the knife to see if it was an offensive weapon. If it was (and one had to assume he was knowledgeable as to what was an offensive weapon!), his intention was to take it to the nearest police station and hand it in so that no innocent member of the public could be injured by it. Commendable! However, to add a touch of reality to the situation, it was difficult (although some might think not impossible) to believe that a young black man with a series of previous convictions would willingly enter a police station in South London in the 1980s and hand over a knife with the explanation that he did not want innocent members of the public to be injured by it. For my own part, if one envisaged that scenario, the defendant's case seemed to stretch credulity. So why did he put forward what I regarded as such an implausible explanation? Why did he admit to handling the knife? Presumably he thought he had to do so because his fingerprints would be on the knife and those fingerprints (because of his 'previous') would be readily identifiable. Except the defendant was not to know that on this occasion the police did not test the knife for fingerprints! So in fact, if the defendant could have foreseen that was going to happen, he could simply have denied all knowledge of the knife, or at the very least he could have denied handling it. An elaborate explanation which in the event was wholly unnecessary. Be that as it may, the jury, by returning a verdict of 'not guilty', plainly accepted the defendant's explanation. I found the whole trial and the series of events related during the course of it to be one of the most bizarre trials I presided over.

Despite some of the more surprising verdicts I have related above, as my career on the Bench continued, I developed increasing respect for the jury system, particularly because the common sense of juries was rarely to be underestimated. Quite often they showed, collectively, a maturity and wisdom that was admirable. For example, I recall being told on one occasion that a case relating to the supply of pornographic films had been put in my 'List'. Such cases are always difficult, and for the part-time judge (maybe even for a full-time one) they represent a minefield. I was concerned that the male members of the jury would not try the case in the serious manner it deserved and that the female members could find it embarrassing. In the event, the jury tried the case perfectly and, in my opinion, admirably. Their verdict of 'guilty' was in my opinion wholly consistent with the evidence.

Although I found sitting as a Recorder very fulfilling, there was one aspect of presiding over criminal trials which disappointed me, and that was that there seemed to me to be very little actual law (as distinct from matters of criminal procedure) which needed to be debated in a criminal case. Although it may be different for a full-time judge, at the level of Recorder a criminal trial is essentially about the facts and, critically, the question of whether the defendant is guilty of the offence as charged. Of course, Counsel may have to make submissions on points of law; the judge has to direct the jury on the applicable law in his summing-up; and during the course of the trial points of criminal procedure may well arise. But in all my years as a Recorder, substantive points of law involving competing submissions as to the correct legal analysis by Counsel were rare. And that is what I missed so much: the resolution of difficult points of law by reference to the relevant statutes and the decided cases. In fact, that only happened to me on one occasion and then Counsel, or at least Counsel acting for the prosecution, based their submissions on the wrong authorities.

Trained as a lawyer, and the lifeblood of my practice being statute and case law, and seeking to reach a conclusion on an issue by teasing my brain as to what was the correct legal analysis, I was left somewhat frustrated by the absence of such daily challenges to my legal skills. Unsurprisingly, therefore, I came to the conclusion after some twenty years of sitting that it was time for me to retire as a Recorder. When I did so, I couldn't help reflecting on what Lord Steyn had said to me in 1984, when he was prompting me to apply for an appointment as a Recorder: "It's all common sense." I harboured some doubts at the time when he uttered those words. But certainly he was right to place so much importance on the value of common sense in a criminal trial, both as regards the judge and the jury.

Overall, sitting as a Recorder had formed a really interesting and worthwhile chapter in my life. But retiring as a Recorder did not mean retirement from the Bench altogether. In 1994 I had been appointed a Deputy High Court Judge, which I found to be a totally different experience. I was assigned to the Chancery Division, which amongst the divisions of the High Court was my natural home. Unlike in the criminal courts, whenever I sat in the Chancery Division, legal issues inevitably arose, on which Counsel on both sides would make their submissions. Those submissions would be based on what Counsel considered to be the relevant statute law, case law, and other appropriate legal sources. That was precisely what I was used to. It was the meat and drink of my practice. Sitting in the Chancery Division, the cases I heard related to very technical, often arcane, points of law. However, that was absolutely fine by me, as the more technical the points of law, the more my legal skills would be challenged. And that was what I wanted. Moreover, I thoroughly enjoyed the experience of hearing Counsel's submissions and then writing my judgment. Indeed, that was one of the critical differences between sitting as a Recorder in the criminal courts, where a summing-up, but not a judgment, was required. Writing a judgment could be a daunting experience, but to me it was always a fulfilling one.

I relate just two cases from my years of sitting as a Deputy High Court Judge. The first was where a point of Insolvency Law and a point of Revenue Law arose. The claimant only had to succeed on one of the two points to win his case. I heard both Counsel on the insolvency issue first and concluded that the claimant was entitled to succeed. But after all those years of writing about Revenue Law, I very much wanted to express my conclusions on the novel tax issue that arose. I was very tempted to do just that. However, the thought then struck me that I would have been very embarrassed if my judgment had been reversed on appeal. So I resisted the temptation, although my fingers were itching to put pen to paper on this new, and to me, exciting point of Revenue Law.

The other case I recall because I was so impressed with the thoroughness of Counsel. The case in question related to a claim for title to a small piece of wooded wasteland (which adjoined the claimant's property), based on his occupation of it. The claimant, as a matter of law, had to show continuing occupation of the land over a period of years. In fact, the claimant alleged his occupation of the land had existed over a period of some twenty years. To support his case, a series of photographs was produced to the court, showing the claimant on this wasteland and marked on the reverse as having been taken in different years. In each photograph the claimant was dressed differently. At first sight, the photographs appeared to be important evidence supporting the claimant's case. However, when it came to cross-examination, Counsel for the defendant pointed out to the court that, although in each photograph the claimant was dressed differently, the leaves on the ground in the far distance of each photograph were in exactly the same position. Under cross-examination the claimant had to admit that all the photographs were taken on the same day, and that he had gone through the elaborate charade of putting on different clothes for each photograph, and then marking each of them on the back with a different date. After hearing Counsel, I indicated that the claim should be withdrawn to avoid further court time being wasted. I also indicated my outrage at the claimant's conduct and said that I would be referring the case to 'the appropriate authorities' for them to consider what further action should be taken. My reference to 'the appropriate authorities' was a time-hallowed phrase used by judges to refer to the Director of Public Prosecutions.

I conclude my references to my history of sitting as a judge with just one further comment. In the twenty or so years that I have sat as a Deputy High Court Judge, I have never had to decide a case where an issue of Revenue Law arose. With a wry smile on my face, I write that this might not have been a bad thing – because I might not have got it right!

CHAPTER 23

TALES OF THE UNEXPECTED

"Oh! what a tangled web we weave
When first we practise to deceive!"
Sir Walter Scott (1771-1832)

In practice at the Bar, one Consultation or informal meeting with a client follows another. Each is usually very complicated and demanding, but there is nothing to distinguish it in one's memory from so many of the others. And nothing that would be of interest to anyone outside the ranks of the Revenue Bar. However, there are exceptions, and those I relate in this chapter. They are all true and I have not sought to embellish them in any way. Naturally I have changed the names of all those instructing me, and of the clients, in the cases referred to below so as to avoid any possibility of identification.

The first case was incredible. It related to a person I shall call Ronnie. At the time of the events I describe below, Ronnie was not a client of mine, although at a later date I was instructed by solicitors on his behalf. Ronnie was flamboyant and seriously rich. To appreciate all the nuances that are to follow, let me set the scene.

We are about to board a large executive jet, one of several owned by Ronnie. Leading the party on board, and in something of a hurry, is his adored dog, Precious, a very large black poodle. As I am soon to discover, the dog's name could not be more appropriate. Precious bounds across the tarmac and up the steps to the plane; she is very eager to be on board. We amble behind.

As we reach the steps, Ronnie turns to me with a huge smile on his face and says with immense pride: "This dog adores flying. In fact, she has her own seat on the plane. Once on board, she makes straight for it and sits there looking very content, like the seasoned traveller she is. Woe betide anyone who takes her seat." I think to myself that this is truly bizarre. A dog which has its own seat on a plane, knows which one it is, and settles down there. I say nothing. I keep my thoughts about this most pampered of pooches to myself.

We board the plane. Precious is already ensconced in 'her' seat, looking smug and proprietorial. Not long after, I learn that she has every right to be so. We take our seats for the flight and start to discuss Ronnie's business affairs. He gazes very fondly at Precious. "That must be the richest dog in the world!" says Ronnie proudly. "I am sure she is a lovely dog – you probably adore her as much as I adore mine."

"No, no, I mean far more than being adorable. She is really rich."

I am puzzled by Ronnie's remark, but he continues in the same vein, with heavy emphasis.

"She is a very wealthy lady. I have taken care of her in every sense, particularly financially."

"You mean you have left her money in your will?" That was something I knew to be possible.

"No, I am not talking about financial provision in my will. I am talking about the here and now."

I am surprised. Ronnie is an extremely successful businessman (his fleet of executive jets was an obvious manifestation of that) and as shrewd and level-headed as anyone I knew. He did not talk in riddles or make foolish statements. When he spoke, he made every word count, and count effectively, so what was he talking about?

"Sorry, Ronnie, you've lost me."

"Well, some years ago, when the top tax rate was 98 per cent, I was paying huge amounts of Income Tax and Capital Gains Tax. I thought that was ridiculous. So one day I was sitting in the bath and the perfect solution came to me. It was so obvious and so simple that I couldn't understand why no one had done it before. I would give all my assets to my dog. No assets, no income, so no tax. All the income and capital gains would belong to Precious, and I thought, how could the Revenue assess a dog for tax? Impossible. Game, set and match to me. Problem solved. So I thought, if this is going to work – and I couldn't see any reason why it wouldn't – I would have to do it absolutely properly. I got my solicitor's advice and he drafted a technical legal document – I think it was simply called a Deed of Gift – which transferred all my assets to Precious."

"So then what happened?" I asked innocently, as I was finding the story incredible, even though I did admire him for coming up with the idea and was curious to find out what happened afterwards. Ronnie continued, "The tax return I submitted for the year I made the gift to Precious consequently showed much smaller amounts of income and capital gains compared with the previous year. Of course I wasn't surprised when I received a letter from my Inspector asking why my income and capital gains had fallen so dramatically. So I replied, explaining the situation to him in some detail. I waited for the inevitable explosion and a reply to the effect that 'You can't be serious!' It duly arrived. He adopted a very simple approach, saying it was not possible to give assets to a dog. The tenor of his letter was that the whole idea was a nonsense and would I now, having had a little bit of fun, please complete my tax return properly so as to include all my income and capital gains.

"I replied that my solicitor had advised me that I could make over assets to a dog and that the gift had been made in accordance with the law. I enclosed a copy of the Deed of Gift, duly stamped. I added for good measure that everything had been done in a legally effective way so that the assets now belonged to Precious. I concluded by stating that my tax return, as submitted, was correct and would he please therefore deal with it accordingly.

"The Inspector replied that he had never heard it even suggested that such a gift could be made to a dog, that it was an invalid transaction, and the assets were still mine. He duly enclosed assessments based on my previous year's tax return. There then followed an exchange of correspondence which was pretty tedious, where neither of us gave an inch. I didn't pay the tax he wanted and, being stumped for ideas, in his final letter he wrote that, as the point was an unusual one, he was going to refer my tax return to a specialist unit of the Revenue, the Technical Division. The Inspector had obviously given up and wanted Precious off his desk and out of his life. As a result, I waited with bated breath for an Inland Revenue response in a letter headed 'Technical Division, Canine Unit'."

The plane bumps around. The stewardess nearly loses the drinks off her tray, and Ronnie is obviously having great fun telling his story. I look across at Precious, sitting there calmly, obviously very happy in 'her' seat, unconcerned about the turbulence. Clearly she is not interested in her tax affairs, believing no doubt that they are being perfectly well looked after.

I am fascinated to hear the outcome of this saga. "Go on, go on," I impatiently say to Ronnie.

"Well, the next step was that I got a letter from some high-ranking official in this specialist unit of the Revenue. All very official and very impressive-looking, with the seal of Technical Division at the top, but to my disappointment no reference to a Canine Unit! The whole matter was obviously being taken very seriously – possibly the Revenue feared an avalanche of gifts by taxpayers to their dogs and the enormous problems that canine taxpayers would present them with. I noticed that the person who had sent me the letter was no less than a <u>Principal</u> Inspector of Taxes. I was impressed, but only until I read the contents of his letter. He merely repeated what the Inspector had said, but he added what he called his 'killer point' in support of all the previously-rehearsed Revenue arguments.

"The Principal Inspector stated, 'Well, you have accepted in correspondence that capital gains were made after the date of the Deed of Gift. If that is right, then someone had made the decisions to sell the assets in question, and a dog couldn't make such decisions; only a human being could.' So, he continued, I must have made those decisions and therefore the capital gains must be mine. This was his killer point – his 'silver bullet' – to show that the whole idea of the assets belonging to Precious was a nonsense. Accordingly, he concluded that the tax was overdue and must be paid immediately.'"

We hit real turbulence now, the plane is being thrown around, but the two of us are entirely unconcerned; Ronnie is enjoying telling his story to his captive audience, and I am totally fascinated by this ludicrous tale. Ronnie resumes his story.

"So I had to deal with the Revenue's so-called 'killer point'. However, that was no problem. I responded to the Principal Inspector by explaining to him how decisions were made to sell the assets. I told him that, as far as selling, or indeed buying, shares was concerned, each day I took out a copy of the *Financial Times* and showed it to Precious. I taught her to place a paw next to the list of stocks and shares. Every day she did this. If she barked once, then the share had to be sold; if she barked twice, the share was to be purchased. Precious always barked once or twice as appropriate, and this is how she managed her portfolio. The decisions were hers, so the capital gains were hers also. It couldn't be more simple. The 'silver bullet' was wide of the mark. Revenue 0 Precious 1.

"However, the Principal Inspector was a determined man. He had no intention of giving up without a fight. He agreed, in light of what I had written, that the income and capital gains were not mine, so the earlier demands for tax would not be pursued. But, and this according to him was a big 'but', what I had written gave him a new and totally different line of attack. Even if Precious made the decisions as I had indicated, I would still have to act on them, which would mean instructing stockbrokers to buy or sell accordingly. Therefore, although I could not be assessed for tax personally, I could be assessed as 'Trustee' for Precious. The Inspector was obviously delighted, as he believed that my explanation had given him a second and more effective 'silver bullet'.

"I wrote back that he was confusing the mere administrative steps necessary to implement the decision with the decision itself. His argument had to be wrong because, if he was right, it would mean that, whenever a stockbroker sold shares, he would become a Trustee for his client. That would be a nonsense. The Deed of Gift was the complete answer. It showed that the assets belonged to Precious. She was the absolute owner. There was no Trust Deed and no Trust. The argument that I was a Trustee for Precious was totally without foundation in law. Another killer argument of the Principal Inspector had bitten the dust. Although, knowing this Inspector, I thought, he still won't give up. And he didn't. Round 3. The Principal Inspector accepted in his next letter that I was not a Trustee for Precious or acting for her in any such capacity. It must really have pained him to write that, but he still had another shot in his locker. He wrote that, as I had maintained I was not the taxpayer, he proposed to accept that Precious was, and accordingly in future he would address all correspondence and tax demands to her."

I burst out laughing. "He wasn't serious?"

"Oh, yes, he was. Thereafter he sent letters and tax demands to Precious. Of course, he didn't receive a single reply to any missive he sent her. The letters, tax demands and threats of action dried up after a while. However, he never formally admitted defeat. Possibly his pride wouldn't let him."

"And how long ago did Precious receive her last demand from the Inland Revenue?"

"Oh, years ago. Maybe six or seven years or so."

"So they really gave up?"

"Yes."

"And did they accept your tax returns showing no income or capital gains?"

"Yes, basically, except for a few small items."

Ronnie was looking very pleased with himself. No doubt he had told this improbable story many times before. But he knew that I would particularly appreciate its nuances, given my professional expertise. Ronnie was looking very pleased; Precious equally so. They didn't realise that I was about to rain on their parade.

"Ronnie, that's an amazing story. However, you do realise that you have a major problem as a result of what you've done." The smile is wiped off Ronnie's face immediately and suddenly he looks very concerned. "What about death?" I deliberately phrase my question vaguely.

"What do you mean?"

"Well, what happens when Precious dies?"

"Ah," he says, and the frown has gone, relief shows on his craggy face and the smile returns.

"I'm surprised you ask that. The answer's simple. The same as for Income Tax and Capital Gains Tax. All the assets will be hers, not mine, and any attempt to get Inheritance Tax in respect of them will fail in the same way as the other tax demands have. No one is going to pay Inheritance Tax on the assets when she dies, or indeed when I die. It's foolproof. It works in exactly the same way as for the other taxes. It's another advantage of the arrangements I have made."

"Sorry, Ronnie, you've missed my point. I wasn't referring to tax at all. I meant, what will happen to the assets when Precious dies? You have said in correspondence with the Revenue, apparently many times, that the assets belong to Precious, so who gets the assets when she dies? Not you. Possibly her puppies," I say somewhat facetiously. "It's a real problem."

"Bloody hell!" Ronnie exclaims. "I never thought of that."

"Well, perhaps you should start thinking about that right now, whilst it's not too late." Ronnie looks downcast.

This story, which he has no doubt told many times with glee, has met a rather different fate on this occasion. He looks thoughtful and somewhat deflated. With that, the plane lands with a thump, rather like Ronnie's wizard tax planning. He pulls himself together a little and says, "What will happen?"

"Well, it might go to any puppies Precious has, or maybe it will go to the Crown as *bona vacantia*."

"What, all <u>my</u> assets?"

"No, Ronnie. Remember, they all belong to Precious. That's what you told the Revenue."

No smiles from Ronnie now, although Precious still looks totally happy. Possibly she does have puppies. She still looks smugness personified; possibly she has a good tax adviser as well.

"Well, what am I going to do?"

"Well, first, get Precious to retain a smart tax lawyer, and secondly, get her to make a will, remembering to put her paw imprint at the end of it," I say with a broad smile on my face. At that point I leave the plane, with Ronnie still sitting in his seat, deep in thought. The words of Sir Wilfred Greene MR in a famous tax case come to mind, "He who plays with fire cannot complain of burnt fingers." Ronnie's fingers are looking distinctly charred.

As I step onto the tarmac, I reflect that I have just heard the shaggiest dog story ever told. And then I think, one day I must write it down, with all its twists and turns. And then I think, no point; no one would ever believe it. You should.

The idea that Ronnie had was simple, innovative and highly entertaining. But, of course, in over forty-five years' practice at the Revenue Bar, there were also the more troublesome cases. Something would arise prior to or during a Consultation that made me concerned, for myself, for my clients or for both. Two cases, both involving 'unusual' proposals, spring to mind.

The first was in the early 1970s when Alfred, my Clerk, came into my room and said that he had received a request from a highly respected firm of solicitors for a Consultation. So far, no problem. "However," he continued, looking clearly embarrassed, "there is an unusual aspect to the request for your advice. They want the Consultation to take place outside Chambers." At that time that was most unusual and could only be justified in exceptional circumstances. Here, apparently, the solicitors had made no attempt to suggest that any such circumstances applied. Alfred continued, "What the solicitors are asking is, would you be prepared to be collected from Chambers by a limousine and, once inside it, to be blindfolded? You would then be taken to a secret destination, which would not be made known to you then or afterwards. I must tell you, sir, that the solicitors said that this is a weighty matter and the fees would be very good."

Weighty or not, good fees or not, I was not prepared to advise professionally in such circumstances, for personal reasons and also because I always want to observe the highest standards of professional integrity. I let no time pass in communicating my thoughts to Alfred. "I am not prepared to accept Instructions on that basis. We would have no idea who the clients actually are. Moreover, once I get into the limousine, I would have no control over my destiny. I am also concerned about the Professional Rules relating to the conduct of practice at the Bar. So for all those reasons please inform the solicitors that Counsel would not countenance accepting Instructions in such circumstances." And so that was that, and the prospect of my making an 'exciting' limousine trip to never-never land disappeared with Alfred as, somewhat disconsolately, he left my room.

Some years later I was surprised again, albeit in a different way, by the course that a Consultation in Chambers took. At the start, and indeed for some time thereafter, the Consultation proceeded in the normal professional way. I had received detailed Instructions from a leading firm of London solicitors. I had prepared my advice as to all the issues that were raised, and was fully prepared when the client entered my room. I then proceeded to deal with all the matters raised, one by one. At times my instructing solicitors asked for elucidation of the advice I had provided, but at no time did the lay client participate in the discussion. Having reached the end of the Instructions and advised accordingly, I believed the Consultation was over. I started tying up the papers with red tape, as would be normal. Suddenly there was an explosion on my right from the lay client. He was obviously very angry. There then followed a tirade which took me totally by surprise.

Almost shouting, he said, "But you have missed the most important point in the case! Indeed, it is the entire reason we are here today."

"Excuse me?" I managed to say at this totally unexpected and irate interruption. My client was so annoyed that his face was red with anger.

"The whole point of this case is that my company is registered in the Isle of Man and therefore is not subject to tax."

"I am sorry. I don't follow what you are saying. There is no reference to the Isle of Man in my Instructions, there is no reference to an Isle of Man company, and there is no reference to what you describe as the whole point of this case."

"But you've missed the point. There are references in your Instructions to a Scottish company, and Scotland is part of the Isle of Man. So it will not pay any United Kingdom tax."

I looked at my client incredulously. Could he possibly have just said what I thought he had said?

"Sorry. Did you just say that Scotland is part of the Isle of Man?"

"Yes. I have spent fifteen years researching this fundamental issue. It is my life's work and, as a result of this, there is no doubt at all that, because of the Viking invasions, Scotland became, and still is, part of the Isle of Man! So my company, being an Isle of Man company, is not liable to UK tax, and that is the real issue in the case."

"Well," I said, trying to gather my thoughts and give a polite response to this ludicrous view that had been raised in Consultation and not referred to anywhere in my Instructions.

It was essential that I retained my professional composure and provided a reply that was professionally appropriate. Accordingly, speaking slowly and with all the gravitas that I could muster, I stated, "The issue you have raised is a novel one. It is, however, not referred to anywhere in my Instructions and therefore I have not been given the customary opportunity to prepare my response in advance. But even if I had been, the point you raise is essentially one of Constitutional Law, and I do not profess any expertise in that subject. I can only advise on United Kingdom taxation, and all the issues raised in the Instructions relate to this. I have accordingly given my prepared answers in relation to them. The status of the Isle of Man is not raised in the Instructions and is a matter of Constitutional Law. So for those reasons, without wishing to be dismissive of the research you have carried out into the status of the Isle of Man, I must reiterate with the greatest regret that I am not in a position to deal with the matter you have raised now."

"That is quite outrageous!" the client spluttered. "I came here to obtain your advice, I will be obliged to pay the significant fees you will doubtless charge for your professional advice, and then you refuse to answer the crucial issue that I have specifically raised with you. I am livid, and I believe you to be both most discourteous and unprofessional."

And with that, he got up and stormed out of my room, leaving my instructing solicitors to gather up their papers hurriedly. They left immediately, looking shamefaced, unsurprisingly. When I spoke to them later that day, they apologised profusely for the behaviour of their client and said that he had behaved appallingly on a number of previous occasions. Although, of course, the whole incident was most regrettable, they said that it gave them the excuse they had been seeking for some time to refuse to continue acting for him.

On that occasion I was dealing with an eccentric businessman who, having become obsessed by a bizarre notion, was seeking my professional approval of it in a tax context. I was being asked to give advice which it was clearly professionally inappropriate for me to provide. The same thing happened again not long afterwards.

This Consultation took place at a time when the party political conference season was in full swing. On this occasion, I was provided with a set of Instructions beforehand and it was clear that there was a very significant political dimension involved. Although not formally instructed on behalf of the political party in question, it was nonetheless clear from the Instructions drafted by a highly reputable firm of solicitors that senior representatives of the party would be present at the Consultation. The Instructions, unlike the previous Consultation I have just mentioned, raised issues which were perfectly proper for me to advise on professionally.

The date and time of the Consultation duly arrived and a large number of people were ushered into my room by Alfred. I recognised one of their number immediately. He was the senior member of the Treasury team of the party, being responsible, amongst other things, for taxation matters. I noticed as he entered that he was only carrying one document. It was green, small, but quite thick. He was clutching it to his bosom in a way that indicated that it contained something vital. I was to discover later, after we had discussed all the issues raised in the Instructions, that it did. The little green book was a highly significant document, and also an extremely sensitive one.

The senior Treasury spokesman then raised the issue that the Consultation was really all about.

"Well, what I want to come to now is a very delicate issue, and I know you will treat it in the strictest confidence. This document," he looked down at the little green book, "is our key statement on one important aspect of our taxation policy. It relates to an area of Tax Law which is being hotly debated at the present time because it is innovative and so raises issues that are not found elsewhere in the UK Tax Code. It is our proposal for a new property tax. And here it is." Again he looked down at his precious little green book, this time clearly with a great deal of pride. He continued, "It has taken a lot of time to devise it; first, because it is revolutionary, and secondly, because we have sought to include all the necessary detail to ensure it is workable. We think we have done that now. And so, at the Conference later today, I will propose in my speech that the Party should adopt 'my' property tax proposal, and in particular that it should accept this document as a basis for legislation as soon as we are able to implement it. That's what I shall say, but it is pure politics and I am just posturing to keep the rank and file of the Party happy. Equally importantly, 'my' property tax proposal will increase my standing with my senior colleagues in the Party. So that's why I say it is all pure politics. But the real world is a very different place and I need practical advice."

Naive as I was, I then thought he was going to seek my professional advice on the policy document and in particular how it might be improved and possibly made more effective. Not a bit of it.

"Well, the thing is this. And I accept what I am going to ask you may be a little unconventional." To say what he then mentioned was "a little unconventional" was putting it very mildly. To me it was totally unprecedented. "You see, I would like your advice on how this property tax I shall be proposing at the Conference later today can be avoided. I shall be most grateful in my personal capacity for any ideas you had on how I personally could mitigate the effect of the proposed tax on my own property."

I was completely taken aback. I found it difficult to believe that a senior political figure, highly respected on all sides, would request my professional advice on how to avoid a tax that he, and his party, were proposing to introduce into law.

I was shocked by his request to provide this advice, not only because I had not even had a sight of the document that I was being asked to consider, but also because the nature of the advice sought troubled me, given all the circumstances outlined above. I did not believe it could be considered appropriate for me to give such advice professionally.

So, in response to his request, I explained first that I could not advise on avoiding a tax set out in a document which I had not perused. I then stated that the only sensible way to proceed was to delay consideration of the scope of the proposed property tax until it had been enacted. Thus, effectively, I avoided providing any of the advice he sought. Fortunately I was never instructed on the matter subsequently, and indeed never saw the Treasury spokesman professionally again. Thankfully.

Over the years in practice I found, as one would expect, that Consultations followed a familiar pattern. Instructions would be sent to Chambers and a Consultation would be arranged. When the time and date of that Consultation arrived, the instructing solicitors or accountants and the lay clients would present themselves at my room in Chambers. The Consultation would similarly follow a set pattern as I went through the Instructions page by page with the intention of advising on all the points raised therein. Afterwards I would prepare an Opinion confirming my advice, or the instructing accountants or solicitors would prepare a Note of Consultation for settlement. That was my professional style and I followed it rigorously throughout my career. So, in four and a half decades, 99 per cent of my Consultations followed that pattern in a totally predictable way. The Consultations I have referred to in this chapter were without precedent, constituting the tiniest percentage of the cases I advised on during the years in question. They were such a departure from the norm that in each instance I was taken totally by surprise. However, such is professional life that any experienced practitioner must be prepared to deal with issues which are totally unexpected, subject always to observing all the professional rules relating to practice at the Bar. As this chapter shows, usually they arise when points are raised in Consultation which have not been included in the Instructions for the Consultation. So such cases can truly be described as being 'tales of the unexpected'.

CHAPTER 24

DISCOMBOBULATING
MEMORIES

'There's nowt so queer as folk.'
Old saying particularly used
in the north of England

"Believe one who speaks from experience"
Aeneid (Book XI, line cclxxxiii)
VIRGIL

The cases I have related in the previous chapter have their light-hearted, even amusing, moments. However, they also had their troubling aspects which gave me real concern in a professional context. This chapter of my reminiscences recalls cases which were quite simply bizarre, and if they had been related to me by another barrister, I would find them very difficult to believe. However, they also are absolutely true and not embroidered in any way. The first two such cases occurred in the course of my advisory practice, the latter two whilst I was appearing in court.

I suppose, in a practice that spanned almost fifty years, there were bound to be many extraordinary professional experiences. In the first such bizarre case, I was completely surprised by the conduct of the client, although on this occasion none of it related to me or my advice. It was the way the client behaved in conducting, or in some respects not conducting, his own affairs. Again in this chapter I am cloaking all names in anonymity, so no identification of the parties concerned is possible.

This client, whom I shall call Eric, owned the entire share capital of a large company headquartered in the northern county where he was born and had lived throughout his life. He was proposing to sell his corporate empire for some £10 million. This was in the 1970s, so it was by any standard a huge sum of money. The problem was that a sale of the share capital would result in a massive Capital Gains Tax charge – something he was determined to avoid at any cost. In his case, 'at any cost' meant that he was prepared to cease to reside in the United Kingdom for one whole fiscal year, i.e. 6 April to 5 April the following year. (In those days it was possible with very careful planning to avoid a Capital Gains Tax charge by becoming non-resident for one year only. That 'loophole' was closed many years ago.) The plan, such as it was, was very simple. Eric would leave the United Kingdom on 5 April and a contract for the sale of all his shares (the critical point of time for Capital Gains Tax purposes) would be signed the following day, 6 April, the first day of the next tax year. As, by that day, Eric would have ceased to be resident in the UK, the contract for the sale of his shares would be signed by his solicitor, John, under a power of attorney. 6 April was a Saturday, but that made no difference to the planning, as John was prepared to attend a meeting with the purchasers on that day and sign all the necessary documents. That meeting was scheduled for 8.30 am at the request of the purchasers.

On 5 April, the Friday, Eric was due to fly off to his chosen destination, Monaco. Everything was going according to plan and continued to do so. Eric was, we assumed, safely ensconced in Monaco, all the necessary negotiations for the sale of the shares had been completed, and all the necessary paperwork was in place. The only thing left to do was to place the appropriate signatures on the Sale and Purchase Agreement on the 6th. (And no, this is not one of those stories where all the planes at Heathrow were grounded by fog so that the client was unable to leave on the 5th, although that did happen to another client of mine.)

So John, having been notified by Eric's PA that he had caught the scheduled plane, met with the solicitors acting for the purchasers and duly signed the contract. He telephoned me to confirm that the contract had been executed. All was done that had to be done. It was all perfect. Or so we thought. Eric in Monaco on the 5th, contract signed on the 6th. The planning was so simple and it had been duly implemented. All that now needed to be done, vitally, was for Eric to remain outside the United Kingdom for the tax year that started on the 6th. No return was possible if the planning was to succeed.

My phone rang. It was 10 am. It was Eric. "I have tried to phone John, but he is not at his office." This was an extremely agitated man who had no time for any pleasantries. Clearly something important had gone seriously wrong. But what? As the planning was straightforward, what could possibly have happened to sabotage it?

"What's the matter, Eric?"

"It's Monaco. It's the most dreadful place. It's full of high-rise blocks of flats, all absolutely hideous. How can people live in such a concrete jungle? I can't live here. I'm coming back immediately." (It is relevant to mention that Eric had lived in the countryside throughout his life.)

I really couldn't believe what I was hearing – not for the first time in my professional career! "But Eric, are you saying that you have never been to Monaco before?"

"No, I haven't."

To me that was truly amazing. I simply couldn't believe that either. Here was a man who had not only agreed to leave the UK, but also to make the positive decision to live in Monaco for an entire tax year without ever having been there.

"So until yesterday you had never seen Monaco or had any idea what it was like?"

"No."

Eric was becoming annoyed with all my questions and sounded as though he was having a nervous breakdown. He was hardly making any sense, but the next thing he said I heard very clearly. "You have got to stop John signing the contract. He must not sign it. Stop him now. I am coming back to the UK today, so tell him the whole plan is dead. I am just not going to do it."

"Eric, I am very sorry to have to tell you this, but it's too late. The contract has already been signed by John. That was the agreed plan and he executed the sale document at the meeting as arranged. So the shares have already been disposed of."

"But there must be something I can do. Please help me." He sounded extremely distressed. "Eric, you have only been in Monaco a few hours, not even a full day. Why not stay a little longer to see what Monaco is really like? You might find it is acceptable after you have been there a while. After all, you haven't given it a chance so far. It really can't be so bad that you feel you have to leave immediately. And remember, your tax planning proposal was very carefully thought out so that, if you return now, there will be a Capital Gains

Tax charge on £10 million. The consequences of your return are potentially disastrous for you. Do think really hard before you return. Surely Monaco can't be so bad that you would contemplate such a dire financial result?"

"It is. I can't stay here. You will think of something. Can I come and see you in Chambers at 10.30 on Monday?"

"Of course you can. But please think very carefully before you come back. If you do, all will be lost and there will be a huge Capital Gains Tax bill to pay."

"No, I have to return. You will think of something. I know that. I will see you at 10.30 on Monday." His voice was breaking with emotion. I felt huge pressure to solve the problem we now faced. My final comment was, "Eric, give Monaco a chance."

He was adamant. "I cannot possibly stay here. I will see you in Chambers on Monday at 10.30."

"If you insist. I will tell John about our conversation, and John and I will see you on Monday. But please do try to think again. This is such a momentous decision."

"I know, but I must return." The conversation ended and for a long while I was simply stunned by what Eric had said.

The more I reflected on his words, the more amazing I found them. It was so surprising that a client who had been planning to live in Monaco for an entire year had never visited the Principality to see whether he found it a congenial place to live for such a considerable period of time. The more so as I had been advising him on his planned non-residence for well over a year, so he had plenty of time to make a reconnaissance visit. Apparently it had never occurred to him to do so. Also puzzling was that at no time during our telephone conversation did he mention his wife and children, who had travelled to Monaco and were going to live there with him. What did his wife think of Monaco? More importantly, what did she want to do? And what were her views on this totally unexpected change of plan? It was all extremely strange. How could a man who had created an extremely successful business empire worth £10 million through his astute financial and commercial skills behave in such a bizarre way? It defied common sense.

Anyway, he was determined to return to the UK and was equally adamant that I had to see him as soon as possible. Hence the Consultation was arranged by John for the following Monday at 10.30, as Eric requested. I was very concerned about the Consultation. The contract for the sale of Eric's shares had been duly signed and of course all the necessary legal formalities had been complied with. There was nothing that could be done to avoid a Capital Gains Tax charge if Eric was determined to abort the non-residence planning and return to the UK. So much was absolutely clear, and I was concerned about Eric's reaction when I told him that face to face.

Monday. 10.30 am. Eric walks into my room in Chambers looking very glum and haggard. He looks a totally broken man. His expression tells the whole story. The atmosphere in my room is emotional, very tense indeed. I am fearing the worst. Almost before he is sitting down, and indeed before I can offer him any consoling words, he blurts out in an extremely nervous way:

"I would like a drink."

"Of course. Tea, coffee or water, or all or any of the above?"

"I mean a drink drink."

His face showed that he was in earnest and would brook no dissent about this or anything else. It is the first and, so far, the last time I have been asked for an alcoholic drink in Chambers. I knew there was no alcohol in my room, so I had to ask my Clerk to see if he could find some. He did, and a bottle of whisky was produced.

Eric had to be in a very bad way. To want, or more likely need, alcohol at 10.30 in the morning indicated how desperate he felt. A conclusion subsequently reinforced by the fact that he had three large glasses of whisky. I had to tell him then, as I had told him on the telephone, that, unless he returned to Monaco or went somewhere else abroad for a full tax year, there was nothing that could be done. However, he totally rejected the idea, even though it would mean a tax liability in millions of pounds. The discussion in Consultation went round in circles, with Eric sipping whisky all the while. The Consultation proceeded inexorably to its inevitable and very sad conclusion, given Eric's adamant attitude.

Eric left my room looking even more depressed than when he arrived, and clearly the worse for wear as a result of his alcohol intake. On his way out he stumbled over a chair and fell onto the floor. It added a final pathetic note to a bizarre and most unfortunate series of events. All the careful planning had come to nought because a supremely successful businessman had not been able to manage his private life with the same skill and common sense that he had applied to his commercial activities. I shall never forget that extremely tense and very sad Consultation, and even more so the request for a "drink drink". I had never heard that expression before and I have never heard it since. A desperate reaction by a broken and, I have to admit, somewhat foolish man.

And indeed an observer might well think that Eric was overdoing the gloom and despondency following his abortive trip to Monaco. After all, even after he had paid tax, he would still be left with many millions of pounds from the sale of his shares. I did point this out to Eric during the Consultation, several times, but he seemed to find no consolation in this. Many others would.

Eric never did become non-resident but took refuge to a large and unnecessary extent in alcohol. Overall, it amounted to a very distressing story. After Eric left my room in Chambers, I was left to mull over the saying which appears at the beginning of this chapter, 'There's nowt so queer as folk', and not for the first time in my career.

The second bizarre case in practice that stands out in my memory at least had no downside for my clients, their clients or indeed, thankfully, for me.

My Instructions sought advice on behalf of a firm of northern stockbrokers who were proposing to establish a unit trust in Jersey for their clients. The Instructions set out in detail the proposal and the United Kingdom tax advantages for their investors. Although the list of such benefits appeared impressive, they ignored the wider uncertain tax consequences of investing in a non-resident unit trust. The balance of advantage was clearly in favour of investing in a resident vehicle because the UK Tax Code conferred specific tax advantages on <u>resident</u> unit trusts.

So at the Consultation I advised my clients accordingly and concluded:

"Well, as you will see, very distinct tax advantages are conferred on unit trusts resident in the UK, and their tax treatment is clear. Non-resident unit trusts do not enjoy those advantages. So it makes no sense for a UK resident person to invest in a foreign unit trust." My clients looked knowingly at each other. The most senior, David Fox, then said:

"I have to tell you, Mr Whiteman, that in all honesty nothing you have said is a surprise to us. We really knew it already. You see, we had to take professional advice before we started advising our clients to invest in a non-resident unit trust. In any event, the only reason we are intending to create a foreign unit trust is that stockbrokers in London are doing so, and if we don't, our clients will believe that we are not at the cutting edge of innovative thinking on investment vehicles. We will then be seen as a Mancunian firm which is second-rate compared with London firms. We risk losing out to our more sophisticated competitors in the south. So we are left with no option. We have to do it, even though we have no faith in it and appreciate the tax uncertainty it creates."

I realised that all the preparation for the Consultation and the detailed advice I had provided was so that my clients could reassure their investors that they had taken legal advice on the creation of the unit trust.

I continued, "Well, at least tell me something about the investment philosophy of the unit trust you are launching."

David Fox began:

"Well, as you know, the market is bounding ahead," (I add parenthetically that this was 1973 and the stock market was enjoying a very strong bull run) "so what we are going to do is establish a 'go-go' unit trust." ('Go-go' was then the 'in-phrase' for a really aggressive investment strategy.) "We will be in and out of the market every day, buying and selling, whenever we see a profitable opportunity. We might well be buying twenty to thirty times a day, depending on market conditions. We will be as active as possible, intending to make profits from quick purchases and resales, or vice versa."

Soon afterwards the Consultation finished and I wished them good luck with the flotation. In due course in the same year (1973) the unit trust was launched in the prevailing booming stock market conditions. Obviously I couldn't resist the temptation to follow the unit trust price quoted in the newspapers. At the start the 'go-go' philosophy was not producing dramatic results – indeed, it was not keeping up with the consistent upward trend of the market. So much for 'go-go' which seemed to have 'gone-gone'.

And then calamity hit the stock market. It was 1974 and the market crashed, but I continued to check the price of my clients' unit trust. Hardly a ripple in the price of the units. Indeed, over the next few months the unit trust price continued to edge, albeit very slowly, upwards. I was lost in admiration for David Fox and his colleagues. Their investment strategy apparently was so brilliant that they had not only avoided the collapse of the market but had actually increased the unit trust price.

When I had my next Consultation with David and his fellow directors, I started by praising their investment skills and stated that they really had done a most brilliant job for their investors by bucking the disastrous trend of the market. I concluded by saying that their investment strategy – their 'go-go' philosophy – was really outstanding in the results it had produced.

David, although looking a little embarrassed, smiled at his colleagues, some of whom burst out laughing.

"Well," said David, "many thanks for the praise, but it isn't really deserved at all. Yes, the price has gone up – by about 4 per cent over the year, which if you look at the market is a tremendous result. But the story behind the curtain is somewhat different. Yes, we did have a 'go-go' philosophy and we did intend to be extremely active in the market. But what actually happened was that we received a huge inflow of funds when we advertised the unit trust – the non-resident aspect appealed enormously, apparently. We were overwhelmed by the response and, as a result, we didn't know what to do with such a massive amount of money. So we never got round to investing it. I feel ashamed to admit it, but all the investors' funds stayed on bank deposit – that's why the unit price went up by 4 per cent. Now it's even worse because, as our unit trust was the only one to increase in price in 1974, the punters are now pouring even more money into it. It's become ludicrous. We didn't do a thing; we never even started to implement our 'go-go' philosophy; and now we are getting rave reviews because we bucked the market!"

I was dumbfounded. This was the world turned upside down. If they had implemented their investment strategy, their investors would have suffered very significant losses, but they hadn't, so everyone was happy. Inactivity had been rewarded and their failure to implement their investment strategy was the greatest blessing for their investors. Life can be very strange.

From the beginning to the end, the Jersey unit trust case was totally bizarre. My clients knew the tax position before they came to see me. They were purely 'going through the motions' and the whole basis of the investment strategy of the unit trust was never implemented. So, given the whole unreality of the venture, I was not surprised to see some years later that a very prestigious financial journal voted them 'Fund Managers of the

Year'. The wheels of fortune can turn in very strange ways. As for my clients' behaviour throughout this saga, again I was left to ponder the saying, 'There's nowt so queer as folk', particularly as David's firm was based in the North.

So much for extraordinary experiences in Consultation. Now for a different type of memorable experience – unwelcome, unpleasant and unjustified comments made by judges. The type of comment that Counsel never forgets. Two cases where I was on the receiving end of such comments are engraved on my mind. The comments were made by Lord Justice Megaw in one case and Lord Justice Staughton in the other.

Counsel must always be courteous, polite and respectful towards judges. Counsel, as it seems to me, are equally entitled to such treatment. In my career at the Bar, that has almost universally been the case. However, I have long since learned, as a member of the Bar, that Monday mornings are when a judge is likely to be at his tetchiest. Some judges obviously find changing to a working environment on a Monday a difficult transition. Both the experiences I now relate occurred on a Monday morning. But I should mention at the outset that the first was in a case which was to prove to be a landmark court appearance in my professional career – and for more than one reason. It had the most terrible start but finished with the most brilliant conclusion. It was a case without precedent, and not just for me!

"No, it isn't!" The words that hit me from Lord Justice Megaw on that Monday morning were uttered in an angry and exasperated way. The man was furious with me. He appeared to be saying it was all my fault. Let me relate how his words "No it isn't" came to be uttered.

I was appearing before the Court of Appeal as Counsel for the British Airports Authority (BAA), who were appealing a decision in favour of HM Customs and Excise. The case related to an arcane point of Value Added Tax (VAT) legislation. It was a difficult point to explain and I was anxious to do so as briefly and lucidly as possible, particularly as all three judges no doubt felt they had drawn the short straw, being obliged to hear a VAT case – an intricate, complex and exceptionally 'dry' subject. What judge, apart from a tax specialist, really wants to hear a case on VAT? So for all those reasons I was anxious as I got to my feet at 10.30 am to address their Lordships: Lord Justice Megaw, Lord Justice Browne and Lord Justice Scarman (later Lord Scarman). However, I knew that once I got into my stride, I would be alright. Once I got into my stride, that is.

I opened the case and explained the point in issue as briefly and accurately as I could. My nervousness was subsiding somewhat as I concluded my opening with the words, "So that is the point in issue in the appeal now before your Lordships."

"No, it isn't!"exploded Lord Justice Megaw. "The point in this case is which government department is going to pay for this litigation. This has happened so many times in the past, and it's litigation I abhor. This is an appeal where one government department is suing another government department. It is perfectly scandalous that there should be litigation like this because, whoever wins, the public is going to pay. This litigation is inevitably at the taxpayers' expense. We have reams of correspondence before us between one department and another and it's all to decide out of which pocket the public is going to pay. Can anyone, as a matter of public policy, justify this type of litigation? Can Counsel tell us what conceivable public interest there is in this litigation? Now I will grant an adjournment and you will go out of court and you will return to court and inform us that you are not proceeding with this appeal. Do you understand?"

I said nothing. I was, however, extremely angry at the judge's outburst. Lord Justice Browne echoed the sentiments of Lord Justice Megaw. Lord Justice Scarman maintained a discreet silence. So, effectively, as Counsel appearing for a very large and well respected public body, I was thrown out of a court by an angry judge. And, moreover, on the basis of an entirely misconceived point he had made.

As we left court, I immediately took my instructing solicitor into a corner of the corridor and said, "I think I know, but I need a complete rundown from you as my instructing solicitor on how BAA is and has been financed, and in particular whether it has ever received any funding from the government. Has it ever received any taxpayers' money?"

My solicitor replied immediately, "The answer is, absolutely not." He then explained in some detail how the BAA was and had been funded, and concluded, "The BAA has never received any government funding at any stage. It is funded substantially by landing fees paid by aircraft arriving at UK airports. That's where its income comes from. Not the taxpayer."

That was all I needed to know. I had been determined to have all the relevant information about the financing of the BAA at my fingertips in case

I met aggressive questioning from the court when I returned. To achieve that result, the adjournment had lasted some fifteen minutes.

"But what are we going to do?" asked my solicitor. "Are you going to abandon the appeal?" I replied, "Absolutely not. We are going back into court and I shall proceed with the appeal. You have briefed me on the finances of BAA. The judge's point is completely misconceived. I shall go into court, explain BAA's finances as far as necessary, and I shall then proceed with the case as instructed." With that, I turned around, thumped the court doors open, and marched to Counsel's benches. I was a man on a mission. I felt I had been treated very harshly and without any justification. I felt aggrieved. I was angry.

When the judges had taken their seats, I noticed that Lord Justice Megaw looked stern, but his expression also seemed to indicate that he was clearly expecting me to meekly abandon the appeal in accordance with his expressed wishes. I had no such intention, whatever brickbats were thrown at me.

I rose to my feet, admittedly feeling a little apprehensive as to what might follow. I then explained briefly how BAA was financed. I concluded as follows: "The Authority is charged by statute to break even each year. In fact, it was expected to make an annual profit of 15 per cent. The Authority has accordingly never received a single penny of taxpayers' money and, if it loses this appeal, it will not affect the taxpayer at all." None of the judges said anything, although Lord Justice Megaw continued to scowl at me. As Counsel for BAA, I had every right to present my client's case, and as I marched back into court, I had made up my mind that, having explained BAA's finances, I would continue with my address to the court. The anger I felt had produced a determination in me that the case for BAA should be heard. I was not going to ask if the judges had any questions. I was certainly not going to seek permission from Lord Justice Megaw to continue with the appeal. I would simply go straight on and open the appeal again. And that's precisely what I did. There was no interruption from the Bench as I went on to explain, without pausing for a second time, the technical issues in the case. And once I had done that, I said with the greatest satisfaction, looking Lord Justice Megaw straight in the eye, "So that is the question which arises in the case now before Your Lordships." The very same words I had used in my original opening, but this time there was no outburst from the Bench.

Indeed, there was complete silence. However, did I detect steam coming out of certain judicial ears?

Soon afterwards, and this was the first gratifying aspect of the case for me, the usher handed me a note. It turned out to be a personal one from Lord Justice Scarman, a missive which I still have and shall always treasure:

"*Dear Whiteman,*

B.A.A. v. C.C. & E.

All my congratulations on the way you handled the sudden and unexpected storm that beset you at the beginning of your argument.

Leslie Scarman

4/11/76"

The day had begun very badly, but I was more than delighted to receive such a complimentary note from such an illustrious judge.

The next aspect of the BAA appeal which I have to mention came from an unexpected quarter. In the lunchtime edition of the *Evening Standard*, and subsequently in the *Daily Telegraph*, Lord Justice Megaw's outburst was extensively reported under the heading, *Judge Condemns Scandalous Litigation*. It was also included in a news report on television. To my chagrin, the harsh words the judge had directed at me were thus fully publicised by the media. This only served to increase my sense of grievance and injustice at the treatment that had been meted out to me.

After lunch, when the appeal resumed, it became clear that Lord Justice Megaw had realised the error of his ways and was beginning to realise the storm that he had whipped up. When he came into court, His Lordship immediately apologised to me, adding that, "because of Counsel's comments about the financial responsibilities of the Authority," it was fair to say that the Authority had a legitimate interest in the litigation. For good measure, he also stated that I should take as long as I felt necessary to develop the grounds of my client's appeal. Needless to say, the apology of the judge, which I accepted graciously, was not reported in the *Evening Standard* or elsewhere. That was not news.

However, Lord Justice Megaw's apology in court in such unreserved terms was not the final surprising twist in the saga of the BAA case for me. There was one more – one which was to my knowledge unprecedented. I come to that in just a moment.

The Court of Appeal delivered judgment the following day and, when I heard the judges delivering their fully reasoned and very detailed judgments, I could hardly believe that this was the same case where I had been subjected to such aggressive judicial criticism the day before. Lord Justice Scarman referred to "the admirably presented arguments of Counsel for the Authority" and Lord Justice Browne stated that he only delivered a separate judgment "in tribute to what I entirely agree with Lord Justice Scarman was Counsel for the Authority's admirable argument". But the sweetest compliment, as far as I was concerned, came (to his credit) from Lord Justice Megaw: "I would join in the tribute paid to Counsel for the Authority for his clear and concise submissions. The question which arises in this case was stated by him at a very early stage of his submissions." Sweet, and of course ironic, that the judge should refer to the "very early stage" at which I had stated "the question".

I had never received tributes such as these before. However, they were not to be the last of the unprecedented aspects of this quite amazing case. There was one more still to come. Again, it was a complete surprise initiated from a quarter which could never have been anticipated. I hasten to add that it did not come from the Bench this time! It may be that it had its origins "in the sudden and unexpected storm that beset [me]" on that fateful Monday morning. And it may have been prompted, in light of what happened next, by others sharing my view that I had been criticised wholly unjustifiably.

Be that as it may, after the members of the court had delivered their judgments in favour of HM Customs and Excise and awarded them their costs, their Counsel, John Rogers QC, stood up again to address the court. The case was over and I was mystified as to what was happening. John had not given me any prior notice of what he had in mind and, in this case of unprecedented incidents, clearly there was going to be another. John had got to his feet, and in the most gentlemanly and fair-minded way he sought to set the record straight in my favour. He drew the court's attention to the reports in the *Daily Telegraph* and other papers and on television, which quoted what Lord Justice Megaw had stated in the morning but without reference to his later comments after lunch.

At that point Lord Justice Megaw intervened and repeated the comments he had made after lunch, no doubt in the expectation and hope they would then be reported and counterbalance the incomplete reports made at the outset of the hearing. They were indeed reported and I was grateful to John Rogers and those instructing him for the courtesy which they had, of their own volition, extended to me. Needless to say, as we left court, I thanked him profusely for his generosity of spirit. As the court doors banged closed behind us for the last time in this appeal, my solicitor looked over his shoulder and said, admittedly with a big smile, "We lost, but you won." I couldn't disagree with his comment – not with Lord Justice Scarman's note tucked firmly in my pocket and the judges' tributes ringing in my ears.

So concluded the most bizarre case I had had in court. It was novel, unprecedented, intellectually challenging and demanding in so many respects. But even as I left court with my solicitor, its impact on my career was still not at an end. Fortunately. And for this reason. Not long after the BAA appeal was heard, I decided to apply for appointment as Queen's Counsel (taking Silk). I thought, in light of the BAA appeal, that Lord Justice Scarman would be an ideal person to ask to be a referee for my application. He had heard me 'on my feet' and had complimented me on my advocacy skills. In due course I asked him and he readily agreed. And the rest, as they say, is history.

In introducing the BAA case earlier in this chapter, I said it was a landmark case in my career, having a terrible start and a brilliant conclusion. The reader can now see why, and the case also illustrates why, when one goes into court, the consequences are uncertain and unpredictable. I could never have foreseen that an appeal on an arcane point of VAT law would have affected my career so fundamentally.

The other case where I was totally taken aback by a judicial intervention was Padmore. The case involved very difficult and arcane points of law relating to a double taxation agreement. They were difficult not only to explain but also to comprehend on a first hearing. The Presiding Judge in the Court of Appeal was Lord Justice Fox, a charming, courteous and softly-spoken man. I had been seeking to outline the taxpayers' submissions in the appeal when suddenly there was a thunderbolt from the judge on the right of the Bench, Lord Justice Staughton.

"Mr Whiteman, I am very tired of this. You start with one whingeing submission and then you follow it up with another bellyaching submission on another point." The words "whingeing" and "bellyaching" rang in my ears. I was furious. That was not the sort of language one expected to hear from the Bench in any circumstances. I also felt that the sentiment they expressed was totally unjustified. I believed I was simply and straightforwardly making submissions on the very technical points which arose in the case, submissions which had been accepted at first instance in the High Court by a very well respected judge, Mr Justice (later Lord Justice) Peter Gibson.

I then used a tactic which I have found very effective in such circumstances. Silence. It is an extremely powerful weapon. When Counsel is on their feet, to stop speaking or allow a silence to descend in court gains more attention than almost any form of words. When silence descends, everyone looks round. Everyone is mystified. What's happened? Why is there a silence? Is Counsel lost for words? Is Counsel ill? And so on. Where there is no immediate explanation for a silence, it gains the immediate attention of everyone in court. "What is going on?" is the communal thought.

After Lord Justice Staughton's outburst, I allowed a silence to descend, which seemed to last for an hour but was in reality no more than a minute. But an unexplained minute of silence in court is a long time. Time it and consider, if that happened in court, what your reaction would be.

I thought the best approach would be not to react in anger and say anything which might be inappropriate, and certainly not to direct any response to Lord Justice Staughton. Instead, I decided to direct it in a 'saddened' way to Lord Justice Fox who, as I said, was a charming and delightful man.

Looking straight at Lord Justice Fox, I simply said, "My, my! I thought I had a reasonable reputation at the Bar. But here I am, making submissions which a senior judge in the Court of Appeal has described as 'whingeing' and 'bellyaching'. My, my! What, in one day, has happened to my reputation as a barrister?"

Lord Justice Fox's face was a study, and I believed he had much sympathy with my position following the comments of Lord Justice Staughton. However, he said nothing. I allowed a short silence to occur thereafter and then continued with my address to the court. There were no more interruptions from the Bench that morning, so I was allowed to make my submissions without any further outbursts.

Again after lunch Lord Justice Staughton found it appropriate to address me.

"Mr Whiteman, I have reflected over lunch on this morning's proceedings and there were certain words that I used when addressing you that were not entirely appropriate. I want to make it clear that you should take as much time as you feel is necessary to present the case on behalf of those instructing you."

Well, I suppose that was as close to an apology as I was going to receive, and given the clear invitation, I was determined, as always, to make certain that my client's case was presented to the best of my ability without feeling in any way constrained by time. More light-heartedly, I can say it looked as though judicial apologies after the luncheon adjournment might start to become routine!

However, this time, unlike the BAA case, my client did succeed. Indeed, every contention I made on behalf of Mr Padmore was accepted by the court. That was exceedingly gratifying, not least because Lord Justice Staughton also accepted all my submissions and found in favour of Mr Padmore. In light of his initial outburst, that was particularly sweet, and something to savour for a very long time. I still do. The pregnant silence proved to be effective. It still does. It is always in my tactical armoury to be used as and when I deem appropriate.

Reflecting on the four cases I have considered in this chapter, and looking back generally over my career, I truly believe that what a senior member of the Bar really has to offer more than anything else is experience in advising his clients. Not intricate knowledge of the law – a much more junior person may have a far superior technical knowledge. In both the BAA case and Padmore in particular, it was my experience that enabled me to adopt a positive approach to hostile judicial comments. I was not going to be intimidated and I was determined, however unwelcome my submissions might appear to the judges, to make my client's interests my paramount concern. I would not be browbeaten into submission. If it meant taking judicial 'stick', my shoulders were broad enough to bear it.

So I do believe, and I say this with an obvious vested interest, that there is no substitute for experience. With experience comes judgement, possibly the most vital attribute of any professional adviser. As the Leader of the Revenue Bar (that is the Silk of longest standing in practice), that is what I would like to believe.

CHAPTER 25

THE WITNESS FROM HELL

"On the make and on the take"
Addressing the court on the behaviour of the claimant
GEORGE CARMAN QC

I am blasted out of a deep sleep. A shrill sound is assaulting my senses. What is it? I try to focus. Not easy. And then I realise it is the phone ringing. But my mind and body tell me it is early, very early. The shrill insistent noise continues. In a daze I reach for the horrid instrument that is the cause of my bewilderment.

"Good morning, this is Stephen Lawford of [he named a well-known firm of solicitors]," says a disembodied voice at the end of the phone. My mind still isn't functioning at all well. The name meant nothing to me. This is a solicitor I have never met and who, as far as I can recall, has never instructed me to advise him professionally.

"I sincerely apologise for phoning you at home at this hour" (it is 7.20) "on a Saturday morning." "Is it an emergency?" I ask. "I think so, otherwise I would not have phoned. It relates to a professional matter where we have been instructed by Mr Al-Fayed. Can we talk about it now?"

These comments concern me. Mr (Mohamed) Al-Fayed had been a professional client of mine for some twenty years. I liked the man enormously. I found him to be charming, kind, warm, very humorous, and most appreciative of the advice I had given him over the years. I found advising him through my instructing solicitors and accountants a real pleasure. The matters on which I was asked to advise were always interesting and challenging in the best professional tradition. The Instructions always called for knowledge, expertise and experience across a broad range of taxation issues. Giving constructive advice in such circumstances was very satisfying and, as I have indicated, really appreciated by Mr Al-Fayed. He always treated me with the greatest courtesy and consideration. I also respected the man for his business acumen, his devotion to his family, and his very substantial contributions to a large number of charities.

"I am sure you are wondering," Stephen began, "why I said I needed to speak to you in connection with an emergency relating to Mr Al-Fayed. I know you have been an adviser to him on Revenue Law for some years. To put your mind at rest, I can say immediately that I am not phoning to seek any professional guidance in relation to matters where you have been instructed to advise Mr Al-Fayed in the past."

Stephen then realised that it was time to tell me precisely what he was calling about. "My phone call relates to the 'cash-for-questions' litigation, that is, the libel action brought by Neil Hamilton against Mr Al-Fayed. I am sure you know about it."

"I do in general terms, but only to the extent that I have read about it in the newspapers. I have never advised Mr Al-Fayed in connection with it because I do not profess any expertise in libel law."

"I know that," said Stephen. "We are seeking your assistance not in relation to your role as an adviser to Mr Al-Fayed, but in a wholly different connection."

In due course I will explain what Stephen was referring to. However, first it is necessary to put the whole matter in context, and by that I mean the events which were at that time being generically described as the cash-for-questions affair. As the reader may recall, it was a major political scandal in the latter years of John Major's Conservative government.

The affair started on 20 October 1994 when *The Guardian* newspaper published an article about Ian Greer, who was the head of a firm of parliamentary lobbyists. It alleged that Ian Greer, acting on behalf of Mr Al-Fayed, had made payments to two Conservative Members of Parliament (MPs) so that they would ask questions in the House of Commons. The alleged payments were £2,000 per question and the two MPs were Neil Hamilton and Tim Smith. Smith resigned immediately after he admitted accepting the payments in question.

Hamilton and Greer then issued libel writs in the High Court against *The Guardian*. In December 1994 Mr Al-Fayed, in a private letter to the Chairman of the parliamentary watchdog, the Members' Interests Committee, confirmed that he had paid Hamilton to table parliamentary questions. Two years later, after three of Mr Al-Fayed's employees stated that they had processed cash payments to the two men, Hamilton and Greer withdrew their libel actions against *The Guardian*. That was on 30 September 1996, three days before the libel actions were due to be heard.

That is only background, but it is essential in order to understand how the critical litigation between the two protagonists, Mr Al-Fayed and Neil Hamilton, began.

A Parliamentary Enquiry, led by Sir Gordon Downey, concluded in July 1997 that the testimony of the three Al-Fayed employees that they had processed cash payments to Neil Hamilton amounted to 'compelling evidence' that he had received the payments in question.

Nonetheless, the following year, 1998, Hamilton issued a writ for libel against Mr Al-Fayed in relation to allegations he had made in a filmed interview on a Channel 4 programme entitled *A Question of Sleaze*. The programme was shown on Channel 4 on 16 January 1997 as part of its *Dispatches* series. In the course of that interview, Mr Al-Fayed stated that he had made substantial cash payments directly to Neil Hamilton on a number of occasions between mid-1987 and late 1989. The payments were made in return for Hamilton's agreement that he would ask parliamentary questions, and otherwise lobby in Parliament, on behalf of Mr Al-Fayed. Mr Al-Fayed stated that he not only gave cash to Hamilton but vouchers as well. In addition, Hamilton and his wife spent six nights at the Ritz Hotel in Paris at Mr Al-Fayed's expense, and some time as his guests at Mr Al-Fayed's house in Scotland and at his Paris apartment. Hamilton admitted that he had enjoyed all these 'freebies' at Mr Al-Fayed's expense.

It was the remarks of Mr Al-Fayed in the *Dispatches* programme that were the foundation of a second libel action. Hamilton issued that second writ on 9 January 1998.

And now we get to what led to that telephone call at 7.20 am. The essence of the defamatory imputation of which Hamilton complained was that he corruptly demanded and accepted material benefits (in particular, cash payments) in return for tabling parliamentary questions and providing other parliamentary services.

This gets us to the very heart of the second libel case. Those acting on behalf of Mr Al-Fayed had to establish that Hamilton did, indeed, corruptly demand and accept material benefits for parliamentary services. Hence the use of the phrase 'cash for questions'. Mr Al-Fayed's defence? That what he had said about Hamilton's demands for, and acceptance of, cash for services was true.

But how could he establish they were true? Mr Al-Fayed would say they were - of course. Hamilton would say they weren't - of course.

Mr Al-Fayed crucially required some 'independent' evidence that the allegations he had made in the *Dispatches* programme were true. But where could his legal team obtain some 'independent' evidence to establish the truth? Even more fundamentally, looking at the matter from a personal point of view, what role could I possibly play in the litigation? I have described the essential events that led to the libel action, but I had not been involved, professionally or otherwise, in any of them. I was mystified. However, it was at that point that Stephen made everything clear as to the role I was being requested to play.

"We want to call you as a witness in the Al-Fayed/Hamilton litigation."

I was still very puzzled and made that clear to Stephen. "But why? How? What evidence can I possibly give, other than that of an expert on United Kingdom Revenue Law, which is obviously not in issue here?"

"No, no - I don't think you understand what we have in mind," said Stephen. "We want to call you on Mr Al-Fayed's behalf as a witness of fact."

I said, "But I have no knowledge of the facts of the case, other than what I have read in the newspapers." Although I was still puzzled, Stephen was about to enlighten me and make it clear that he believed he had the right person. He believed I could fulfil the allotted role absolutely perfectly. The enlightenment from Stephen came, but only to a somewhat limited extent. The detail was missing.

"You will be giving similar fact evidence." Of course I knew what similar fact evidence was, but it may be helpful to the reader if I give the textbook definition of such evidence:

"*Evidence pertaining to similar conduct of a litigant (or an accused) on other occasions, or of the commission by the accused of similar acts.*"

"Stephen, I am still puzzled. What similar fact evidence could I possibly provide from the witness box that is relevant to this case?"

"Well, it is in relation to your role as the leading Tax Counsel to the Mobil Oil Corporation," said Stephen.

"Mobil? I still don't understand."

At long last Stephen decided that the time had come to explain precisely what he had in mind and why my evidence would be relevant.

"Well," he said, "we discovered very recently that, when you were advising Mobil Oil, Mr Hamilton telephoned you about his being paid by Mobil for an amendment he had tabled in the House of Commons on the Company's behalf in 1989. It was an amendment to the Finance Bill of that year. This information came into our possession a week before the trial was due to start. Lawyers for Mr Hamilton tried to exclude the evidence, but after three days of intense legal argument, Mr Justice Morland ruled that the evidence could go before the jury. It was that ruling of the judge that meant evidence as to the Mobil affair was live. That happened yesterday, and that is why I have made the telephone call to you today. It is urgent that we take the matter forward as soon as possible.

"The information we received was that there was a Consultation in your Chambers in May 1989 which was attended by representatives of Mobil Oil and by Mr Hamilton. The Consultation was principally about the retrospective legislation in the Finance Bill and the possibility that Mr Hamilton might table an amendment to it in Parliament. We understand that there was no discussion at that meeting about whether Mr Hamilton should be employed or paid in any way."

At that point, Stephen paused. I was amazed by the level of detail that had come into the possession of Mr Al-Fayed's lawyers. I was trying to cast my mind back ten years (Stephen's telephone call was on 27 November 1999). These were events I had not had to consider for such a long time, but, as far as I could recall, the details that Stephen had recounted were all correct.

"Am I right, so far, in relating what happened?"

"Yes."

"Now we come to the crucial part. Is it correct that it was Mr Hamilton who subsequently raised the question of being remunerated for tabling the 1989 parliamentary amendment on behalf of Mobil?"

"That's correct."

"How did that happen?" Stephen asked.

"Soon after the Consultation, but I can't remember exactly when, I received a telephone call from Mr Hamilton. After brief pleasantries, he got straight to the point:

'What do Mobil pay?' he asked bluntly."

"Are you sure that those were his words? After all, it is now ten years ago."

"I do distinctly remember Mr Hamilton asking, 'What do Mobil pay?' I am absolutely certain those were the words he used."

"Because?"

"It was imprinted on my mind because I was so shocked by the question."

"Do you remember anything else from that conversation?"

"Yes. I responded that, if he wished to raise any question relating to money or payment of any kind, he had to speak directly to Mobil."

"Well," Stephen continued, "we know that he subsequently corruptly demanded and was paid £10,000 by Mobil."

This was news to me. But now I realised the role I had to play and the evidence I was required to give that was crucial to Mr Al-Fayed's case. It was obvious to me how the 'similar fact' issue arose. The demand for, and indeed the receipt of, money from Mobil would be said to be 'similar conduct' constituting the 'commission of similar acts' by Hamilton. So if the demand for payment to Mobil by Hamilton in 1989 was corrupt, then it would be just as corrupt for him to take money from Mr Al-Fayed for asking parliamentary questions. The demand for money from Mobil would constitute 'irresistible evidence of corruption'. It seemed to me that Hamilton's claim would fail completely on the Mobil affair alone because it established corruption on the part of a Member of Parliament. If he had acted corruptly once, the jury would be asked to infer that this was a man who was capable of acting corruptly on a second occasion. On that basis, Mr Al-Fayed's evidence would be accepted and Hamilton's claim for damages would fail.

It was now clear to me, after being mystified for so long, that I was being asked to give the critical evidence, something which Stephen confirmed immediately.

"Well," said Stephen, "the best possible person to give evidence on the Mobil connection is you. And it will have to be given next week, to fit in with the closing of the witness evidence given on Mr Al-Fayed's behalf. That is why I had to disturb you at the weekend. It was essential to speak to you as soon as possible. So now there is only one question: are you prepared to give evidence of the Mobil connection for Mr Al-Fayed in the libel case?"

"Yes, I certainly am, subject to one qualification, which is that my evidence will relate to professional advice that I gave to Mobil Oil. I will therefore need their permission to give such evidence, and in particular their consent to waive legal professional privilege."

"Agreed. We had assumed you would insist on that condition being fulfilled," Stephen interjected. (In the event, Mobil gave their consent and waived legal professional privilege.)

"So your answer is that, subject to Mobil's consent, you will give evidence in the litigation as a witness for Mr Al-Fayed?"

"Yes."

The die was cast. I had one further related question.

"Who has Mr Al-Fayed selected as Counsel to represent him in Court?"

"George Carman QC will lead for him, and Julian Bevan QC will be in court with a watching brief on Mr Al-Fayed's behalf to provide him with a general overview of the proceedings."

I was delighted by this news. George Carman was the outstanding libel QC of his day. His reputation was immense, particularly in his ability to 'work' a jury. In addition, I was very pleased to learn that Julian Bevan would be in court to observe the proceedings. An eminently successful and very talented QC, he was my Co-Head of Chambers. I had found him in that capacity to be a person who was a pleasure to work with.

That telephone conversation with Stephen was the precursor to a week of the most intensive preparation for the hearing and then my appearance in court as a witness of fact. The telephone conversation with Stephen took place, as I have mentioned, on 27 November and, in the event, I gave my evidence on the following Thursday, Friday and Monday (2, 3 and 6 December). So it was a very compressed timetable within which my evidence had to be prepared. It was absolutely essential that I carried out detailed research which confirmed my recollection of the events of the Mobil affair.

There was one further task I felt I had to undertake before I gave evidence. That was to collect every document in my possession which corroborated the evidence to be included in my witness statement. In that way I would be prepared for any matters which might be raised by Hamilton's legal team in cross-examination. It was a long, somewhat tedious, research exercise, but in the event it proved to be absolutely invaluable.

Unusually, Mr Al-Fayed, even though he was the defendant, was to give his evidence first. When the hearing had started, and indeed even before then, the libel case became the hottest news story in London. *The Guardian* wrote on 22 December 1999:

"Liar v. Liar, as one tabloid paper billed it, has been the best show in Town, with the queues outside the public gallery more closely resembling those for a West End musical, rather than a fight-to-the-death libel trial."

I had read about the hectic scenes outside the Royal Courts of Justice, where the trial was taking place in Court 13. Pressmen, photographers, television crews, all the media were there in force, completely taking over the pavement outside the Royal Courts.

When the hearing did start, Mr Al-Fayed gave evidence that he had paid Hamilton handsomely for his parliamentary efforts on his behalf. He told the court that Hamilton had received more than £50,000 from him personally and another £40,000–£60,000 indirectly. In addition, he had provided Hamilton with a six-day stay at the Ritz Hotel in Paris, which he valued at £6,000.

Mr Al-Fayed gave very detailed evidence to support the statements he had made that Hamilton had taken cash for asking questions in the House of Commons, and generally for providing parliamentary services. Whenever appropriate, Mr Al-Fayed injected a humorous note into his evidence. At one stage in his cross-examination he was asked why he called himself '<u>Al</u>-Fayed'. He replied that he didn't care what he was called. "Call me Al Capone, if you like!" was his witty impromptu response, said with a huge smile. The court erupted into laughter.

After Mr Al-Fayed's evidence had concluded, a series of witnesses was called on his behalf to substantiate what he had said. All that evidence related to the allegation that Hamilton had received money and other benefits from Mr Al-Fayed. None of it did, nor could it, relate to the Mobil connection. That whole vital chapter was about to be unfolded before the jury.

So at the eleventh hour, when the court had heard all the evidence about the Al-Fayed cash-for-questions affair, George Carman sprung his major surprise on the jury and pulled his rabbit out of the hat - me! I was the said rabbit. So then it was my turn to play my part in the case by giving the critical evidence on the Mobil affair. In the event, as the jury found, the result was the destruction of Hamilton's character. When I was in the witness box, George Carman took me through the series of events that I had discussed with Stephen Lawford on that fateful Saturday morning when he had phoned me at home.

"Do you remember a telephone call that Hamilton made to you after the Consultation in Chambers?"

"Yes."

"What did he say to you?"

"He got straight to the point and asked, 'What do Mobil pay?'"

"Are you certain he said that?"

"I am absolutely certain those are the words he used because I was so shocked by the question. I had never thought that an MP would ask for payment for tabling an amendment to the Finance, or indeed any other, Bill. I was completely taken aback by this demand. It had not been mentioned at the Consultation and it was a complete surprise. I was really shocked."

The court gasped at this evidence. And then it was totally silent, hanging on my every word. The atmosphere in Court 13 was electric as the drama played out. It seemed that everyone appreciated how significant this evidence was. There was much headshaking and note-taking by members of the jury. They were completely absorbed by this 'similar fact' evidence and its obvious importance in considering whether Hamilton was the kind of man to take cash for tabling parliamentary questions. Simply put, would he act corruptly?

George Carman continued: "So payment for Hamilton's services had not been discussed at the Consultation?"

"Definitely not!"

"How did the telephone conversation continue?"

"I responded to Mr Hamilton that, if he wished to pursue any question relating to money, or payment of any kind, he had to speak directly to Mobil. I could not become involved in any matter of that nature."

George Carman continued with my examination for some time longer, but the critical part of my evidence – the 'silver bullet' – had already been delivered.

My evidence on behalf of Mr Al-Fayed completed, George Carman sat down. Mr Desmond Browne QC, Counsel for Hamilton, rose to his feet to cross-examine me. He was (and is) a highly respected member of the Bar with a formidable reputation. However, I found no difficulty in answering Mr Browne's questions, except in one somewhat surprising respect.

I have referred to the 'questions' from Mr Browne, but in fact, on a number of occasions, I found the 'questions' to be more in the nature of monologues or perorations. They were more like speeches (which seemed to go on for some while) than questions. I found it difficult at the end of each peroration to know what question or questions I was being asked. So a number of times, after Mr Browne had delivered what I regarded as a speech, and silence had descended on the court, indicating that the monologue had come to an end, I asked, in what I believe was a respectful manner:

"And your question is?"

I was not for a moment seeking to be impertinent but genuinely trying to discover what I was being asked. Certainly the judge did not take any such response to be inappropriate or unjustified because he never intervened. Each time, Mr Browne then dutifully rephrased what he had previously 'asked', but in a more succinct way. I, of course, duly answered the reformulated question to the best of my ability. However, it did seem very strange to me that such unfocussed questions should be asked in relation to many matters which were so straightforward. But even more important was that, by reformulating his original 'questions' in the way he did, Mr Browne allowed me to take the initiative by asking him questions. That put him on the back foot because he then had to explain his 'questions'. In my view, Counsel should never allow that to happen. His demeanour indicated he was uncomfortable with this development. On the other hand, it meant that I became more relaxed in the witness box and felt entirely comfortable giving my evidence. I knew I had the upper hand.

And then Mr Browne sought to question the evidence I had given on behalf of Mr Al-Fayed. On nearly all such occasions I was able to corroborate my oral testimony by picking up my trusty briefcase, which I had taken into the witness box with me, delving into it and producing a document or documents from it. I have already related that, in preparation for the trial, I had undertaken the task of collecting all the documents which might be relevant to my evidence. In the event, it proved to be a vitally important and most worthwhile exercise. To answer a question positively from the witness box is one thing. But to be able to produce contemporaneous written evidence which corroborates it is quite another. Often Mr Browne would put a question to me based on paperwork he had in court. As I recall, each time I was able to counter it with a document that I was able to produce. These skirmishes essentially became a game of cat and mouse. My reaction to a question, supported or not by Mr Browne's paperwork, became familiar to the court. Each time, I would reach down from my seat in the witness box, pick up my briefcase, open it, select the relevant written evidence and then read it (without interruption) to the court. Such an approach countered any point that Mr Browne was hoping to make by his question and supporting paperwork. It also meant, in my view, that the cross-examination was unlikely to make any impact on the jury because my documentation countered any point Mr Browne was trying to make. His approach, therefore, if it achieved anything, was only to support George Carman's submissions. Indeed, *The Times* wrote on 22 December 1999 that Mr Browne was *"not a natural with the jury. He seems slightly pompous, even plodding, and his questioning was bogged down by his reference to documents."* This was indeed confirmation from an unexpected source that my meticulous approach to my evidence, supported by appropriate documentation, was destabilising Mr Browne's cross-examination.

Indeed, on the evening of the second day I had been giving evidence in court, something very gratifying to me occurred at our annual Chambers' Christmas Party. My Co-Head of Chambers, Julian Bevan QC, who, as I have mentioned, held a watching brief at the trial for Mr Al-Fayed, was at the party. He had, of course, witnessed the day's proceedings and in particular Desmond Browne's cross-examination of me. With a huge smile on his face, he came bounding up to me and exploded with the words:

"I just couldn't believe what happened today. You really were the witness from hell. I would hate to cross-examine you. Every question Desmond Browne asked you, you always had a convincing answer, and worse still for him, each time he asked you a question, you produced a document to support what you had just said. It completely destroyed his line of questioning. Document after document produced by you killed him. You really were the epitome of the witness from hell. I just hope I never have to cross-examine you. I couldn't imagine there would be a worse experience for a barrister in court!!"

With that, he burst out laughing. However, what he had said made me feel very pleased. That such an experienced and outstanding Silk, so used to cross-examining witnesses in criminal trials, should take such a view of my cross-examination was immensely gratifying. Indeed, that day I had really started to enjoy being cross-examined. I found sparring with Desmond Browne very stimulating. Particularly when I asked him to rephrase his questions. With not a single critical intervention from the judge when I asked for such rephrasing, and Julian's view of my approach to my evidence, I felt I had at the very least held my ground and done all that could have been expected of me. As a result of my conversation with Julian, I started the weekend in an upbeat mood, even though Desmond Browne had not finished his cross-examination.

I returned on Monday to continue giving my evidence. It was more of the same, except for two dramatic developments in court. The first related to a tactic adopted by Desmond Browne to establish through my cross-examination that I had once advised Hamilton on a tax matter at a cocktail party. It was alleged that this occurred at some time in 1995, the precise date being unknown. Certainly the allegation made by Desmond Browne was, I knew, completely without foundation - I would never give formal advice at any party or social occasion. However, to substantiate the allegation, he sought an order from the Presiding Judge, Mr Justice Morland, that I should produce my 1995 Professional Diary to the court.

Mr Justice Morland turned to me and said:

"Mr Whiteman, you have heard what Mr Browne has said, so I am formally directing you to produce your 1995 Professional Diary so that he might inspect it."

My response resonated round the court. "No!" I replied.

There was murmured surprise in the court at my unqualified refusal to comply with the judge's direction.

"Well," said Mr Justice Morland, "if you won't produce your diary for Mr Browne, will you produce it for me so that I can inspect it?"

"No," I replied firmly but politely.

There were mild gasps in court, and the previous murmur when I refused to provide my diary for Mr Browne's inspection became a distinctly incredulous buzz. The reason was obvious. A barrister was refusing, politely but firmly, to accede to a direction of the judge in the clearest of terms.

Mr Justice Morland appeared to be taken aback by my refusal, however respectful it was. Indeed, not expecting the question, I had surprised myself by my quick and negative response. My tone indicated that "No" really meant "No".

"Why?" the judge asked politely. And in a way that did not indicate irritation or indignation.

I responded in a courteous and professional way.

"Because, My Lord, my Professional Diaries contain, as you would expect, the names of solicitors, accountants and their clients attending a Consultation, the name of the matter on which I am advising, and a brief indication of the advice given. My Lord, I cannot deliver up to the court a diary containing such highly confidential information relating to my practice. I am sure you will understand that." He did. Mr Justice Morland accepted my submission and my 1995 Professional Diary was never produced to the court for inspection by the judge. As a Queen's Counsel, I had had the temerity to say "No" to the direction of a High Court Judge. No wonder the court gasped. There had been, of course, no such cocktail party, no such tax advice had been given, and consequently there was no such entry in my 1995 diary. So its production to the court would not have assisted the judge, nor Desmond Browne. Indeed, production of the diary would only have established that what Hamilton had alleged, namely, that I gave him tax advice at a cocktail party in 1995, was completely untrue.

The second incident that occurred on the Monday was that, at the very end of my cross-examination, Desmond Browne asked me a question that I regarded as deeply offensive. Also, in my view, it was a most unwise question for him to ask. The question that caused me such offence was as follows:

"Has the fact that you have been Mr Al-Fayed's adviser for over twenty years in any way affected the evidence you have given before this court?"

My response was immediate and I declaimed:

"I find that question offensive, and I am surprised you should ask it. The answer is, of course not."

I considered at the time, and I still do now, that it was a most ill-advised question to ask. Obviously a Queen's Counsel, giving evidence before a court of law, would tell 'the truth and nothing but the truth'. The unwise question meant that Mr Browne's cross-examination petered out, leaving it flat and without any devastating conclusion. So ended my evidence in cross-examination, and I believed it finished on the same upbeat note as all my previous evidence had. That may be regarded as a somewhat biased view, but I have the words of Julian Bevan ringing in my ears to vindicate my conclusion on the quality of my evidence. As I relate later, however, there was more to come to reinforce that view, and it came from a variety of significant sources.

The high point of the trial for me was now over, but the case continued with the evidence of other witnesses and the presentation of Hamilton's case by Desmond Browne. Of course, Hamilton denied all the allegations, but George Carman's cross-examination of him was masterly and completely devastating. George was famous for the 'one-liners' he invented to describe the litigant on the other side. As I have said at the start of this chapter, he described Hamilton as "on the make and on the take". As Hamilton gave evidence, I could only think of George's vivid, and indeed wholly accurate, description of him. It very aptly described this major player in the cash-for-questions scandal.

The jury started their deliberations. It became obvious how critical the evidence on the Mobil connection was to the jury. As the *Daily Telegraph* wrote under the heading *The Mobil Connection* (22 December 1999):

"[The Mobil connection] proved the undoing of Neil Hamilton in his libel battle with Mohammed Fayed. It was devastating evidence of corruption … The potential damage to Mr Hamilton's case was obvious. Here was a man who, while denying that he took cash from Mr Fayed, was apparently prepared to demand a £10,000 fee for trying to change the law."

Certainly the jury seemed to interpret the Mobil connection in that way, as did the *Daily Telegraph,* whose article continued:

"The £10,000 payment Mr Hamilton received from Mobil Oil ten years ago clearly bothered the jury. It returned to court while considering its verdict and asked the judge to go over Mr Hamilton's explanation again."

Interestingly, the jury only ever asked for clarification from the judge on one piece of evidence: the Mobil connection. In his address to the jury, George Carman had said Hamilton's claim "falls, and falls completely, on Mobil alone because it establishes corruption on the part of a Member of Parliament." (Under ancient parliamentary rules, taking cash solely for parliamentary action is corrupt.)

The jury agreed. After almost nine hours of deliberation, they returned to court to deliver their verdict. Asked whether the members of the jury had found "on the balance of probabilities" that Mr Al-Fayed had established corruption by Mr Hamilton "on highly convincing evidence", the forewoman replied, "Yes."

There was a collective sharp intake of breath in the court; Hamilton crumpled. *"Mr Hamilton and his distraught wife looked on in disbelief"*: *The Guardian* 22 December 1999.

Outside court, Hamilton seemed to share the view of *The Guardian* that the Mobil connection was the crucial factor. Hamilton said, "It may well be, from the questions the jury asked the judge during the trial, that [the Mobil connection] is what secured this verdict."

After the verdict of the jury, others reflecting on the outcome of the case seemed to share the view that my "devastating" evidence had been critical to the outcome of the case; it was the 'silver bullet'. One commentator (Ian Dales) wrote, *"There is no doubt that the Mobil allegations were the killer blow to Hamilton's defence of his character."*

Another commentator wrote, in somewhat colourful language (although it was right on point), *"It was the man for Mobil who did for him."* That was to prove to be the general consensus, certainly at the Bar. I remember a member of my Chambers calling out to me as I mounted the stairs to my room after the jury had delivered their verdict, "It was your evidence that won the case for Al-Fayed."

So the trial that had lasted five weeks was over. Overall, I had actually enjoyed giving evidence, and the fact that what I had said in the witness box was *"the clinching piece of evidence"* (*The Guardian*) was extremely gratifying. So, although not acting as Counsel or as a presiding judge, my participation in this trial was one of the most dramatic experiences of my career.

Although Counsel frequently give expert evidence, it was, to my knowledge, without precedent for a Queen's Counsel to give evidence of <u>fact</u> relating to his professional practice.

POSTSCRIPT

Interestingly, the day after I gave evidence in the Hamilton trial, I appeared as Counsel in the High Court in another case, and the day after that I sat as a judge. So in three consecutive days I fulfilled the three distinct court roles: as a witness, as Counsel and as a judge. No doubt the reader will not be surprised to learn that I asked myself, "Is this also without precedent?"

CHAPTER 26

PARTYING WITH THE IRON LADY

*"Though the sex to which I belong is considered weak
you will nevertheless find me a rock that bends to no wind."*
QUEEN ELIZABETH I

*"It is not where a person comes from that counts,
but where he can get to."*
21 October 1959
MARGARET THATCHER

In 1985 the Prime Minister, Mrs Thatcher, and her husband, Denis, purchased a house in Dulwich. In 1986 I decided to establish a new society to protect and preserve the amenities of Dulwich and promote the interests of the residents. The two events soon became connected, for reasons I will explain in this chapter. But first a little background to the creation of the new society, in the event called the Dulwich Village Preservation Society (DVPS), which is vital to understanding much of what follows.

As I have related, Kate and I moved into our house in Dulwich in 1978. There was then, and is now, a Scheme of Management for the Dulwich Estate, which imposes numerous and strict controls over what residents may and may not do with their property. The authority entrusted with the management of the Scheme was a body of trustees, then called the Estates Governors. The more I became involved in local community affairs, the clearer it became that there was considerable and deep-rooted discontent with the way the Estates Governors administered the Scheme of Management and, in particular, their behaviour towards residents. Their attitude was seen by many as high-handed and arrogant, and their management of the Scheme as unfair and inconsistent. A particular cause of irritation was the adoption of a double standard towards

Above: As President of the Dulwich Village Preservation Society, delivering a petition
to Mrs Thatcher

Photograph © Daily Telegraph

development and building works on the Estate. On the one hand, the Governors rigorously enforced the Scheme of Management in respect of the most minor building alterations which residents proposed, whilst on the other hand they undertook large scale construction of new buildings on their own land, which was outside the terms of the Scheme of Management.

On a practical level, backed by the Scheme of Management, the Governors were extremely powerful and were very firmly in control of everything of importance, particularly development, which occurred on the Estate. The only organisations in being to protect the interests of residents were amenity societies which, although well-intentioned, did not, in my view, adopt a sufficiently proactive stance in their dealings with the Governors. The perception of many, including me, was that the amenity societies were too ready to accommodate the proposals of the Governors and to fall into line with their ideas on the overall management of the Estate. Many, if not most, of the residents I spoke to felt their interests were not being sufficiently protected.

So in 1986, feeling that positive action was needed to ensure that in future the wishes of the residents were fully taken into account, I called a public meeting at the Village Hall. It was well publicised, and the response far exceeded my expectations. My estimate at the time was that there were more than five hundred people crammed into the Hall – a true measure of the dissatisfaction of the residents with the management of the Estate. Following such a turnout, and having heard trenchant views expressed at the meeting, it was obvious that positive and far-reaching action needed to be taken as a matter of urgency.

As a result, I, with others, set about the task of forming a new society, which would not be supine in its relations with the Governors, but, on the contrary, would be proactive in vigorously protecting the interests of the residents. Clearly a well-thought-out legal framework for the new society had to be created, so I drafted the Constitution for it, the DVPS, and registered it as a charity with the Charity Commission. I ensured that everything that needed to be done was done as meticulously as it should be. As a result, we were now in business, the business of ensuring that the Governors behaved in a way which was more appropriate to the late twentieth century, rather than the eighteenth. I was determined that the Governors' attitude, which had been more suited to a feudal society, should be brought to a swift end. Obviously, the incorporation of a new society, with a widely-publicised progressive stance, ruffled many feathers, notably amongst the Estates Governors and the other amenity societies. So be it, I felt. The relationship between the Governors and the amenity societies had, in my opinion, been too 'cosy' for far too long and in a way which was not beneficial to the residents. Action, positive action, was needed, for example, to stop building developments, 'infilling' and the erosion of open spaces. Now the DVPS would be there to promote the protection and preservation of the amenities and character of Dulwich.

And here's the link between the fledgling society and the Prime Minister. The Constitution I had drafted for the DVPS provided for a Chairman (a post to which I was elected), a Vice-Chairman and other appropriate Officers. There was, however, one somewhat unusual feature that I had incorporated into the DVPS Constitution. It provided that, in addition to the other Officers, there would be a President of the Society. I had very deliberately included this post in the Constitution because I had a cunning little plan in mind, which was to invite the new, most famous resident of Dulwich to become the Society's President. In the circumstances, and given the overwhelming obligations of the Prime Minister, my intention was that she would not be invited to discharge any duties in that post, but that she would be an illustrious figurehead of the nascent society. That would, of course, be a real coup and bring an enormous cachet to the Society.

Then, at just the right moment, luck played into my hands. I had been acting unofficially as the legal adviser to the recently-formed Dulwich Village Business Association (DVBA) and had started the process of drafting a Constitution for it. Because of the role I was playing in their affairs, the Committee members invited me to a buffet and drinks reception to be given in honour of the Prime Minister and Denis Thatcher. The reception was on 30 November 1986. This was manna from heaven, giving me the opportunity to approach Mrs Thatcher about the possibility of her becoming the President of the DVPS.

At the DVBA party, I was introduced by its humorous and enthusiastic Chairman to the Prime Minister with the words, "May I introduce you to one of the movers and shakers of Dulwich, Prime Minister?" Mrs Thatcher asked me about the part I played in Dulwich community affairs. I very briefly outlined the purpose and activities of the DVPS and my ideas, as Chairman, for its future. A brief discussion about conservation followed, but then she was whisked away to speak to other guests. But, as far as I was concerned, the groundwork to entice her to become the President of the DVPS had been laid. I had seized the opportunity that had fortuitously presented itself and was delighted with the progress that had been achieved. Subsequently the DVBA organised another drinks party, to which I was also invited, and which the Prime Minister attended. Again I took the opportunity during a brief conversation with her to refresh her memory about the work of the DVPS. She appeared more than politely interested and, being thus encouraged, with some trepidation I invited her to consider the possibility of becoming its President. She was charming in her response but, as one would expect, suggested that the best way to take matters forward would be for me to write to her in detail, which of course I did. In her amusing reply she said she had considered my kind invitation carefully, but she had come to the conclusion that she must decline my offer, explaining light-heartedly that "at the present time I have one or two other little things to do!" More seriously, she then said she was concerned that, if she accepted the post of President, it might give rise to a conflict of interest. The DVPS would obviously from time to time be involved in planning appeals, which might eventually go to the Department of the Environment. She stated that, as all parts of the government are one, she could not appear to have a conflict of interest, being the President of a Preservation Society and a member of the government which had to decide the outcome of a planning application. It was for that reason she had reluctantly concluded that she could not accept my invitation. She added, however, that she had discussed the matter with her husband and that Denis would be writing to me. This he did, in equally charming terms, stating that he supported the work of the Society and wished to become a member and, to encourage us on our way, enclosing a contribution to our funds. The contribution was very significant, far in excess of the annual membership fee – a most generous gesture.

After Mrs Thatcher indicated she was unable to become the President of the DVPS, I was elected to that post. (As an aside, I mention that I held the Offices of President and Chairman for the next eleven years. During that time I worked hard in furthering the aims and objectives of the Society, and I believe it was very successful in fulfilling the purposes for which it had been created.)

After my two meetings with Mrs Thatcher, I did a certain amount of research into her background and realised that, quite apart from our discussions concerning the DVPS, we had other areas of common interest. Naturally I knew that the Prime Minister had been elected a Bencher of Lincoln's Inn in April 1975. My researches enlightened me as to her career at the Bar. I had not appreciated that, as a barrister, she had practised at the Revenue Bar for some five years in the Chambers of Sir John Senter QC, which specialised in Revenue Law. As a result, I discovered, we had a number of mutual acquaintances, including Hubert Monroe QC and Michael Nolan QC (later Lord Nolan). On a subsequent occasion, which I shall refer to in detail later, Mrs Thatcher and I reminisced about these two distinguished members of the Revenue Bar, whom we both knew so well and held in high regard.

My first two meetings with Mrs Thatcher at the DVBA parties, although both fascinating and enjoyable, were a mere prelude to the far more significant social occasion when we met for the third time. But before I tell you what took place on that third occasion, it is appropriate to describe the stage Mrs Thatcher's premiership had reached by then, and her status and reputation at that time.

I take myself back to the somewhat heady days of 1987. Earlier this year Mrs Thatcher has been convincingly elected Prime Minister of the United Kingdom for a third time. She is riding a wave of popularity with the electorate. She has established a reputation for single-mindedness, strong leadership, and faithfulness to her convictions. She has always used the audacious language of change and followed it through with decisive action. Almost single-handedly, she has changed the country from the muddled, depressed and near chaotic state it was in in 1979 to one that is dynamic, efficient and extremely successful. She has set the standard of how to wield Prime Ministerial power and, in the process, has become the epitome of a strong and determined Prime Minister. For eight years she has dominated the United Kingdom political scene and also cut a very powerful figure on the global stage. There can be little doubt that history will judge her as one of our greatest Prime Ministers.

My third meeting with the Prime Minister turns out to be one of the most exciting and meaningful experiences of my lifetime. I am thrilled when I receive an invitation from the Prime Minister and Mr Denis Thatcher to a drinks party at their home in Dulwich. As a result of my first two meetings with her, and our limited correspondence, I believe that I have established something of a rapport with them both. Nonetheless, an invitation to a private party at their home is something I could never have expected.

In the event, I am to spend three spellbinding and totally fascinating hours in her company. Beforehand, I resolve to remember every detail of this meeting with the Prime Minister. I expect it to be amazing. It is. And indeed I do remember every aspect, every word, every mood change and every minute of those three hours.

The invitation I receive to the Prime Minister's drinks party is sent to me, I assume, because of our previous meetings and correspondence and in particular because I am President of the DVPS. Indeed, the invitation is so marked.

As Mrs Thatcher owns a house in Dulwich, I assume that she is seeking to offer hospitality to a large number of her fellow Dulwich residents. A drinks party would, of course, be an ideal way to achieve that objective. With the invitation firmly grasped in my hand, I come running down the stairs from my study to tell Kate. I explode into the kitchen with the exciting news. She is as thrilled as I am. "What a fantastic experience this is going to be. I'm sure it will be one we will remember for the rest of our lives," I blurt out. Kate agrees.

"Well, as I want to remember every second of such a wonderful occasion, I am not going to have a single alcoholic drink at the party. If I am going to recall everything about it, I will have to be stone cold sober!"

So when the day comes, we walk from our house to the Prime Minister's, a distance of about a quarter of a mile. Her house is within a guarded estate, but even so I am amazed at the minimal amount of security – we are able to walk through the gates of the estate, which are open! And this is the entrance to the home of the Prime Minister of the United Kingdom.

We duly arrive at the front door of Mrs Thatcher's home. She is standing in the hallway to meet her guests. We introduce ourselves. Not a single footman or flunky in sight. She obviously wants her welcome to be personal. A good indication of the nature of this thoughtful woman. After a brief "Hello", Mrs Thatcher asks me, "Did you drive here?" "No," I respond. She looks sternly at me and then, in the tones of a headmistress addressing a pupil, says, "Then you can have a drink." And then she adds as a humorous comment, one I am told she regularly makes, "DT is mixing the drinks today." This mildly amusing comment is intended to be a pun on her husband's initials and at the same time a reference to delirium tremens. Anyway, she continues: "You will find him in the kitchen, mixing champagne cocktails." I keep to my resolution and never try one. Kate does, and says it is three-quarters brandy and one-quarter champagne, and not, as it usually is, the other way around. The sacrifices one makes to live (and recall) a memorable experience!

Almost immediately afterwards, Mrs Thatcher arrives by my side. "I will introduce you to the other guests." I look around. At a quick glance there appear to be only about a dozen people present. Beforehand, I had assumed that there would be a very large gathering. After all, Mrs Thatcher is the Prime Minister and I anticipate that all 'the great and the good' of Dulwich will be here – or at least 'the great and the good' of the Dulwich Tory Party.

And then I am truly astounded. Mrs Thatcher does exactly what she said she would. She introduces me to the other guests. But what an introduction! She takes me over to Lord McColl and then proceeds to describe my background, almost as if she were reading from my curriculum vitae. It is all there: student at the LSE, being awarded LLB and LLM degrees, teaching at the LSE, member of the Bar (naming the Chambers of which I had been a tenant), author of the leading textbooks on Revenue Law, establishing my own Chambers, Professor of Law at the University of Virginia, Queen's Counsel and part-time judge. She omits nothing of significance. And all of this without a single note. I am so very impressed and flattered. She has either done her own research into my life (and remember this is before the days of Google) or she has asked an aide to do so, who has informed her accordingly. Either way, she has taken the time and trouble to become completely acquainted with my life history and to memorise it so that the other guests at her party will be totally au fait with my background. I find that attention to detail very impressive, and this, it has to be recalled, is at a time when she is the Prime Minister. I think to myself, no wonder she has a reputation for having such a grasp of detail and controlling every situation. Moreover, she (or her aides) has no doubt carried out the same sort of research into the background of the other guests. It is clearly Mrs Thatcher's intention to put all of us entirely at our ease. Being so relaxed, I remain determined to adhere to my resolution that I must remember every detail of this occasion, and also that I am going to enjoy it to the full.

Having introduced me to Lord McColl, Mrs Thatcher moves away to meet and introduce her other guests. This is becoming a very enjoyable occasion. Once again I have to pinch myself that this is happening to me. I don't believe one ever really forgets one's background, and for me to be at such an intimate party given by the Prime Minister in her own house is incredible. And such fun. That I hadn't expected. And I tell myself to enjoy and remember every moment of it.

Denis Thatcher wafts past the guests with two of his special champagne cocktails in his hands and pauses at my side. I keep to my resolution and don't take one. I had met Denis previously, at the drinks parties of the DVBA and at Southwark Crown Court, and I had always found him to be affable and utterly charming. True, he was not averse to the odd 'tincture' or two, but this did not affect him adversely in any way. He would continue to be entirely happy listening to others and making his own contribution, usually witty, to the conversation. A very pleasant social companion on every occasion I met him.

Denis then starts to tell me and two other guests that the following week he is to accompany the Prime Minister on an official tour of East Africa. "I am so looking forward to visiting East Africa and seeing Kenya."

At that precise moment, Mrs Thatcher walks across the room, passing behind her husband's back, and she hears his reference to East Africa. Without altering her purposeful stride, she says in a resounding voice, over her husband's shoulder, "West Africa, not East Africa. Denis, do get it right. And it's Nigeria, not Kenya!" Her correction made in passing, she continues on her way. Denis does not look scolded at all and simply shrugs his shoulders. There is the slightest sheepish grin on his face, as if to say (to use a modern American expression), "Whatever!"

All of this only increases my enjoyment. I continue my conversation with two other guests as Denis drifts away. Then Mrs Thatcher sails into view. There is no mistaking it. She has set her sights on our little group of three and, as she approaches us, it is clear from her face, particularly her eyes, that she is a lady on a mission. I am soon to discover why, but not before she makes a very illuminating comment. She reaches my side and proclaims proudly: "I made these myself!" "These" refers to a plate of smoked salmon sandwiches. Prepared, I am sure, to make us feel very welcome, they are piled high, inelegantly high.

"I made these myself," she repeats. That, I think, is obvious. The bread is sliced so badly – often thin at one end and gradually becoming thicker at the other – they look as if they have been cut from a slate mine rather than prepared on a breadboard. I immediately realise my thought is a churlish one and not worthy of me. Here is the Prime Minister of the United Kingdom, who could easily have arranged to have sandwiches brought in by outside caterers, but no, she has gone to the trouble of making them herself. Very impressive.

I do not have to wait long for the next memorable incident, when I discover that I have a shared passion with Mrs Thatcher. I delicately take a sandwich. I want no repetition of the disastrous occasion when my millefeuille flew across the tablecloth and landed on Dean Edwards' 'flies'! "I do love smoked salmon," proclaims Mrs Thatcher, "and it is so good for you. I could almost live on smoked salmon. I love it."

Message received loud and clear. And not for the first time I find myself in complete agreement with the Prime Minister. I stand there, almost to attention, waiting for Mrs Thatcher to continue. Naturally she will lead the conversation. She has a purposeful look on her face and it is clear that we are now going to move on to more serious matters. As she might ask for my views, I need to be in a position to respond without showering her with crumbs from the ill-cut sandwiches.

"Now, Professor Whiteman, you are the President of the Dulwich Village Preservation Society." This sounds like the start of what might become a gruelling cross-examination. Her determined look and the tone of her voice leave me in no doubt that I am in for a difficult time. My light-hearted state of mind evaporates. The Prime Minister is now in serious mode and I need to adopt a like-minded approach.

"Now, of course, as I have mentioned to you in the past, I realise that there has to be conservation and I believe it has a role to play in many situations. But I do get annoyed with some conservationists who, without thinking, blindly want to conserve everything and oppose any form of development. Houses have to be built for the people. I particularly become incensed with all those 'townies', who move into villages in Sussex and, as soon as they are there, oppose any form of change or development, however sensible the proposal might be. They move in and want to pull the drawbridge up behind them."

I am not sure to whom she is referring when she alludes to "all" these people moving to Sussex. Indeed, I am not really able to follow the logic of her argument. Certainly, the tone of her comments is very different from the one she adopted when we were talking about conservation in Dulwich at the DVBA drinks parties. Maybe she sees conservation in Dulwich as being of a different order from conservation campaigns in the countryside led by townies.

Whatever the tone of her comments, however, I stand there listening politely. I say absolutely nothing. After all, she is the Prime Minister, and I am a guest in her home. Moreover, I am concerned that, if I say something which doesn't find favour with the PM, I might be 'handbagged'. At this time it is not impossible because she has the plate of sandwiches in one hand and the famous handbag hanging over her other arm.

The peroration continues, whilst I stand there holding the smoked salmon sandwich I had originally taken, still uneaten. Whatever she might say, I am still determined not to shower her with breadcrumbs or, worse still, a piece of her beloved smoked salmon. Then suddenly out of nowhere, and it seems as if she is in mid-sentence, she turns to me and says, "Eat your smoked salmon!" It is not advice; it is not a request. It is an order, barked out in stentorian tones. I rather assumed (foolishly) that that tone of voice was reserved for Denis or her Cabinet colleagues. Without pausing for further breath, she continues straight away with her criticism of some townie conservationists. Her comments are basically more of the same, but in case I have to respond, as before, I still hold my sandwich in my hand. Same reason, even though I have not said a word. Indeed, there is no way to get a word in edgeways. The monologue continues and then suddenly she points at me and says even more sternly, "I told you to eat up your smoked salmon sandwich. Why haven't you done so?"

This is the headmistress calling a recalcitrant pupil to order, not polite advice to a guest. Before I can answer, she turns to my fellow guests and (apparently forgetting she herself is a lawyer) says, "That's the trouble with these lawyers, they never stop talking!" Me? I haven't said a word, and the only reason my sandwich is still untouched is out of respect and consideration for her. So ironic. But before I can say anything, her lecture completed, she sweeps off to pastures new, no doubt convinced that she has got her message across about certain conservationists. Well, at least I haven't been handbagged! Duly chastised, I resume my conversation with my companions. But that conversation with the Prime Minister is not the most insightful incident that day relating to Mrs Thatcher's character. That comes later.

First, I want to refer to something very different. There had been one question relating to the composition of Mrs Thatcher's Cabinets over the years which had, given my background, intrigued me for a long while. So when the Prime Minister approaches me again, I think this is a good moment to raise the matter in question.

"Prime Minister, it has always interested me, being Jewish, that over the years there have been a significant number of Jewish members of your Cabinets, for example, Sir Keith Joseph, Nigel Lawson, David Young, Leon Brittan and Michael Howard. Without, I hope, being insensitive in any way, may I ask whether there was any particular reason as to how that came about?"

"Well, there is a very interesting background to those appointments, which goes back a long way, in fact to before the Second World War. My sister, Muriel, corresponded with a young Jewish girl called Edith Muhlbauer who lived in Austria. They were what one would call pen pals and they wrote to each other very regularly. In the 1930s life gradually became more and more difficult for the Jewish community in Austria, especially after the Anschluss (1938). So Edith's parents decided that it would be sensible for her to leave Austria, travel to the United Kingdom and, if it were acceptable to my parents, for her to live with us. My parents readily agreed and shortly afterwards Edith arrived at our house with a large number of trunks filled with clothes. I remember the three of us – Edith, Muriel and I – unpacking the clothes, particularly the dresses. They had been so lovingly packed between sheet after sheet of tissue paper. The clothes, and especially the dresses, were so pretty and so very sophisticated. I was mesmerised by the sight of them. I had never seen anything like them before. I never knew that clothes could be so beautiful. From then on, Edith lived with us. As time passed I realised that, although originally she had been Muriel's friend, Edith and I had become very close friends, more so than my sister and Edith were. I developed a real fondness for Edith and I grew to like and respect her enormously. She was a lovely, kind and lively person who was highly principled. From that relationship I developed a real respect and liking for Jewish people, a view I have had ever since. So it was natural, when I was appointing members of my Cabinet, if everything else was equal and it was otherwise appropriate, to think, why not appoint someone Jewish? Edith had shown me how hard-working, caring and trustworthy Jewish people can be." It is obvious that relating this story has brought back fond memories for Mrs Thatcher and I detect that, as a result, she has become somewhat emotional.

I find the Prime Minister's explanation fascinating and a great credit to her open-mindedness in a world where prejudice still prevails. It also shows how one experience can so influence a person's approach to any issue. The question that has intrigued me for a long while has been comprehensively answered by the only person who can provide the definitive explanation. (However, the reader may care to note that the account the Prime Minister gave of her friendship with Edith and how it developed is somewhat at odds with the version of events related by Charles Moore in his excellent authorised biography, *Margaret Thatcher Volume 1: Not for Turning,* at pages 20–21. It is intriguing to speculate why there should be two versions of such events, although it has to be said that Charles Moore's account is less flattering to the Roberts family's hospitality in welcoming Edith into their home.)

By now, the party is in full swing. There are several conversations going on in the room, which now has a real 'buzz'. A little later, I find myself in a huddle with the Prime Minister and Sir Robin Butler (later Lord Butler). Sir Robin is Secretary to the Cabinet, and he is also a Dulwich resident. For either or both of those reasons, Sir Robin is currently one of the Estates Governors. In that capacity I have come to know him and I have great respect for him. But before I continue with this narrative, a little technical background is necessary to enable the reader to comprehend the matters I am now going to relate. At a number of meetings of the Advisory Committee of the Dulwich Estate, Sir Robin and I have found ourselves, metaphorically speaking, on opposite sides of the table, he representing the Estates Governors and I the DVPS. From time to time, difficulties arise as to the correct interpretation of various clauses of the Scheme of Management. The established way of resolving such difficulties is to have 'friendly' litigation between the Estates Governors and the amenity societies, which settles the correct interpretation of the clauses in question so as to bind all parties.

At the moment, one such piece of friendly litigation is afoot between the Estates Governors, where one of the named litigants is Sir Robin, and the amenity societies, where I appear as one of the named litigants. As I talk to Sir Robin, I have that very much in mind today. Clearly, so does Sir Robin because, when there is a lull in the conversation, eager that it should not last, he mentions the friendly litigation now pending before the courts. Pointing at me, albeit in a gentlemanly fashion, he looks in Mrs Thatcher's direction and says, "He's suing me and ...", but before he can continue, he is cut off in his prime. He has touched a raw nerve with the Prime Minister. She is not going to allow Sir Robin to finish whatever he is about to say. She is clearly furious with me and determined to tell me so. She has gone white – with anger. Cutting across Sir Robin is a matter of no consequence to her. Out comes the finger, jabbing at me repeatedly, emphasising how angry she is.

She looks me straight in the eye and it is obvious from her expression that she is enraged. She then explodes, saying, "You should know better. You're a barrister. You should know how expensive, pointless and futile litigation is. You are being totally irresponsible. It is a complete waste of time, and here you are suing the Cabinet Secretary. I don't know what you must be thinking of! And ..."

But just at that moment the cavalry arrives in the form of Sir Robin, no doubt very used to mollifying the Prime Minister in Cabinet meetings. I can see he is terribly embarrassed at the storm he has unwittingly whipped up. He is obviously desperate to prevent the unjustified attack on me from continuing. His first words are uttered hesitantly. "Prime Minister, with respect, may I just explain what the position is with regard to the litigation because it is not what you appear to think it might be. The litigation is purely technical, it is not acrimonious at all. It is simply that I am one of the Governors of the Dulwich Estate and Professor Whiteman is Chairman of the Dulwich Village Preservation Society, and we are jointly applying to obtain clarification of the Terms of the Scheme of Management. Professor Whiteman is behaving perfectly properly and he is, in fact, assisting us to obtain resolution of some very complex legal issues."

Mrs Thatcher is totally taken aback. "Oh!" she utters. The jabbing finger is lowered and relaxed. It is laid to rest – at least for the time being. The anger drains from her face. She realises that she has totally misunderstood the situation. All she says is, in a somewhat softer voice, "That's rather different." Sir Robin looks very relieved. The comment he had made to keep the conversation going had created a storm, something he had of course never intended. But the whirlwind that had engulfed all three of us had caused great embarrassment.

A half-smile returns to Mrs Thatcher's face and Sir Robin starts to relax. The panic is over. And then I think, if Mrs Thatcher can become so angry over one small, innocuous comment, what would be her reaction to a point of real substance with which she disagreed? Maybe all those stories of members of the Cabinet being taken apart by a displeased Mrs Thatcher could be true. After a major difference of opinion between the Prime Minister and a Cabinet member, there would no doubt be blood everywhere. And it wouldn't be Mrs Thatcher's!

And then something happens which is very surprising. At least to me. Not only for its substance, but for the total change of atmosphere in this part of Mrs Thatcher's sitting room. There is a real calm after the storm. The contrast could not be more striking.

Just after Mrs Thatcher had stated in muted tones, "That's rather different," there arrives at her side a middle-aged woman with a pleasant, relaxed expression on her face. Mrs Thatcher being the accomplished and caring hostess she is, she immediately introduces us. "This is Mrs Barratt, my next-door neighbour." Mrs Barratt smiles graciously and, before the Prime Minister can say anything more, she interrupts her. She immediately goes to the top of my class for being able to beat Mrs Thatcher off the mark. No mean feat.

"Prime Minister," says Mrs Barratt, "I have to tell you something I would very much like you to know. It's about your chauffeur, David." Mrs Thatcher completely recomposes her face from the irate visage of a few minutes ago. It is now the face of a kind, gentle, indulgent aunt, gazing affectionately on a relative. "You see, Prime Minister," continues Mrs Barratt, and by now she has Mrs Thatcher's complete attention, "David absolutely adores you." At this point I see a little misting of the Prime Minister's eyes. "Well, you see, whenever you come down to your house here and David is waiting for you in the car,

I always take a cup of tea to him and we have a little chat. He says he is lost in admiration for you." The eyes are definitely misting up now. "The reason is that, whatever affairs of State are on your mind, whatever political crisis there might be, you always ask him about his wife and children by name. You ask him how his children are doing at school and about other aspects of his family life. You never fail to do so. He thinks that you are wonderful because clearly you care about him and his family. It means the world to him." Now there are clearly tears forming in the corners of the Prime Minister's eyes. Obviously she is very moved by this story of her chauffeur's affection for her. That she is so touched by what she has heard shows a very caring side to her nature. I find it almost impossible to believe that this is the same person who had barked, "Eat your smoked salmon sandwich!" at me, castigated inflexible conservationists, and become furious with me when she was informed that I was suing the Cabinet Secretary. The difference is incredible. Now she stands before me with tears in her eyes, the picture of sentimentality. She clearly has a very soft centre.

"Well, Mrs Barratt, thank you so much for telling me that. David is a lovely person and I am very fond of him. And you see, the reason I ask about his wife and family is that I really care about people. And the family is the backbone of this country, and people very often forget that. And they shouldn't!"

I think the Prime Minister is gearing herself up to deliver another little homily – this time on the family. I have the distinct feeling that it only takes a word, a phrase, a sentiment, an idea or whatever, to set in train the Prime Minister's concluded and indisputable view on any particular topic. When her gaze is fixed on one, it is clear she will brook no dissent. Expressing a different view is not a wise path to tread. But this time there is no sermon on family values. Perhaps Mrs Barratt's comments had struck too deep an emotional chord with her.

I had seen the emotional and kindly side of Mrs Thatcher. I am now to see yet another volte-face. She has decided, so it seems to me, that she will don the mantle of the omnipotent Prime Minister. In that role, she decides to target the head of the government of Nigeria, the country she will be visiting early in the following year.

In measured terms she delivers what sounds like a lecture, as she speaks slowly and deliberately with real feeling.

"The President of Nigeria has just sent me the speech he will make when he welcomes me to his country." At this point her lip distinctly begins to curl as she continues, "Of course, there are the usual comments about the evils of apartheid. And that from a man who is the head of a military dictatorship! I can see my meeting with him will be a very difficult one." Not for the first time that day, she appears to be very angry, more incensed than before. "Can you believe it? He is going to lecture me on the benefits of a multiracial, democratic society, and that from the President of a military government. The hypocrisy of it makes my blood boil!"

With that, she seems to come to the end of her diatribe on the military government of Nigeria. But that is not the end of her monologue. The PM has by no means run out of steam, and her attention is now to be focussed, highly critically, on the leaders of Europe.

"In this country the great thing is that we can make decisions. I have always been lucky as Prime Minister because I have always had a working majority. This country is an oasis for decision-making." The finger comes out and starts stabbing the air again. "That's what it is, an oasis. The Europeans are hopeless at taking decisions. The Belgians take six months to decide anything, however trifling. The French have a divided government. And as for the Germans, they are impossible to deal with. Getting a decision out of them" (there was heavy emphasis on the word "them") "is nigh on impossible. Kohl [the German Chancellor] can't make any decisions without Genscher [the German Foreign Minister], and as for him, he's a real turn-off."

Well, that was Europe dealt with and duly despatched as not having any capacity to make decisions, except of course for her oasis, the United Kingdom. By now, she is in full flood and her comments are not to be limited to the competence of European leaders. The United States, and even her dear friend President Reagan, are not to be immune from criticism. "More than once I have had to tell President Reagan to get his house in order. The most recent occasion was when I had to send messages to him saying he should deal with the global financial situation. I told him that, at a time when I have an important foreign visitor [Mr Gorbachev, the Soviet leader] coming to my country," ("my" was emphasised) "I shall make sure everything is in shape before he arrives. So I told President Reagan to sort out the financial crisis before Gorbachev comes to London."

The monologue we were hearing constitutes a wonderful insight into the Prime Minister's view of world events and leaders. By now, she has recovered her composure and is smiling. She politely excuses herself, without giving anyone the opportunity to gainsay her on any of the views she has expressed.

The party is starting to wind down. The guests are saying their goodbyes. It has been the most fantastic experience. Kate and I are both exhilarated by all we have experienced. I knew it would be one of the most memorable occasions of my lifetime. I had been determined to recall every moment of it, and I have.

As we start to walk back to our house, one thought strikes me: the way that Mrs Thatcher seemed to be in control of, and observing, everything in the room. Her gimlet eyes seemed to be everywhere, and her ears missed nothing within audible range. This view of Mrs Thatcher's ability to control and assess what was going on in her presence was confirmed, as I am now about to relate, by a highly-placed person who was in one of the best positions to observe her behaviour on numerous occasions.

POSTSCRIPT

Some twenty years after the drinks party at Mrs Thatcher's house, I was at a bankers' dinner where the speaker was Douglas Hurd, principally known for his role as Foreign Secretary in Mrs Thatcher's Cabinet. I had the very good fortune to be seated next to him at dinner. After he had made his eloquent and very impressive speech to the assembled guests, I found him a most interesting and informative dinner companion, and he told an anecdote that struck a real chord with me. It related to the way the Prime Minister controlled a room full of people, in the manner I have just described.

"One of the things I most admired about Margaret Thatcher" (as he somewhat formally called her) "was that she never missed a trick. She knew everything that was happening in a room and even, somehow, seemed to be aware, fully aware, of what was happening behind her back. Let me tell you what happened on one occasion. There was a meeting at Downing Street to hold discussions with the Japanese Prime Minister. There were only three of us present, Margaret Thatcher, the Japanese Prime Minister and me. Margaret Thatcher and the Japanese Prime Minister were in deep, intense conversation about some highly sensitive issues, including the denuclearisation of the Pacific. Margaret Thatcher had her back half turned towards me, paying no attention to me whatsoever, and I was a complete supernumerary. In all honesty,

knowing that I had no part to play in the discussions, I was bored. Relief arrived in the form of the tea lady with her trolley of pastries. I decided that I would devote myself to enjoying my tea with pastries; after all, there was nothing else to do."

He then proceeded to tell me the story which touched such a deep chord with me. The reference to the pastry trolley had brought back those embarrassing memories of my tea at the Strand Palace with Dean Edwards. I was eager to discover whether the Foreign Secretary had replicated the faux pas that I had committed with my millefeuille.

Douglas Hurd continued, "So I perused the pastry trolley at length while the two Prime Ministers were solving the world's problems. I decided to take a millefeuille." I thought this was an amazing coincidence. Where would this story end – possibly with the millefeuille in the Japanese Prime Minister's lap?

Douglas Hurd then said, "When the millefeuille was on my plate, I realised I had made a terrible mistake." (I instantly felt a close bond with this man.) "I found I could not cut it. Either I pressed the fork gently on it and all the cream oozed out, or I tried to cut it with the edge of the fork and it jumped across the plate." I felt like saying, "I know, I know! I really know the problem!" Obviously this story was bringing back the most embarrassing memories for me. The curse of the millefeuille had struck again. I started to perspire, but I tried to look totally composed. Douglas Hurd went on, "In all honesty, I wasn't quite sure what to do. Squeeze it, cut it or even leave it." (Oh, how I understood his dilemma.) "And at that moment, Margaret suddenly turned round to face me and said, 'Douglas, will you stop fiddling around with that pastry! It is really so annoying. Just pick it up with your fingers and eat it now.'" So the memory of my tea with Dean Edwards was supplanted with another different memory: "Eat your smoked salmon sandwich!" at Mrs Thatcher's house in Dulwich. Douglas Hurd concluded his story: "And then, having delivered her reprimand, she turned her back on me again to face the Japanese Prime Minister and said in the most gentle of tones," (here I thought of Mrs Barratt) "'Now, Prime Minister, as I was saying, I regard the denuclearisation of the Pacific as a most important issue and …'. And so she continued her conversation with the Japanese Prime Minister as though she had not spoken to me in such a harsh way. From then on, she ignored me. I had no option but to follow her order. I picked up the millefeuille and ate it."

As I parted company with Douglas Hurd that night, I reflected on how the experiences of life have a habit of repeating themselves. I found his story really amusing, stirring, as it did, memories of my past, particularly the tea at the Strand Palace and the drinks party at Mrs Thatcher's home.

I shall always treasure the memory of being entertained by Mrs Thatcher, one of the most outstanding figures of the second half of the twentieth century. It was a great experience to meet her, if at times somewhat intimidating. But intimidating or not, I would not have missed it for the world. I feel I shall never have a better treasure trove of stories of meeting such a famous and important personality.

CHAPTER 27

CAPTURED BY THE PRESIDENT'S BODYGUARDS

"I don't know if I want to be a Secret Service agent.
In the movies, it is exciting and romantic and all that.
Really, most of their job is standing in a hallway for twelve hours,
making sure somebody doesn't come through a doorway off a stairwell."
DENNIS QUAID (1954–)

I am in heaven. I am in New York, one of my favourite cities in the world. But this has to be the most amazing experience I have ever had in the 'Big Apple', and that's saying something, as I have had some pretty fantastic times here before. It is a beautiful clear October night – no clouds, and the stars are scintillating, lighting up the sky. The Manhattan skyline, not to be outdone by the stars, is ablaze with light – hotels, skyscrapers, lit up like giant Christmas trees. The slow, rhythmic purr of the engines brings me down to earth, or rather water, as we are on an evening cruise, moving slowly along the Hudson River. But it is better than that, as this is no ordinary river cruise. It is a private, very private, voyage to celebrate the conclusion of a client's deal. The hostess has thought of everything for this elegant occasion. When we arrived on board, we were all given name badges which, rather formally for such an exclusive event, stated our full name and title. Formal or not, at the time I was presented with my badge, I was not to anticipate the important role this small piece of plastic was to play in my life the following day. How could I guess that it would be the catalyst for an incident which would remain in my memory bank forever?

I am standing on the afterdeck, enjoying the soft evening breeze. Waiters, elegantly dressed, buzz round the cabin below and also up here. A seven-course dinner will soon be served in the cabin. So I feel I must absorb every moment I can, mesmerised as I am by the sight of the Manhattan skyline lit by a myriad of stars. The chief steward tells us that dinner is served in the saloon and, as each guest enters, their name is announced to the hosts. At dinner I am seated on the right hand of the hostess and I feel really flattered. After we take our places, the conversation flows, amusing stories are told, laughter erupts. Everyone seems very happy, and for good reason. I lose myself in thought and reflect that life cannot get much better than this, and so I promise myself that I will remember every moment of this evening. I am not to know that very soon life is to become even more exciting. Exciting beyond my wildest dreams. But more, much more, of that later.

The evening passes. Everything is perfect. The company, the food and the entire ambience are all just stunning. I am still young enough, fun-loving enough, to be transported into heaven by such beautiful experiences. However, soon (far too soon it seems) the party is over, it's time to call it a day. Being the sentimentalist I am, and an opera lover too, I can only think of Zeffirelli's film of *La Traviata* with Placido Domingo and Teresa Stratas, where, at the end of Act I, Alfredo leaves the most opulent party, held in the most gracious surroundings, having met Violetta for the first time. Although there is no Violetta for me this evening, the opulence, the absolutely stunning surroundings and the whole party have left me 'on cloud nine', just like Alfredo. I float back to my hotel.

As I enter my suite on the forty-eighth floor (courtesy of my clients), I see a sheet of paper on the floor. It is a 'Note from the Management'. I pick it up and what is stated on it excites and intrigues me in equal measure. It announces somewhat baldly and impersonally:

"Dear Client,

Tomorrow there will be a very important person coming to the Hotel. Accordingly, there will be the most stringent security measures in force in the Hotel from 8 am to 5 pm. The Hotel will be in lockdown for that period and, although leaving the Hotel should not be a problem, entering it will be subject to the tightest security procedures. Anyone entering the Hotel, including guests, will be subject to screening and will have to produce proof of identity. In addition, the fifty-eighth floor of the Hotel will be closed to guests for the entire day, as a private function is being held on that floor.

The Management apologise in advance for any inconvenience which may be caused to our guests."

Having read this, I felt that, in true American fashion, this note should have commenced with the words 'Now, here's the thing!' and ended with the valedictory 'Have a nice day!' accompanied by a smiley face symbol. But as I was to discover, the following day's events were far too serious to be trivialised by Whiteman's quirky sense of humour.

Of course, my mind is now racing about the identity of the "very important person" whose presence requires "the most stringent security measures". I conclude it must be the President. It has to be, to warrant putting one of the most prestigious hotels in New York in total lockdown for an entire day. However, surmise is not enough for me. On a 'need-to-know' basis, I definitely do – to satisfy my curiosity. But it is more than that. Once I am told the identity of this VIP, I will know how exciting tomorrow's events are going to be. As it turns out, the excitement I imagine will be mine tomorrow misses the target by miles. After all, there is excitement, and then there is EXCITEMENT.

I decide to phone Reception for this critical piece of information, but I hit a brick wall. The concierge politely but very firmly refuses to put me out of my misery when he replies to my question, "Sir, I am afraid I am not allowed to give out that information. It is strictly forbidden."

I am temporarily defeated, but only for a moment. If the official channels won't give me the answer, how can I find out the identity of the VIP? I answer my own question with a rhetorical one. Who knows anything and everything that goes on in a hotel? The chambermaids! So I leave my room and go in search of my selected quarry. Being the efficient hotel this is, I find a chambermaid very quickly. I ask the question that is burning me up. Rosie (as I discover her name to be) looks puzzled when I ask her what she knows about tomorrow's visitor. The answer to my question is obvious to her. Her expression indicates total surprise that I don't know already. Unlike the concierge, she has no qualms about imparting this sensitive piece of information. "The President, of course!"

My excitement level reaches a new high and all I need ponder now, as I return to my suite, is what that reference in the note to a "private function" alluded to. I go to bed and rest my head on the pillow with only thoughts of happiness and excitement in my mind. At that time I am not worried about anything, nor are any of those acting for the President concerned by my presence on the forty-eighth floor. As I am to learn later, all guests staying at the hotel on that and the following day (as well as all staff) had, unbeknown to them, been subject to the most stringent security vetting by the Secret Service and FBI, to ensure they did not present any threat to the President.

I sleep well and wake early. I know this will be a day full of surprises, and the first, which I could never have imagined, is both imminent and alarming. It happens just as I leave the bathroom in my suite and enter the bedroom. To appreciate why I am concerned, the reader should recall that my suite is on the forty-eighth floor. Its advantage: the most wonderful unobstructed view of Central Park, which is particularly stunning on this beautiful sunny morning. However, being on this floor, it means there is a sheer drop to the ground past all forty-seven floors below. When I first arrived in this suite, I looked at the view of the Park and then down to the ground – a big mistake for someone who suffers from vertigo. But hold on to the vision of that drop as I relate what happens next.

Leaving the bathroom, I am still stark naked. Why not? I am in my own suite, and my room is at a height where no one can see me. And then I notice (how could I not?) the most bizarre sight outside the window. Walking along the window ledge, edging their way very slowly, inch by careful inch, are two men. I see them. And almost at the same moment, they see me. They turn to face me. I freeze at the sight of them. Their faces are grim, very grim. These are two very tough individuals. Their faces look very 'lived-in', they have seen everything. Survived everything. And they can, as a result, deal with any situation. I am terrified, as they are dressed from top to toe in black. Are they part of a terrorist cell, here to assassinate the President? I must call Reception and alert them to this potential risk to the President's life. But I am frozen by fear. I can't move. And then, ludicrously, I am terrified for them. Why? They are forty-eight floors up, on a narrow window ledge, with no safety harness. One false step and they will be history. My fear of heights makes me feel sick for them at the thought of that horrendous drop. Random thoughts pass through my mind. How can I feel sick for 'terrorists'? For that is what I believe them to be. They remain motionless, staring at me. And then they turn almost 90 degrees as if, now being parallel with the ledge, they are about to inch forward again. And it is that turn which saves New York from the major terrorist alert that would have been triggered, had I phoned to report two men in black jumpsuits on my window ledge. It was a call I had up to then intended to make, but now I am not going to phone anybody because the movement of the men in turning has revealed something which has changed everything. That 'something' is just two large letters in white. No more. As one man made his 90-degree turn on that death trap of a ledge, I caught a glimpse of two white letters on his black jumpsuit. The fateful letters were PD. Obviously there were other letters I could not see, which preceded PD. No prizes for guessing that the unseen letters were NY. My vivid imagination, which had created a terrorist cell in the heart of New York, where the President would be present, had in overdrive mode completely misread the situation. For 'terrorists in black jumpsuits' read 'NYPD officers in uniform' checking out the hotel and its guests. But was my initial fear so outrageous? They were outside the building, not inside; they were all in black, and from what I could see originally, with no markings or identification whatsoever. They were also in the most precarious position, without any safety equipment. No wonder I had been shaking with fear throughout. Now, however, it was different. The men, being, as I now assumed, NYPD officers checking out the building, no longer terrified me. My pulse rate returned to something like normal. However, the story does not quite end there. The men were now looking intently at me. One of them raised his hand and then moved his index finger a circular motion. Looking fixedly at me, it was clear what he meant me to do. Satisfied that, because of my total nudity, I was not in possession of any weapons on the front of my body, he wanted to check there was none attached to my posterior and no gun taped to my back. I didn't hesitate. His granite face, his stare, his circular sign, left me in no doubt what I had to do, and if I disobeyed him, I did so at my peril. I duly turned. I thought at the time that I did so not only slowly (so as to ensure a full inspection by 'NYPD's best') but also somewhat elegantly. Whether the officer appreciated the latter, he was certainly grateful for the former. He gave me a double thumbs-up, although, with all due modesty, I thought my performance was worthy of a high five. Whether it was or not, the next thing that happened was totally unbelievable and could only occur in the US: the granite-faced officer smiled and mouthed the words, "Have a nice day!" Somewhat bizarre, but it did show that, whatever his appearance, this officer had a human side. The two officers then moved further along the window ledge to continue their hair-raising task to ensure the President's safety.

After their departure, I pace up and down my bedroom. There are decisions to be made; first of all, what do I do to soak up the atmosphere of the President's visit to the full, or even better still, to see him? Obviously, as a member of the public, I will not be admitted to the private function or any other special events. So I ponder what to do. My mind clears and I make my plans. First, I shall stay inside the hotel all day. If I go out, I may well find it difficult to get back to, and then re-enter, the hotel. The surrounding roads will no doubt be crowded beyond belief. Next decision. The note pushed under my door spoke of "stringent security measures" and doubtless these will be most strictly enforced at the place of entry to the hotel – the lobby. So that will be my first port of call. I must get dressed. I shall look as smart as possible so that I will cut an impressive figure and not give the Secret Service agents any cause for concern. I put on the same smart suit that I wore the previous night for the party. I leave my room and head towards the elevator to make my inspection of the security measures for the most important person in the world. I turn the corner from the corridor where my suite is to reach the bank of elevators. What I see next completely surprises me. I do a double take. It is my first encounter with what the expression lockdown really means. There, standing by the elevators, are three men who are obviously Secret Service agents. 'Obviously' because they are dressed in formal suits, they are huge in stature, they have coiled earpieces, no doubt linking them to a central control room, and all have a massive bulge under their jackets, which I am sure is not caused by a packet of popcorn. One of the three, a very tough-looking individual, speaking through his teeth, leaves me in no doubt that anything I did which caused him a problem would be dealt with promptly and very effectively. I decide to be as compliant as the occasion and the agent demand. The agent says, "Please step aside to be searched." He directs me to a colleague for 'the necessary' to be done. That completed, the first agent then motions to me that I may proceed to the elevator. I do, and when the elevator arrives, I descend to the lobby, where the sight is unbelievable. It has been totally transformed; yesterday it was a large, spacious, opulent hotel entrance, where only hushed conversations were taking place. As a result, it was calm, relaxing and very welcoming. Today it could not be more different. I see a seething mass of humanity, which is creating the most horrendous noise. This is sheer pandemonium. I am surprised and shocked by the transformation.

With the President's forthcoming visit, I expected everything to be orderly and tranquil. Not so. Dominating the centre of the lobby, three metal-detecting scanners, such as are found in airports, have been erected, and all baggage has to be passed through them on conveyor belts. The line of people to pass through the screens is so long that it backs up into the street. Many of those waiting to be processed are becoming very impatient. In particular, those attending the private function must be concerned that they will be late for the President. Tempers are running a little high. I decide I have seen enough of the stringent security measures and I leave, congratulating myself on my wise decision not to leave the hotel and subject myself on re-entry to the screening process.

Arriving at the elevators, even before being asked to step aside for security, I raise my arms to be searched. By now I am familiar with the procedure and, the search over, I get into the elevator, joining a large number of people wearing lapel badges indicating that they are delegates attending the private function. The elevator operator is well-dressed, tough-looking, huge, has an earpiece and a bulging jacket – no question who his employers are! He asks what floor the assembled company wants. With one voice they shout out, "Fifty-eighth!" – the floor where the private function is being held. I decide, literally and metaphorically, to go along for the ride. As I glance at my reflection in the elevator mirrors, I notice that I am still wearing my lapel badge from the party last night. I had totally forgotten to remove it before I went to bed. I also notice that it is a less significant lapel badge than the ones the others in the elevator are wearing, which proclaim 'Democratic National Convention'. I am worried I will not be allowed out of the elevator, although I hope that my different badge will not be noticed in the rush to attend the meeting on time. I will stay with the 'herd' in the hope of satisfying my curiosity about what is taking place on the fifty-eighth floor and because it will be fascinating to see the President. The doors open, the Secret Service agent masquerading as an attendant announces we have reached the fifty-eighth floor, and I am carried along by the tide of humanity discharged from the elevator. There are Secret Service agents everywhere. Will they notice an interloper amongst the authorised delegates? I do not have to wait long for my answer.

"Will you please step aside?" The difference between my 'party badge' and the official badge for today's meeting has not escaped the eagle eye of at least one agent. He stares suspiciously at me and appears ready to take any necessary action to deal with the situation. He asks, "What are you doing here?" "I am staying in the hotel." "What floor?" "The forty-eighth." "What name?" he demands. I give it. He whispers into a microphone attached to his wrist. He must have been satisfied by what he was told through his earpiece because he relaxes, but only a little. "This is the fifty-eighth floor, not the forty-eighth. Why did you come here?" I say somewhat lamely, "I must have misheard the elevator attendant when he stated the floor number." He gives me a cynical look and, no doubt as a result of his training, does not believe a word I have said. As we are talking, I find that another agent has come up and is about to frisk me. He does, and the first agent then says, "Please return to your room immediately."

Having originally been in a curious frame of mind on hearing about the President's visit, then in a really excited one at the possibility of seeing him, my mood has changed again. Now I am apprehensive, if not a touch alarmed, as I am surrounded by four Secret Service bodyguards who have isolated me from all the delegates. Their tough, unsmiling faces indicate they really mean business and that business is to get me off the fifty-eighth floor as soon as possible. The four agents usher me back to the elevator; there is no option other than to comply. However, I do look to one side and see an enormous banner bearing the words 'Democratic National Convention. Welcome, Mr President.' Some *private* function!

The agents quietly but firmly shepherd me closer to the bank of elevators. We seem to be heading for Elevator 2 when a whole phalanx of bodyguards streams past me in a Gadarene rush to join colleagues who have stationed themselves around the doors to Elevator 1. They all have their backs to the elevator doors, looking outwards, not inwards, preparing to guard whoever may emerge from the elevator. I suddenly realise that all this movement around the elevators must be because the President is about to arrive. The bodyguards surrounding me seem unsure what to do. Elevator 2 has not arrived and I am still in what is (to me) forbidden territory. The agents are now engaged in fraught conversations through their wrist microphones, presumably seeking instructions as to what they should do. For the moment they are motionless and then suddenly the doors to Elevator 1 slide open – and, yes, it is the President! He is instantly recognisable with that charming broad smile. He steps briskly forward and moves to pass close by me. Obviously he realises from years of being protected by bodyguards that something is amiss. He pauses. His first words, glancing at me, are, "What's the fuss about?" He doesn't wait for a reply. He certainly is not perturbed by the possibility of any "fuss". And then, with words that are full of warmth, he says, "Good morning, Professor Whiteman!" For a moment I am mystified by the greeting, as I have never met the President. How on earth does he know my name and title? And then I realise the obvious: he has spotted my lapel badge. How delightful of him to greet me that way; he has made me feel a million dollars. Although meeting the President is the most jaw-dropping experience, I do manage to reply, "Good morning, Mr President," and I return his broad smile before he is swept away towards the podium. I am, of course, on cloud nine. My exchange of words with the President may have been brief, but this has truly been the experience of a lifetime and one I will never forget. When in the past I had ruminated about my 'American Dream', so many thoughts, hopes, ideas, aspirations and much else about that country had flooded through my mind. But never in my wildest dreams did I ever contemplate that I would have such an amazing experience as I have had today. I am truly overwhelmed.

What a fabulous two days I have had – God bless America!

CHAPTER 28

HURTLING TOWARDS THE PRECIPICE

"It was the best of times, it was the worst of times."
A Tale of Two Cities
CHARLES DICKENS

"In the middle of my journey through life
I found myself lost in a dark wood
With no straight path I could see anywhere."
The Divine Comedy: Inferno (Canto I, lines i–iii)
DANTE ALIGHIERI

By 1990 the focus of my professional career had changed. The balance of time that I was devoting to the various activities of my working life had altered fundamentally. My practice at the Bar was even more demanding and, in particular, numerous appearances in court on highly complex matters were making life very hectic. My time spent sitting as a judge was also becoming more challenging because, as time went by, I was being allocated more serious criminal trials to preside over. 'Serious' nearly always meant more complex, requiring in particular more preparation and close attention to everything that happened in court.

That the focus of my professional career had shifted very significantly to the Bar and the Bench was emphasised by two events which occurred in the 1990s. First, the Bar. By the beginning of the decade it was apparent that the developing trend was that sets of Chambers needed to be large if they were to be very successful. The thinking was that, given the technological innovations that had occurred and the economies of scale that would be possible, a set of Chambers would be more efficient and offer a better service to clients if the Chambers were large. It was essential, so this fashionable thinking went, that a set of Chambers was not only modern in its approach to professional life, but also that it was seen to be so by its clients. This was particularly important to me because, from 1989, accountants and other professionals were granted the right of direct access to the Bar. That meant that, in addition to solicitors, members of the Revenue Bar would have contact with a far greater number of accountants than previously. They also had to be convinced that a set of Chambers was modern, progressive and efficient and provided the services they required. All these factors provided a strong impetus for Chambers to grow, and grow quickly. None of this was lost on me. I had been thinking of a merger of our set with another for quite some time, long before it had become fashionable. Indeed, I entered into long and protracted merger negotiations with the Chambers of Richard Southwell QC, a highly regarded set of Commercial Chambers. In the event, for various reasons, after months of negotiation, the merger did not come to fruition. I was not daunted, however, and remained convinced of the benefits of a merger. But while I was musing, others were acting – not an unusual occurrence in my career! Thus it was that, out of the blue, I received a letter from Daniel Hollis QC, the Head of an outstanding set of Chambers also in Queen Elizabeth Building, inviting me to have a 'chat'. By the phraseology of his letter I had little doubt what was in the offing. So I replied accepting the invitation but suggesting that our meeting should not be in either of our sets of Chambers. The Temple is such a gossip shop that, if we had met in QEB, word would have been out on the street in no time. The gossipmongers would have had a field day.

My ready acceptance of Dan's invitation highlights another aspect of my approach to life. Part of my mantra that "anything is possible" is that I rarely reject any offer, invitation or suggestion from others which might lead to better things, even if at the time I have serious doubts about my ability to carry it through. Here, however, the invitation was not in any way tainted by doubts. If what was being suggested was a merger, then, subject to agreeing terms, I would be wholly in favour. That is why I accepted Dan's invitation with the greatest alacrity. I knew Dan extremely well as a friend of Kate's family and had the greatest respect for him. He is an outstanding barrister with a wonderful sense of humour. His set, as I have mentioned, had an enviable reputation, and a merger would create a set of Chambers with some sixty members. That would be ideal.

Dan and I met for tea at The Howard Hotel in Temple Place to have our discussion. It was a meeting of old friends and the atmosphere could not have been more cordial. Dan was indeed proposing a merger, and for the reasons I have mentioned I was very receptive to the idea. Although Dan is a down-to-earth, practical person, he always expresses himself in the most charming way. Never could merger negotiations have been concluded so quickly. In twenty minutes we decided everything of consequence, including that the two of us would be Joint Heads of the merged set and that it would be called 'Hollis Whiteman Chambers'. The negotiations may only have lasted twenty minutes, but we so comprehensively covered all the relevant issues that we never needed, nor had, a second round of discussions. It was all over before we had our second cup of tea!

To me, and I am sure to Dan, the merger was manna from heaven. It not only created a new set of some sixty outstanding barristers, but, as our sets were on the third and fourth floors of QEB respectively, the new Chambers would also have spacious accommodation on adjacent floors. It was not surprising therefore that the merger was agreed on both sides very quickly and without any hitches. And so Hollis Whiteman Chambers came into being on 5 August 1991 and opened its doors to solicitors and accountants from that date. We received many letters of congratulation, many saying that the merger was an "obvious fit".

The rest, as they say, is history. The new set was outstandingly successful from the start, and there were none of the usual problems of integrating two different entities. Indeed, the set ran like a well-oiled machine from the day it came into being. For my own part, I have always regarded the merger as an excellent idea (of Dan's) and I have been extraordinarily happy being a part of Hollis Whiteman Chambers throughout.

In my new happy home, as Joint Head of Chambers, my focus was even more on my career at the Bar. I was, of course, determined to make the merger a success, and I put every effort into ensuring it was. It meant more work of an administrative nature, but that was a very small price to pay for this brilliant new development in my career.

So, as I mentioned earlier, the Bar and Bench were occupying more of my time in the 1990s. The Bar for the reasons I have outlined above, and the Bench because, in 1994, as I wrote earlier, I was appointed a Deputy High

Court Judge in the Chancery Division. So I was combining my practice as a member of the Revenue Bar with sitting as a Recorder, presiding over criminal trials, and with hearing Chancery cases in the Royal Courts of Justice as a Deputy High Court Judge. It created a hectic schedule which gave my Clerk severe difficulties at times, fitting all my commitments into a very busy diary.

It was fortunate that, given all my commitments, especially the new ones at the Bar and on the Bench, the time I had to devote to my other professional activities had reduced significantly. As far as authorship was concerned, I had produced new editions of *Whiteman on Income Tax* and *Whiteman on Capital Gains Tax* in 1988. Those editions were based on the new consolidated tax legislation, so they were completely up to date and new editions would not be required for some time. My commitment to my duties as Professor of International Tax Law at UVA had reduced very significantly, and finally, the legislation I had drafted for the Unitary Tax Campaign had been passed and placed on the Statute Book. My principal task for the UTC had thus been achieved, although until 1996 I was still acting as their legal adviser on international tax and attending all their meetings as a committee member. But the essential object of the UTC had been achieved and, following the enactment of 'my' retaliatory legislation and President Reagan's initiative in supporting the abolition of Worldwide Unitary Taxation, it had all but ceased to exist in the United States, as I have related in Chapter 20. State after State had formally abandoned it by passing appropriate legislation.

So the decade of the 1990s was one I essentially devoted to my Bar practice and the Bench. At the Bar, one high-profile and long-running case seemed to follow another. The first such case was advising the Executors of the Estate of Sir Charles Clore, which required detailed advice over many years. Secondly, in 1990 I was instructed by Exxon Oil to provide advice on their upcoming litigation with the US Internal Revenue Service. I was to advise them and subsequently to appear in the US Federal Tax Court in Washington DC as an expert witness on the United Kingdom's Petroleum Revenue Tax. I provided such advice from 1990 until the final outcome of the litigation in 1998. It was a fascinating case to be involved in, as I saw the US litigation process at first hand. My expert evidence was accepted by the US Tax Court in its entirety, which was most gratifying, and Exxon resoundingly won their case. All those involved in this long-running case were, naturally, delighted.

Thirdly, in 1992 I embarked on a most interesting, but extremely technical, tax appeal for J Sainsbury plc. It was very complex and required the mastery of a huge amount of detail. There were over seventy lever arch files of evidence! The case was heard over a three-year period 1992–1995. It was a challenging but exhausting experience. Finally, on the list of high profile cases where I was briefed in the 1990s, I was instructed in the Al-Fayed Tax Appeal in 1999, which related to the powers of the Inland Revenue to enter into 'settlement' agreements with taxpayers.

These four headline cases were all very challenging but at the same time absolutely fascinating. I felt that my experience and expertise of Tax Law and practice were being expanded significantly. And it was a joy to work with so many talented and experienced lawyers on both sides of the Atlantic. In addition to these cases, there were many other significant pieces of litigation, and of course there was also my advisory practice. Again, the more senior I became at the Bar, unsurprisingly the more detailed and complicated became the advice required. Sets of Instructions to advise in Consultation regularly ran to 100–150 pages, with appendices and lever arch files of supporting information in addition. Consultations frequently lasted four to five hours. Such a large practice threatened to overwhelm me, so I came to the conclusion that I had to organise my practice like a military operation. That was the only way I would be in total control of it. First, I realised that I would only be able to manage the mountain of work if I spent six and a half days a week on it. I regarded Sunday afternoon as time I had to spend relaxing with my family, recharging the batteries for the week ahead. However, efficient management of my practice required more than just working long hours. My practice necessitated significant advance planning at the beginning of each week so that there was a clearly established structure in place for the coming week(s). Litigation obviously established its own timetable, which had to be complied with. However, when there was no litigation pending in the following week(s), I had to plan my advisory practice most carefully. I would decide, for example, to prepare on Monday for the Consultation scheduled a week later (Monday week). Then Tuesday would be allocated to the Consultation taking place the following Tuesday, and so on. Thus, at the beginning of the week, I knew exactly the preparation I had to undertake each day. Even then, that was not the limit of the planning I thought necessary, as, obviously, my timetable for that week would also have time allocated to the Consultations for which I had prepared the previous week. It did work, and it worked well. I was never caught out by not having sufficiently prepared for a Consultation. To me it was a matter of honour and professional obligation to ensure that I had done all the necessary work for a Consultation, and I know from the comments of my instructing solicitors and accountants that they appreciated the time and effort I had put in to ensure that I covered all the issues raised in my Instructions. The same, of course, with even greater emphasis if possible, applied to my court appearances.

The timetable I have referred to also had to take into account the fact that very often I was travelling abroad professionally, including to Paris to advise on the Sir Charles Clore Estate, and later to consult with my American clients (including Exxon Oil) on transactions which involved both United Kingdom and United States tax considerations. The latter I found particularly challenging and exciting. I really looked forward to my frequent professional visits to the US, although fitting them into an already crowded timetable was not easy. However, my military-style planning also coped with this additional demand on my time. Indeed, it had to. Given my passionate interest in anything which involved my two favourite tax jurisdictions, there was no alternative. As a result of all my strategic planning, the possibility of being overwhelmed by my practice in the 1990s was averted. That decade was a supremely successful one for my practice. 1990 started with a very full professional diary and so it continued throughout the decade, reaching its zenith in 1999 with the most thrilling case of my career. It was such an exciting case that (as I hope the reader will agree) it justified devoting the entirety of Chapter 25 to all its unbelievable twists and turns.

Everything I have written above about the 1990s, particularly the extent of my practice and the need for meticulous planning, applied equally to the years 2000–2006. This meant, of course, that, like so many other members of the Bar, I remained under enormous pressure. I had no option (or so I thought) but to continue working six and a half days a week throughout that period.

I have written at some length about 1990–2006 because the work I undertook in those years led to my being where I am now. Where is that, you may ask? Well, grotesquely, it is in a hospital bed. To be more precise, in a hospital bed in Room 314, overlooking a river. I watch the tide ebb and flow each day. No more six-and-a-half-day working weeks for me now. I am forbidden to work at all. Absolute rest is everything, so I am told, after having two heart procedures, an angioplasty and an ablation, after six months of stress, anxiety, chest pains, staccato breathing and palpitations; six months of sheer hell – what a price to pay! It never even crossed my mind that I was hurtling towards the precipice, with the blackest abyss down below waiting for me.

The angioplasty was necessary as, after many months of tests, it was discovered that my arteries were 90 per cent blocked. And this despite the fact that for some thirty years I had exercised regularly, running six miles daily, and always followed a healthy diet. Nor was I ever a smoker. The more I discussed my health and background with my doctors, the clearer it became that the obvious root cause of my current condition was stress. But now there was a real and imminent risk of a heart attack. Immediate medical action was essential. I was told that there was nothing to be concerned about with an angioplasty, as it was a routine procedure carried out time and time again. The medical team risibly dismissed any risk as totally insignificant, stating that statistics showed that in only one in five thousand cases did this procedure give rise to complications. In the event, all I could do was envy the other 4,999 such patients. Why? Because I was to become the 'one' in the statistic that had been quoted to me. The reason? The procedure went disastrously wrong. The insertion of a wire to guide the three stents into place in my arteries, the essential purpose of an angioplasty, resulted in that wire puncturing my main artery, the aorta. As it was taking place, that is, when I was on the operating table, I knew that things were not going as they should. The procedure was carried out under a local anaesthetic, so I could see everything that was happening in the theatre. I was aware that the medical team was very concerned about the procedure and that it was not going as it should; the cardiologist looked a very troubled man. Matters seemed to be out of control, a conclusion which was reinforced when the anaesthetist took charge of the proceedings – always a very bad sign. I was told afterwards that I almost died – twice. But they saved me – just.

The angioplasty took not the anticipated hour or so, but four hours. When I emerged from the operating theatre on a trolley at 8.15 pm, Kate was there. She was beside herself with worry because of the delay and because she had been told there were complications. She looked ashen-faced. I felt so sorry for her.

However, even that ghastly occurrence was not to mark the end of my medical problems. I was told that I was also suffering from arrhythmia, so I needed an ablation to treat my abnormal heart rhythms. That meant a second procedure and a return to the ghastly operating theatre which had been the scene of my previous traumatic experience. In the event, at least there was no problem with that operation. So all I need to do is ensure that I have absolute rest.

Now I lie here each day watching the river ebb and flow. It is very calming. And it gives me plenty of time to read, as the doctors tell me I should. Except I do not want to read. I want to reflect; because I think I was, and possibly still am, staring death in the face. Or maybe because I want to think about my life. Not for one moment to engage in self-pity as to how I came to be in Room 314 overlooking the river. Indeed, just the reverse. I want to reflect on so many good things that have happened to me. And the one that rises to the very top of my list is that I have been so lucky in my life. So lucky to have been encouraged, supported, advised, call it what you will, by so many kind and thoughtful people. People who were so generous with their time in guiding me through life, and without whose support I would never have become the man I am. It is only now, when I have the time to think about it, that I can truly appreciate how long my 'list' is. It is worth recalling some of the many wonderful people I have referred to in this book and who merit inclusion in my list: Paddy Clinch (advice as to my future career and life), Ash Wheatcroft and Basil Yamey (my mentors at the LSE who taught me the skill of academic writing and teaching), Mr Pilkington (ever-supportive at Lincoln's Inn), Hubert and John Monroe and Charles Potter (three barristers who inspired me), Lord Oliver (a crucial role in enabling me to take Silk and establish QEB), Lord Steyn (advising me to become a judge), Bill McKee (opening the door to UVA), and Michael Grylls (introducing me to the UTC).

All of these people, at critical stages in my life, saw in me some skill, talent, attributes and as yet unrealised potential that they wished to encourage and assist as far as they could. And they did so magnificently. Moreover, the most gratifying aspect of their encouragement is that, in the main, they all took the initiative in approaching me. Their support if I had asked them for help would have been truly amazing. But that they approached me with their diverse but crucial offers of guidance, support and assistance touches me beyond measure. The more so when I recall that, by offering their advice to me, they were genuinely interested in promoting my career. There was not in any one of the instances referred to above any question of self-interest on their part.

So the question arises, if it was not out of self-interest, why were all these individuals prepared to give so generously of their time and contacts to help my journey through life? As a friend said, "Peter, the question is not how they helped you, but why they helped you?" A particularly pertinent question when I bear in mind that I never heard of my mentors (particularly Ash Wheatcroft) providing such outstanding encouragement to others in my position.

Since the comment was made, I have thought about that question so much. I find it difficult to answer. The only way I can even attempt to provide any explanation is to analyse my own character at the time and, in so doing, try to form a view as to how other people would have seen me. Certainly in the critical years, as I was trying to make my way forward in life, I was full of energy, full of drive, full of determination. I was like a butterfly in its chrysalis waiting to burst forth into the sunshine. I was also full of ambition and ready to work as hard as necessary to realise my goals. And those goals, as each new one succeeded the last, were always very clearly focussed on the realisation of a particular idea or concept. So it was ambition, based on carefully-laid plans which were realisable. My ideas and concepts were innovative and in some cases, I believe, could be described as visionary. In every instance, however, they could only be brought to fruition if other well-placed people were there to provide the necessary support and guidance. And on each occasion they were, and, remarkably, of their own initiative. So if this is a correct summary of how I saw myself in the critical years, perhaps it is not totally unreasonable to think that others may have formed a similar view of my qualities and attributes.

On that basis, they may have believed that to support and guide me in realising my objectives would be a very worthwhile thing to do. In every single case it was. Perhaps the most outstanding example was the critical help that the six exceedingly distinguished judges – Lords Oliver, Scarman, Templeman and Steyn, Lord Justice Parker and Sir John Arnold – gave me in setting up my own Chambers, supporting my application for Silk and encouraging me to become a judge. At each step they took the initiative in ensuring that my dream would become a reality. They believed in me. They showed that it was not only barristers, or at least some of them, who could be visionary, but judges as well. Their modern, forward-thinking approach was extremely refreshing and particularly impressive. I owe them a huge debt of gratitude.

For my own part, all I can throw into the balance is that I have never hesitated to grasp any opportunity that has been held out to me. Even though I may have had real self-doubt, I have always embraced all such opportunities with the greatest enthusiasm.

It is a beautiful sunny day; the crest of each little wave is lit by the sun. A single sculler on the river glides past my hospital window like a silver knife slicing through grey silk. The wake he leaves on the sunlit water twinkles in a V-shaped pattern. But then he stops rowing. I go on looking at this peaceful sight. Why not? There's no need to rush anywhere to do any footling task. They are all a thing of the past. They seemed so important at the time. And perhaps many of them were. But now, in retrospect, seen from my hospital bed, they seem of such little consequence. No need to formulate any more military-style operations. All I need to do is take my cue from the oarsman and rest. Rest for a long while.

Where did it all go wrong? It was all so wonderful as I achieved one enormously satisfying objective after another. One unbelievable high after another. And now I am in a hospital bed, having almost died twice. I did what I criticised other barristers for doing – working ludicrously hard. I look up again. The sun is shimmering on the river; the rower is still resting on his oars. Surely this is a sign. I take it. I vow that, if I survive, I will never work at such a furious, wholly unnecessary pace again. I will never sacrifice my life to work again, and never neglect my family again. I regard these vows I make in Room 314 as solemn oaths. I shall never break them. If I survive. Never. My resolve is totally firm. I have been very, very foolish and it will never happen again. Like the oarsman, I shall rest. My vows shall govern my life hereafter and I shall never break them.

But they don't, and I do. Such a very foolish man. Within three months of leaving hospital, as 2006 turns into 2007, I am working as hard as ever. It is only when the unseen hand of fate intervenes two years later with a cataclysmic event that I change my lifestyle. Or rather, my lifestyle is changed for me. By that time 'the man upstairs' has completely lost patience with this foolish man who will never learn his lesson. So my life is changed forever by events outside my control. But did they have to be so dramatic that they almost destroyed me, albeit in a horrifically different way? Indeed, my life as I knew it was torn away from me. It was shattered, and I did not know how to exist in a world which terrified me. I was in a hellish black tunnel, with no light at its end, and from which I could see no escape.

CHAPTER 29

AMBULANCE

"Shock-headed Peter"
Struwwelpeter
HEINRICH HOFFMAN

"A Traveller betwixt life and death"
WILLIAM WORDSWORTH

The paramedics help me up the steps of the ambulance. I am almost unable to climb inside because I am shaking so much. As I ascend, I nearly fall over, but the paramedics grab me. But still I bang my head on one of the doors. They take me inside the ambulance and help me onto a stretcher which has been placed on top of a trolley. I sit on the stretcher and then lift my legs so that I can lie flat. Pain, dizziness. The interior of the scruffy ambulance is swimming before my eyes. The paramedics attach tubes to my body. I am on my back and I study the faces of the two men. They look very grim and I feel very strange. It is stiflingly hot. There is a strong smell of antiseptic. The paramedics are still standing as the ambulance moves off. Then there is a shrill sound. I realise that it is the ambulance sirens. They are howling and the sound is so loud it is piercing my ears. The paramedics on either side of the stretcher are holding it steady, as the trolley is not properly secured to the floor. As we go round each corner, it feels as though the stretcher will fall off the trolley. I am terrified I will crash onto the floor and suffer more injuries. More pain. I am also frightened it will tear out the tubes which have been attached to my body.

The ambulance is going at high speed to get me to a hospital as soon as possible. The vehicle jolts each time it goes over a bump in the road, which adds to my discomfort and my fear of crashing to the floor. I have no idea where we are. I have no idea of the extent of my injuries, and presumably neither do the paramedics. I feel completely dazed and confused. I know I am in a state of shock.

I am totally isolated. There can be no conversation; I do not speak Spanish and the paramedics do not speak English, so I cannot find out any more about the extent of the tragedy that has occurred. I am adrift on a silent sea of grief.

I look at my clothes. I see that I am still shaking uncontrollably. I look again. I am shocked to see blood all over me. I do not know whether the blood is mine, or Kate's, or both.

The ambulance is still speeding along. There are more corners now, more discomfort, more pain, more fear. Intermittently, I am hit by flashes of the horror of what has so recently occurred.

In my confused state, so many questions run through my mind as I struggle to make sense of what has happened. What has occurred? How did it happen? Why now? Why in the middle of this country, so far away from home, where I can't speak the language and I feel totally isolated? Is Kate really dead? I simply don't believe it; everything is all such a blur. In my shocked state, I can't really remember what has just happened. I know there was an accident; I think I can remember cradling her in my arms and talking to her. Or am I imagining this? Did she really die there? I don't want to believe that she did. My inability to communicate with anyone makes me feel so helpless, so useless, completely lost. For better or worse, my life is completely in the hands of others.

The ambulance slows. Is it stopping? I am not sure. Have we arrived at a hospital? I don't know. And there is no one I can ask. I keep on thinking, how did it happen? Am I dreaming all this or is it really happening? However, the blood tells me, screams at me, yes, it did happen. But what now? I realise that life will never be the same – assuming there will be a life for me to live. And what have they done with Kate?

The ambulance has almost come to a complete stop. Are we at our destination? The possibility that we are shakes my befuddled brain into some sort of activity. There is something I must do if we are here. But I cannot remember what it is. Think, think. I remember it is very important. Then, suddenly, I do remember. How could I have forgotten something so vital? It is my first priority – it has to be. I must tell Victoria and Caroline about the accident and the tragedy that has befallen all three of us. It will be the worst telephone call I shall ever make – totally shattering for my daughters, and for me. But I must do it – tell them that their mother has been in a car crash, grievously injured, and I do not yet know if she is dead or alive. There will be no gentle way of breaking this horrific news to them. How will Victoria and Caroline begin to cope with it? I have never dreaded doing anything in my life more than this – not for me, but for them. I am desperately worried about the effect it will have. I fear that receiving such horrific news, out of the blue, may well have a devastating effect on them. And somehow we must share our shock and grief together, even though we are currently separated by thousands of miles. I am consumed by these thoughts as the ambulance comes to a complete halt. I hear the driver getting out and slamming his door. I have arrived – I know not where – but in a state of total despair and with my mind in complete turmoil. As soon as the wheels of the ambulance stop moving, the paramedics throw themselves into a bout of the most frantic activity. The doors of the ambulance are thrown open and crash against its sides – another ear-splitting sound. Now I am really terrified – the crashing of the doors brings back the ghastly sounds of the accident. But as I try to control myself, I am hit by sunlight flashing into the interior of the ambulance. It blinds me. Quickly, quickly, the paramedics grab the trolley and start to pull it, and the stretcher on top of it, out of the ambulance. I suppose they do it as carefully as they can, but speed is of the essence and so, in their haste, they bang the trolley – and me – against the side of the ambulance. It increases my feeling of helplessness and vulnerability even more. I see the roof of the ambulance passing above my head and then, without any warning, the trolley goes down a slide to reach the ground. It is a terrifying sensation. The whole journey has been a terrifying sensation. Being thrown around on the trolley in the ambulance, the ambulance twisting and turning as it went round corners on the road, and the terrible feeling of insecurity and isolation. All of that replicated the sensations I experienced as the car rolled over and over, plunging towards the gully. But now it is even more frightening, with all the deafening sounds, the bangs, the crashes, and then the nerve-racking feeling of being tipped out of the ambulance. This, and the sensation of having no control over what is happening to me, and being exposed to everything that I suffered in the crash all over again, is beyond endurance and I feel I am sliding deeper into an even worse hell. I am trying so hard to be calm, even though I am trembling with shock. I am struggling not to cry. The terrible ambulance journey has forced me to relive this most appalling and tragic event. When will this all stop? Possibly never, I think in total despair.

I cannot see the paramedics' faces, as they are backlit by the sun. They are mere silhouettes to me, so I cannot have any idea what they are thinking. But as they reach the ground and turn the trolley round, I see their faces in full sunlight and I don't like what I see at all. Not one little bit.

CHAPTER 30

HOSPITAL

"If you're going through hell, keep going."
Attributed to
Sir Winston Churchill (1874–1965)

They are panicking. As I look up at them, panic is written all over their faces. And they look grim, very grim. But their previous silence has ended. They are jabbering away to each other at a furious pace. In Spanish, so I can't understand a word. Each paramedic is holding one side of the trolley. They are running at full stretch, pushing the trolley as they rush me towards the building. They are talking, almost shouting at each other, over my inert, bloodstained body. Suddenly amongst all the Spanish I hear the word *"muerte"* ring out from one of them. Did he mean I am dying? Or did he mean Kate is dead? I am so confused. Maybe I am dying. There is blood on my clothes, most of it dried by the sun.

The paramedics hardly look at me. They know what the score is; they were with me in the ambulance for what seemed like hours on a twisting, curving, bumpy road. A very uncomfortable journey for me and for them. They are aware that what has happened is very serious. But they know what they have to do: get me inside the building as soon as possible. They run with the trolley; they talk; occasionally they point at me; everything is moving at lightning speed. But there is nothing for me to do; there is nothing I am capable of doing. I don't know where I am; I don't know how serious my injuries are. I don't even know whether I am going to live, or if I want to. There is only one thing I know I have to do.

It is so important that I must try again to see if they understand any English. I try to summon up the words I want to say, but I can't. They simply won't come out of my mouth. In my head they are all in the wrong order. But I have to try. I must articulate the thought that is driving me mad. I say to the paramedics, "I must talk to Victoria and Caroline. I must talk to them. They are my daughters."

Their faces go blank. They stop talking but don't respond to what I have said. They haven't understood me at all. Their first task is to get me to the hospital as quickly as possible, so they don't stop running. My words are of no importance to them. Once they have decided what they will do with me, then I can do what I must do – phone Victoria. Will she answer the phone? What is the time in England? How do I break the news to her? Indeed, what is my news? I know we have had a car accident; something terrible happened to Kate, but I can't remember what. I am so confused. Martha said she would stay with me all the time. Or at least I think that is what she said. Where is Martha now? No sign of her. A million thoughts, all jumbled up, race through my mind. I just can't sort them out. One thought is halfway through my mind when it is pushed aside by the next. In its turn, that one is jostled out of the way when a fourth muscles into my head.

The building is much closer now. One of the paramedics takes my right arm, which I have lifted to take some dried substance (blood?) off my face. As gently as he can while he is running, he places my arm by my side. I want to thank him, but the words won't come out. I realise I am crying because these two men have been so kind to me.

It seems to take an age to get to the building. There is no sign on it that I can see. But then, lying flat on the trolley, I can't see very much. The run across the forecourt seems to take forever, but probably it only takes a minute or so.

We enter a hallway. Antiseptic hospital smells assault my nostrils. I see a cracked, white ceiling high above me as the trolley rushes me through the hospital. The paramedics are shouting in very stentorian tones. Are they shouting at people to get out of the way of the trolley? Are they calling for assistance? I don't know. I never will. Everything is being done in such a rush.

The paramedics stop running. The trolley comes to a complete halt outside two doors. A pause. The doors open. Two nurses with grave expressions peer out. They beckon the paramedics in. I am wheeled into a large hot airless room. One of the nurses points to a machine which is clearly some sort of X-ray equipment. Neither of the nurses seems to speak English. One of them takes some cotton wool to dab my face and arms and I can see she is wiping blood off me. And then slowly, carefully, they help me off the trolley and walk me to the machine. This is the first time I have been upright since I boarded the ambulance at the scene of the accident. At least I remember that, however insignificant it may be. One of the nurses helps me onto the X-ray table. She doesn't ask me to change into a hospital gown, or indeed to take off my shirt, trousers or shoes. Very slowly the X-rays are taken and then, after a while, I am helped off the X-ray table and walked to a second machine, where they carry out more X-rays. In moving from one machine to the other, I realise that I am in a lot of pain. It really hurts me.

No sooner are the X-rays taken than one of the nurses indicates with gestures that I am fine. Even in my exhausted, confused state, I wonder how she could know so quickly, after such a cursory inspection, that everything is fine. But today I am not in a condition to question anything. I am just grateful to receive whatever treatment is offered. So I let the moment pass and allow my addled brain not to be troubled further.

The two nurses look as though they are very nice people. They smile. One brushes my hair away from my forehead and swabs it again. The other also starts to clean me up, but again, surprisingly, without taking off my clothes. There is even more blood than I realised. The nurses finish wiping the blood away – eventually. Then they carefully put me in a wheelchair and push me out of the X-ray room. As they do, a doctor in a white coat sees me in the corridor. He comes up to me and asks, "How do you feel?" I don't even realise for the moment that at last I have found someone who speaks English. "All right, I think." I lie. I have never felt worse. "I must speak to Victoria. I must talk to her. Victoria is my daughter, you see." I start to sob again as I think of Victoria and Caroline and the news I must break to them.

But this doctor is in a hurry. He speaks to me in a somewhat brusque manner. A man who does not believe in breaking bad news gently or slowly. No bedside manner. Despite the fact that I am crying and in a state of shock, he jumps straight in and confirms the news I have been dreading. "First I must tell you what has happened. It is bad news, I am afraid. You have had a very bad car accident and your wife has been killed. She didn't suffer."

I go totally numb. This is not happening to me. It is happening to somebody else. Then I start to cry uncontrollably. It was such a lovely morning when we got up in the hotel bedroom; we were so looking forward to seeing the

Argentinian Lakes. It was all so perfect. How could such a wonderful morning turn into the most ghastly, tragic afternoon? All in one day. Unbelievable. This can't be happening. It is a nightmare.

I look at the doctor's face. Very grim. No, it's not a nightmare; it's true. I can't stop crying. Between sobs I say, "I must speak to Victoria." The doctor pushes me in the wheelchair to the main reception desk, where I see a telephone. He says, "Patients are not allowed to use this phone. But I suppose," he adds grudgingly, "your circumstances are exceptional." Exceptional! That's for sure, I think to myself. With Kate dead, and me still to make what will be the worst telephone call of my life, they couldn't be worse. I rise unsteadily from my wheelchair – my legs still feel like jelly – and stand to use the telephone. Unbelievably in my confused state, I somehow remember Victoria's number. Despite my worst fears that the phone will not be answered, I get through to her first time. Very slowly, amidst my crying, I have the overwhelming urge to tell Victoria my horrific news as soon as possible. "Victoria, this is Dad." No response. My distressed tone and my crying tell her something appalling has happened. "I am sorry, but I have some terrible news. We have had a car accident and Mum has been killed." I so wish I had had more composure to break the news to Victoria much more sensitively, but there was this stone in my heart which had to be pushed out as soon as possible.

The response is not the one I would have expected. It surprises me. She replies almost immediately, "Well, that's terrible news, but it could have been worse. I could have lost both my parents." She seems so very stoical. There is no sound of her crying. She is clearly in shock. Maybe I expected a much more emotional reaction, but then how anyone will react to hearing about such an appalling event can never be predicted. We are two stunned people and we find it impossible to know what to say in such ghastly circumstances. Although punctuated by silences and some questions from Victoria about the accident and whether I am in hospital, the conversation doesn't last long; there is everything to say and there is nothing to say. I am finding it very difficult to gather my thoughts together and then express them sensibly. But one thought is so important that I must pass it on to Victoria immediately. It is so important that I have no difficulty in articulating it. "Victoria, please tell Caroline about the accident as soon as possible. She has to know what has happened." Of course she promises to do so immediately. And then she adds, "Caroline and I will fly to Buenos Aires as soon as we possibly can. I will let you know the details of the flight as soon as I have arranged our tickets." (Victoria had a copy of our itinerary and knew where I would be staying that night.)

To me, at that time, that was the most important thing in the world. I was going to see my daughters very soon and we would be able to comfort each other in our grief. That thought causes the dam to burst – I collapse into floods of tears, shaking uncontrollably. Victoria tries to console me from the other end of the phone, but, strange as it may seem, these are tears not of grief but of gratitude that I will see Victoria and Caroline as soon as it can be arranged. Amidst my tears, I say goodbye to Victoria, asking, almost begging, her to telephone me as soon as she knows the details of their flight. And then, almost maniacally, I keep repeating to myself again and again, "I am going to see them very soon. I am going to see them very soon …". Was I sane at that moment? I doubt it. But this was not to be the last time in the coming months that I doubted my sanity.

Never, never shall I forget the exact spot where I made that dreadful telephone call – the corner of the main reception desk – and the precise words of our conversation.

I shall also never forget that exact spot for another reason, a horrid crushing reason. The nurse who had left the desk returns with a small, tatty, crumpled paper bag. She hands it to me without saying a word or showing any understanding or sympathy. I have no idea what it contains. I open it as the nurse disappears. She does not wait to see my reaction or my emotions on glimpsing what is inside. I am completely and utterly devastated by the sight of its contents – my body shudders with the shock. They are Kate's personal belongings, taken by the medical staff from her body – her watch, her engagement ring and, most poignant of all to me, her wedding ring. Will the horrific experiences of this day never end? One follows another, playing total havoc with my feelings. Here's another which crucifies me, perhaps more than any other because it brings home to me so vividly the end of a life and the end of our marriage. I stand there looking into this pathetic little bag. Amidst yet more tears, I think, is this what life comes to – Kate's world stuffed into a small, scruffy, anonymous paper bag? A life which, at its end, is represented by no more than three items, not wrapped, not separated in any way, but thrown together without thought into this disgusting wrapper which can be fitted into the palm of a hand. Ghastly and so unfeeling. Is this what all life comes to? Is this how all life ends, with a miserable insignificant little curtain drawn over all that has gone before?

I stand there lost in thought, trying as best I can to control my emotions. They have been so unbelievably battered, I retreat into my own world – again. So much so that I do not notice the doctor leaving. There were so many questions I would have liked to ask him. But he had gone at the first opportunity, without saying or waving goodbye. No one in the hospital makes any attempt to keep me in for observation, despite the events I have witnessed, the blood they have seen on my body, and the obvious pain I am in. Later on, I reflect on the rudimentary treatment I received in the hospital. It was quite appalling to carry out such a cursory inspection of my injuries and then discharge me so quickly, when I had suffered so much and was still in great pain. Nor did they give me any medication to take later to help with the aftermath of the accident. It was another ghastly piece of the horrific jigsaw that was 4 January 2009. However, at least the call to Victoria had been made and that huge burden had been lifted from my shoulders. But then I notice the wheelchair has been taken away. So, without any assistance, I stagger and find the hospital exit, largely by trial and error. I realise again as I leave the hospital that I am in great pain, that I am confused, and that I am exhausted. Even my totally befuddled brain realises that my world has come to an end. My life is over. I should have died with Kate. There is no point in living. There is nothing left for me. Game over.

CHAPTER 31

HOTEL

"So long as we can say, 'This is the worst.'"
King Lear (Act IV, sc. i)
WILLIAM SHAKESPEARE

I had worried so much about making the telephone call to Victoria. Now it was done. To that extent I was relieved. Even more importantly, she had said that she and Caroline would fly to Buenos Aires as soon as they could. Since the accident, I so wanted Victoria and Caroline to be around me. For us to hold each other, give each other support and share this terrible grief together. So, the telephone call made, the desire to make it satisfied, that overriding thought was replaced by another: I couldn't wait to see Victoria and Caroline and hug them with every fibre of my body.

I have no memory of leaving the hospital. The fog had descended and totally overwhelmed my brain. That fog would not start to lift for a very long while. Martha must have been with me as I left the hospital; after all, she had promised at the scene of the accident to stay with me the whole time I was in Argentina. She said she would never leave me while I was in her country. But she did, as I shall relate later. She kept on promising me that she would do everything she could to help. And she did. She became my guardian angel for the rest of the time I was in Villa La Angostura. Whatever Martha suggested, I did it because, with her, I felt protected. I never thought, protected against what? I followed Martha like a puppy follows close to the heels of its new owner. The only difference, of course, is that a new puppy is full of life. I was full of death. There was no life in my inert body. So I trudged along beside Martha, shoulders drooping, hunched over, dragging my feet across the ground. No doubt I would have appeared to any onlooker as the picture of despair and the epitome of hopelessness. And that would be a fair indication of how I felt at the time.

The fog having descended, I have no real recollection of the order in which subsequent events happened in Angostura. Although I recall, or I think I do, the detail of some of the experiences I then went through.

After I leave hospital, Martha takes me by car to the local police station in Angostura. We go in. At the reception desk, the police officers are courteous, polite and, I detect, sympathetic. I am sure they know what has happened. They must do, although there was no police car at the scene of the accident. Martha and I are escorted to an interview room and there sits a police officer with a very understanding expression. As I am about to sit down, I notice a fan whirring round in the corner of this very scruffy room. I am mesmerised by it. I immediately think of the film *Casablanca* and the scene where Humphrey Bogart is being interviewed in a police station in Morocco. I think the film was *Casablanca*. I am lost in thought. It all adds to the unreality of the situation. Where am I? What am I doing here?

The police officer gestures to us to sit down in the two vacant chairs in front of his desk. Facing the police officer, I sit at the left-hand corner of the desk, Martha the right. (I wonder why I remember such inconsequential details, when I cannot recall matters of real importance.) My thoughts, such as they are, are broken when Martha starts to speak to the police officer at length in Spanish. He listens patiently and makes some notes. At this stage, I have no part to play in the proceedings. I am lost in my own little world. I see the lips of the policeman and Martha moving, but I don't take in anything. I don't hear anything. I feel like an observer, an outsider removed from the world where I am. It is as though I am watching a film or television with the sound turned down. But even though my mind (or what is left of it) has detached me from the world, nothing rushes into the void that has been created. Nothing. My brain has shut down. This is a real out-of-body experience. I feel as though I am watching myself from above as some kind of celestial being. I am the audience watching these three performers on stage. I watch, I observe, but I am not participating. As I look at the kind police officer and Martha talking to each other, there is not a thought in my mind. I am so confused by what has happened that I am now an automaton. I sit huddled at the left-hand corner of the officer's desk, hunched over. My attention drifts away to the fan again. Whirring away. I look at it. I continue to be mesmerised by it. Eventually I become bored with it. I now have no thought process at all. I don't even think what time it is. In fact, after the accident, it never crosses my mind to think what the time is. My brain must think it is a total irrelevance. Of course it is! What on earth does time matter today? My clock has long since stopped.

The police officer turns to me, the expression on his face full of sympathy. By now he must know that my wife has died and that I was not driving. Even so, he has a number of questions to ask. As he does so, Martha translates each one. I am not excited or excitable. I am not angry. I am not shouting. I am not crying. Like the confused man I am, I sit there quietly while he asks each question and Martha translates it. I show no emotion. I feel I have been given medication which has totally tranquillised me. I have been eviscerated. There is nothing left inside me to produce any form of emotion.

In my subdued state, everything that is happening around me seems so unreal. If the accident had happened in England, in familiar surroundings, possibly I would not have behaved in such a dull lifeless way. Maybe I would have been angry, shouted and screamed like someone demented. I don't know, and the speculation, like so much speculation in such circumstances, is pointless.

However, here in Villa La Angostura, I don't really believe what has taken place. I don't really believe I am in this police station in the middle of nowhere, in a country I know little about. Possibly I am intimidated by the 'foreign-ness' of my situation. Everything around me is all so unfamiliar. My only touchstone is Martha, who, despite the fact that she is looking after me so wonderfully well, does not diminish my feeling of being in a wholly 'foreign' environment. I need personal comfort, personal reassurance, and the hugging that only a relative or friend can give. This 'foreign' environment is not, and is not capable of, giving me what I really need now. Like a time warp, I am in a 'place' warp. This is not me. I am not here. That person down there is here, but that person is not me. That is somebody totally different. It is vital that I am not confused with him.

The questioning over, the officer having written down all my answers, Martha explains to me that I now have to sign the statement. I do so. Despite the fact that I am so confused, my legal training comes to the fore. I must have a copy of that statement. I must. At that time, I have no idea why I must have a copy, but I know I must. I ask Martha to ask the officer for a copy of my statement. Martha translates my request. The police officer looks very embarrassed and, with a very apologetic look on his face, gives his answer to Martha. She translates: "The officer says that unfortunately he is unable to give you a copy of your statement. Under the law of Argentina, he is forbidden to do so. If it were within his power to do so, he would."

"But I must have a copy of the statement. It is very important that I do." I say the words, but I have no idea why it is so important. But every instinct tells me it must be. He must give me a copy. I look the officer straight in the eye, pleadingly, and simply say, "Please." No need for any translation there. He hesitates. Many times during the interview he has looked at me sympathetically, but never in such an understanding way as he does now. He says something in Spanish to Martha, who translates for me. "He says that under Argentinian law he should not give you a copy, but this time, because of what has happened, he will. But you must not tell anyone that he has given you a copy, even if you are asked, because he will be in trouble."

I smile at the police officer and look him straight in the eye again, nod my head in obvious acceptance of his condition, and say, "Thank you." Again, no need for any translation. He looks moved.

Martha gets up from her chair. Puppy follows her out of the room, escorted by the police officer. We leave the station after I have thanked the police officer again, and also his colleagues at the front desk. We get into the car. Still no fear of getting into cars. I put on my seat belt. I don't know where we are going. Martha will look after me. She will take me wherever I should, or need, to go.

We arrive at the hotel – the Corrientes – where I had reserved a double room. I get out of the car unsteadily. I stumble slowly, thoughtfully, to the hotel entrance. This is terrible. This is absolutely horrendous. Horrific event follows horrific event. Absolutely unbearable. This is where Kate and I should have arrived, full of happiness, full of enthusiasm, full of anticipation of the wonderful sights we were going to see, particularly the Argentinian Lakes. It should have been the most joyous of arrivals. We had started the day full of enthusiasm and excitement, and it should have finished on the same note. But it is not to be. Instead of a happy couple arriving at a delightful hotel to continue their fabulous holiday, it is me, just me. Martha and the driver may be there, but it is just me – alone. I feel I am a broken man. I think of what it should have been. And instead it is this. This will be the first time on a holiday that I stay at a hotel alone. But it will be the first of many. Possibly it will never be otherwise. Instead of joy as I stand outside the hotel entrance, there is unmitigated grief. Thinking of what this arrival should have been like destroys me. And although I don't realise it then, I have just endured a 'first' – a 'first' in the never-ending series of 'firsts'. It is shattering, and so will all the others be, as they hit me like a succession of Atlantic waves hits a swimmer. Only later will I start to realise that the 'firsts' are a nightmare which destroys any progress on the road to recovery. Survive this wave, try to get your breath back, and then the next one will come crashing down on you. And flatten you.

Martha walks into the hotel, puppy follows at what is becoming his usual (safe) distance. Instead of Martha with me, it should have been Kate, full of energy, full of life and full of *joie de vivre*. No energy, no life, no *joie de vivre* tonight. Or at all. The receptionist clearly knows what has happened. The expression on his face says it all. Martha talks briefly to him. I say not a word. In my totally despairing frame of mind, there is nothing to say. I just want to grieve – with my children.

The receptionist hands me the key to Room 303. After making certain there is nothing more she can do, Martha says goodnight to the receptionist and to me. She leaves. It doesn't occur to me then, but she too has had the most appalling time, and she has had to carry the responsibility of dealing with everything that needs to be done after the tragic events of that day.

I am not hungry. I don't want to eat. Anyway, how could I possibly eat, let alone enjoy, food? And sit at a table alone? My thoughts every minute would be of Kate, who should be sitting there with me. Seeing an empty chair staring at me would be yet another unbearable experience. That 'first' can wait for another day.

The receptionist summons a porter. As I stand there waiting, I realise that I am in pain, something I haven't noticed for a while – possibly because I have been so traumatised by the events going on around me. Now, for the first time since the accident, I am truly alone. The porter arrives, picks up some of the suitcases, and heads towards the stairs. I climb the stairs slowly, some way behind him. Today seems to have been a day where at every turn I am following someone. The stairs are of highly-polished wood, as are the banisters. As I climb the stairs alone, I look at them. They are shining so brightly. Highly-polished shining wooden stairs, wherever I see them in the world in the future, will always remind me of the end, or almost the end, of that day of horror. They will haunt me forever. By that time, I am not only in a state of despair, in real pain, but I am also exhausted. My mind simply cannot cope with what it has had to endure today.

The porter arrives at the door of Room 303. He opens it. I follow him. I enter the bedroom. The porter puts my suitcases on the luggage rack. I look at the bedroom where I am going to have to spend my first night without Kate beside me. The porter leaves, to bring up the rest of the luggage. After he has gone, I look at the bedroom carefully. It is spacious, delightful, and beautifully furnished. It has a large double bed, which is next to the French windows, giving a spectacular view of the lake below. Kate was meant to be next to me here, admiring the bedroom, enjoying the view, and looking forward to our dinner. She would have absolutely adored it. This is yet another 'first'. One that, every time it happens, reduces me to tears. This night it produces cascade after cascade of tears, with my shoulders shaking with the grief. This 'first' is, "What would Kate have thought of this if she was here?" Always a deeply emotional experience, but tonight it is even worse because I know that she would have been ecstatic about the hotel, the bedroom, the view, everything. Why has she been denied all that pleasure? What did she do to deserve her horrendous fate and have this wonderful moment snatched from her? More floods of tears.

I am shaken out of my thoughts by the quiet footsteps of the porter returning; this time with Kate's luggage. I stare at it. I can't move. I can't think. I am mesmerised by that luggage. It brings home to me so forcefully the tragedy that has occurred. I manage to mumble some words of thanks to the porter. He departs. Now I am not just alone, but very lonely. I have no idea what to do. But then, suddenly, something occurs which is so bizarre as to be unbelievable. It can only have taken place because my brain has decided to shut itself down on the events of the day. What happens next will haunt me forever. I go to the suitcases on the luggage rack. Move one, open the other. And then I solemnly unpack every single item, one by one, and put them neatly in cupboards, on hangers, or wherever I consider their duly-appointed place to be. I do not stop until each item has been put away. There is a job to be done and I have to do it. Now. What amazes me, on reflection, is that, while I am pursuing my self-inflicted mechanical task, I do not succumb to any emotion. I do not weep. I do not think of what this evening would have been like if Kate had been here. I do not think that Kate is no more, that she has died at a tragically young age, that our forty-year-old partnership is over. I do not think, "Why did this happen to her, not me?" In fact, I do not think at all. My 'calm' phase has replaced my emotional phase, as it often does if I stop that wretched thinking. My brain has shut down to such an extent that, even when I catch sight of the most symbolic and heart-rending sight of all – Kate's suitcases in the bedroom, standing upright and proud on the wooden floor – I still do not succumb to emotion. My brain seems to treat it as just one more vision – one more horrific vision – that has to be taken on board. Nothing more than that. Such a sight in the months to come will reduce me to floods of tears. But not tonight. My brain seems to be saying, "Oh, yes, Kate's suitcases, so everything is here as it should be." Nothing more than that. Well, at least I don't need to unpack them – what a callous thought! I leave them exactly where the porter put them. This evening they will continue to stare at me all night. They seem to be taunting me. I deliberately avoid looking at them.

But I am still 'calm', or what passes for 'calm' today. After all the emotion that has preceded it. And so, again, I learn something new. That a period of profound emotion, producing floods of tears, can suddenly stop and be replaced by apparent calm with no moist eyes at all. I will find, in due course, there is no rational explanation as to why one phase replaces another, but now I am in a period of (apparent) calm, which will so often happen when I stop beating myself up with highly emotional and totally pointless provocative questions.

The unpacking painstakingly done, I move on to the next task. The bath is in the middle of the room. It is huge and delightfully old-fashioned, with beautiful bath furniture. Obviously the time has come to use it. I remove my bloodstained clothes. As I do so, I realise I have even been wearing them whilst unpacking and putting away all my clean clothes. Strange that. But, on second thoughts, maybe not. I believe that everything that has to be done today must be done in a set order because, I say to myself, "I am an orderly man." It is obvious what I must do next. Put all the bloodstained clothes in a neat pile and place them behind a sofa in the bedroom so that they cannot haunt me. No crying when I do so. No reflections when I do so.

I climb into the bath and find I am covered in cuts and bruises. They are unimportant. I pay no attention to them. I mechanically devote myself to the task of washing.

The next part of the evening I totally fail to understand. It is the most bizarre part of a totally bizarre evening. Having dried myself, I put on my pyjamas and, with no emotion and no thought of the day's events, I climb into bed. A double bed. Although I do not think about it then, indeed I am not thinking about anything, it is another of those dreadful 'firsts'. One of the most appalling experiences of the months to come will be getting into a double bed alone. That never really changes. But tonight I do not even think of this being a 'first'.

And then, having done my unpacking, had a bath, and climbed into bed, I go to sleep – immediately. Unbelievable. How could this happen, when I have experienced the horrific events of that fateful day, unless – and this has to be the explanation – my brain has returned to its 'shut-down' mode? It is rejecting anything more. It has had enough.

I wake up. I don't know this room. I look at the clock on my side table. I don't know why. What conceivable relevance does time have for me now? It is 7.30 am. Then I realise that I must have slept undisturbed throughout the night; some eight hours or so. I never stirred. No dreams. No nightmares, but now the horrific memories of yesterday start to invade my confused mind. I try to push them aside. Go back to thinking how long I slept last night. That's safer ground. But it's not, because then I think, how could I have slept so long, and so deeply, after what I saw yesterday? So then I feel guilty. Kate is dead, and I am so callous, so indifferent, that I can sleep, not troubled by the tragic killing of my wife. Callous bastard, I think to myself. Just stop it. Stop beating yourself up. You were exhausted, totally annihilated by what you experienced. Yes, that's it. You're not a callous bastard. I have to stop thinking. Thinking is torturing my brain. I know – be positive! I must make a plan and immediately afterwards I will get up and get on with this day. I formulate my plan. One. Get up. Two. Shave and have a bath. Three. Repack all the items I unpacked, except the ones I am going to wear. I shall repack them one by one. I shall do it meticulously, repacking each item in the place it had in the case last night before I unpacked it. I am going to make Kate proud of my packing today. Four. Get dressed. Five. Call Reception and tell them I would like my (our?) luggage taken down. But then I worry. I might forget one of these steps and then all will be lost. I've got it. I shall make a list. Then I won't forget anything vital. But already I have. I forgot to include in my steps taking my money and passport out of the safe. I proudly add it to my step plan. It goes on the list as step six.

The list made, I get out of bed; step one. I am groggy, very groggy. Did I take a sleeping pill last night? Not surprisingly, I can't remember. I start to implement my plan. I keep the list in my hand as I go through my tasks. I take it everywhere. It is an aide-memoire. It is more than that. It is my friend. Nothing will go wrong if I do everything that the list tells me to do, and in the order in which it appears on the list. As I do each step on my list, I say to myself each time, "This is step one, this is step one, this is step one …", "This is step two, this is step two …", and so on. Although this recitation of these few words is amazingly tedious, it means that I can't think of anything else while I am articulating them. That is a real blessing. "Concentrate on your plan," I order myself. I do. At step three I slightly change my formulation of the words for each step: "This is step three. This is a very important step. Step three, this is a very important step… . It is very important because it must be done so carefully." I feel good. Reciting the steps of my plan is stopping me thinking of anything else. That's good. It takes pressure off my mind. Emboldened, I go further with my next recitation. "This is step three. This is a very important step. Those blue socks were in the top right-hand corner of the case. This is step three…". I finish step three, the very important step. I do not go near, or even look at, Kate's luggage. It will be such a relief not to have it sitting there defiantly on the floor of my bedroom. Glaring at me. Jeering at me. It has stared at me the entire time I have been in this room. Goading me to such an extent that at times I have felt compelled to look at it and inflict more misery on myself. I have come to hate that luggage. It is such a devastating reminder of yesterday's tragedy. I shall look at it no more. I forget my nemesis, and look, with pride, at my suitcase, more beautifully packed than ever. I can almost hear Kate's words of approval.

Step five. I call Reception. Step six. I retrieve my money and passport from the safe. My steps are completed and have gone precisely according to plan. I am so pleased. "Whiteman, you did that extremely well. Well done." I repeat it. "Now," I say to myself, "all you have to do is be ready to leave the hotel when the car arranged by Martha arrives to collect you." I realise that I am talking to myself a lot, but I convince myself that there is nothing wrong in that because then I will get everything right. If Kate were here, I would be talking to her about the same things. So what's the difference? Anyway, it's fine because I realise I am not talking to Kate – yet – and so my list and my conversation fill perfectly the otherwise empty void.

The porter arrives. He speaks some English. "Would you please take those cases," pointing to Kate's luggage, "downstairs first." I want those wretched cases out of my sight as soon as possible. The porter seems to understand what cases he is to take away first and he picks up Kate's luggage. I feel immensely relieved. It was such a great idea to make a plan. I feel on top of the situation. Pause. Silence. Thinking. I reflect. How could I have duped myself into believing such ludicrous nonsense? I wasn't on top of any situation. But I suppose it did provide comfort to my addled brain, and I console myself with the thought that I did fulfil my hope of not thinking about yesterday's events.

The porter returns for the rest of my luggage, and I leave the room which received me on the worst day of my life. I leave it without any emotion. It had a part to play in this nightmare, and it did just that – no more and no less. As I leave the room, I take a mental photograph of it, which I shall never forget.

I go downstairs and reach the reception desk. The receptionist is a solemn-looking girl, no doubt having been made aware of my circumstances. A pleasant "Good morning" is followed by a question which completely throws me, "Would you like to have some breakfast?"

My first thought is so grotesque as to be unbelievable. I think to myself that I can't have breakfast because it is not one of the steps of my plan before I leave the hotel. Pause. I stutter, "I can't." Not surprisingly, the receptionist looks puzzled. I recover my composure to an extent and mutter, "No, thank you." Leaving aside my 'plan', I could not possibly eat anything now anyway. I have not eaten for a long while – I can't remember how long – but I am not hungry. Kate can't eat. So, in my demented and totally irrational state, I believe I can't eat either. I walk away from the receptionist, who looks bemused. My only hope is that, if she knows the background, she will understand and make the necessary allowances. But then I think, how can anybody start to understand how I feel? For the moment, I am totally lost, in every sense. I am in despair. I wish I could crawl into a hole and disappear.

Now I see Martha for the first time this morning. She is waiting for me in the lobby. She looks very grim. She says, in somewhat ominous tones, "Let's sit down over there," pointing to a sofa. I notice that there are four men with Martha, all of whom, I later discover, work for the Argentinian travel agent. One of the things that stands out so much in my mind about my stay at the Corrientes Hotel is being seated on a sofa, talking to Martha, with a huddle of these four men speaking in low voices some distance away. It is as though they want to create a cordon sanitaire between us and them, which they only cross when they have some important piece of new information or when they can provide me with some advice. They are extremely sensitive to my situation, behaving in an absolutely impeccable way, and providing assistance which, as I explain below, is absolutely invaluable.

I walk to the nearby sofa with Martha. We sit down. I don't know why Martha is looking so grim, and I am very apprehensive about what she is going to say. "There are several things I have to tell you, one good, the others not so good," Martha says. Now I am really on edge. I cannot take any more bad news. It will push me over the edge – that edge which is already perilously close. I know that. So whatever the good news may be, I am fearful of what the bad news may be. Surely I have already had enough bad news for one lifetime. My worst fears are, of course, about Victoria and Caroline. Until I know they are alright, I am going to be on tenterhooks, whatever the good news may be.

The good news is, as Martha explains, that Victoria and Caroline have got their tickets for their flight to Buenos Aires and, weather permitting, they should arrive at the hotel in Buenos Aires (not the one that Kate and I stayed at) at around seven o'clock that evening. Weather permitting is, however, a big proviso, as Europe is covered by a huge blanket of snow. And, moreover, they have to fly via Frankfurt. It will be the most dreadful journey for them in every way. Despite my real concern for them, my overall feeling is relief, knowing that they are on their way. I so desperately want to see them – hold them. Not only for them to comfort me, but also for me to comfort them. It is vital for me to know that everything that is so dear to me has not been snatched away. I still have my daughters and I want to be with them so much. With them, holding them, possibly I may keep my sanity. This news, that they are on their way, opens the floodgates again. The tears that possibly I should have shed before, and many more, stream down my cheeks. 'An Englishman doesn't cry' is the old adage. Well, this one does. My emotions are so overwhelming that I am shaking uncontrollably as I cry.

But now I know I have to face the bad news. Martha looks very grim as she starts to impart not just bad, but really bad, news. "I am sorry to tell you, but there are a number of problems which have to be dealt with under Argentinian law. First, your wife cannot be taken out of the country without the formal consent in writing of the Provincial Judge, and he is on holiday 200 miles away. We do not know, as yet, how we will be able to obtain his consent. Worse still, all the official papers relating to the death of your wife have to be filed at the provincial capital, Neuquén, and that is also 200 miles away, but in the opposite direction. The papers will have to be taken there for registration. We are also dealing with the local undertaker and, although his company can transport your wife to Buenos Aires, it has no facilities for onward transmission to take her from there back to London. So we will have to instruct another undertaker for the journey back to London, and the two firms will have to liaise with each other to ensure your wife is transferred from one to the other without any problems."

Problems, problems. But my worst nightmare is one of Kate's body being lost or abandoned by the Angostura undertakers in some soulless depot in Buenos Aires, the undertakers in the capital not knowing where she is. I am totally distraught by the thought of this possibility.

"We will try to deal with all these problems," says Martha, "but it will take time." With my thoughts still dominated by the prospect of Kate's coffin being lost in Buenos Aires because of the lack of contact between the two firms of undertakers, I burst into tears. I manage to splutter out, "How long will it take?"

"You have to stay in Angostura for three weeks or so while we deal with all the official formalities." Three weeks! I can't bear the thought. Victoria and Caroline will be in Buenos Aires tonight and I have to see them. I can't spend three weeks in this frightful place, in the middle of nowhere, being constantly reminded of the disaster that has befallen us. "I can't be here for three weeks.

It would be horrendous. Please will you do something. I must be in Buenos Aires tonight to see my daughters. I can't cope if I don't see them. I can't cope if I have to spend three weeks here."

"The official formalities have to be complied with," says Martha, "but I will see what I can do." She goes scuttling off to talk to the four men, who are still in a huddle some distance away, talking in soft tones but very animatedly. I see her speak to them. There is much shaking of heads. They are looking very grim. Martha talks to them for what seems to be an eternity. She also has a very depressed look on her face. Eventually she returns. "My colleagues have been in touch with the firm of undertakers. They will take the body …". Body! The word hits me like a hammer blow. Body! Since the accident, I have referred to, and thought of, Kate by name. I have done so subconsciously, no doubt because I have felt she was in some way still living. She was still with me. This was to be the first of many references to 'the body'. Such a harsh word that brings home to me so vividly and so cruelly what an appalling tragedy has occurred. That dreadful word means there is no escape from accepting what happened yesterday. No place to hide from the dark thoughts of a life that has been extinguished.

That word shakes me so much that, although Martha's lips are moving and she is talking directly to me, I do not hear a word she is saying. I am fast descending into a very deep bottomless pit. Martha continues to talk to me. I understand that Kate will be taken to Buenos Aires and that arrangements will be made to transfer her directly to the undertakers there. It would seem that the fear, the horror, of her being abandoned in some place in a foreign country has now been dealt with.

However, there are still other problems Martha has mentioned that remain to be resolved. During the morning, the 'huddle' of men in the corner of the reception area never disperses. They are talking all the time. Martha goes across and converses with them many times. Often she returns to me looking depressed as she sits down on the sofa next to me. Sometimes less so. But overall she looks a very troubled woman. She tells me of the many phone calls that have to be made to ensure that all the requirements of Argentinian law are complied with – nearly all of them relating to taking Kate back to London. But eventually, after this group of people have gone to such lengths to help me, the problems that seemed insuperable are somehow resolved. The tour company will send a car with the necessary papers to the Provincial Judge so that he can sign them where he is on holiday. They will be brought back to Angostura and, together with the death certificate to be issued locally, Martha will then take them all herself, by motorcycle, to Neuquén, where, contrary to all usual procedures, they will be registered today – and not in three weeks' time, the normal period required for registration. How Martha and her colleagues have arranged that, I will never know. She will then take a plane to Buenos Aires, provide all the necessary papers to the authorities and undertakers there, and give me copies of all the documents. She will do all this herself. Bless Martha. What would I have done without her? However, because I am so relieved, so emotionally drained by this good news, I miss the vital word. She says again, "I will do that all today." Today! I had missed that crucial word, being so relieved to hear that all the problems concerning the formalities in Angostura and Neuquén could be overcome. Today! The word rings in my dull brain.

"Does that mean I don't have to stay here for three weeks?" I ask. "Yes." "Can I leave here today?" Same wonderful answer. "Yes." I realise that miracles must have been performed on my behalf. I am overwhelmed by the news. I cannot control myself. Once again I sob my heart out. That I can leave this place, with all its dreadful memories, today, having had to contemplate the prospect of a three-week enforced stay, is the best news I could have received from Martha. I want so desperately to get away from here. I want so desperately to be with Victoria and Caroline when they arrive in Buenos Aires. The thought of seeing them, being with them, is keeping me sane – just. And now Martha is telling me I will see them today. I simply cannot stop crying because of the enormous relief. All these people have worked so hard for me and have achieved the impossible. I kiss Martha's hand. I thank her again and again and again for what she and her colleagues have done for me. The emotions of the last twenty-four hours rise to a crescendo. I make no sense when I talk to Martha. I don't hear what she is saying. I have heard all I need to hear from her today. I will be with Victoria and Caroline. God willing. I just go on crying for a very long time. Martha puts her hand round my shoulder. We sit there, huddled together, tears streaming down my cheeks. For a very long time.

Finally, I recover some semblance of composure. I kiss Martha's hand again and thank her so much for all she has done, and will do – especially going to Neuquén and then to Buenos Aires. But now, although incredibly fragile, I have a little control over myself and my emotions. "There is, however, one thing that you must do so that you can leave today. You, as the husband, must register your wife's death here in the local civic office." Although the outcome is what I desperately desired – to leave Angostura as soon as possible – this morning has been yet another appalling chapter in a terrible book. This morning my fate has been entirely in the hands of others. But worse than that, my emotions have been pulled this way and that. At times Martha would say something that was encouraging – that this could be done, or that would happen. And then in a few moments bad news would follow the good. And so on. Once again in this nightmare, my head is in turmoil. I feel totally exhausted, unable to play any meaningful role in my own life, or provide any constructive thoughts on what should be done in the future. A piece of flotsam on a dark sea of misery, being tossed in whatever direction the waves dictate. I am in control of nothing.

So the next decision taken for me is that I should be ferried to various municipal offices to register Kate's death, to obtain authorisation to move her out of the province, and so on. After hours in the hotel lounge discussing the most distressing consequences of the tragedy, it is time for us and the 'huddle' of men in the far corner to disperse. Martha, of course, stays with me, but her colleagues have done all they can at the hotel, and any further planning can be done from their respective offices.

Martha and I embark on our trek to the relevant civic offices to obtain the 'permissions'. That is the word that comes up in conversations, English and Spanish, all the time. In the event, it means visiting, on this extremely hot day, a series of dreary, airless, characterless offices and being interviewed by minor civic officials. One civic office is some distance outside Angostura – twenty minutes by car. We go there. It is closed. Closed for another hour. So we have to wait outside this small ugly hut – so small it reminds me of the prefabricated structures erected in England after the Second World War. But much smaller. It is in an open country area, with no buildings around it, sitting on dried, fissured ground. This is going to be a hellish hour. It is scorchingly hot, with no cover anywhere, and nowhere to sit. I trudge up and down the baked earth for an hour. I ask myself repeatedly, what am I doing in this barren, desolate wasteland in the middle of nowhere? How have I come to be here? Very sadly, of course, I know the answer, but it is so impossible to accept. The civic official arrives late, naturally. She is a short fat elderly woman, who looks the epitome of a clerk in a third-rate civic office. Without any grace whatsoever, she admits us into her tiny office. She produces a huge book, which looks like the sort of ledger one envisages in a Dickens novel. The 'ledger' is about 4 inches thick. She opens it and the front cover slams onto the desk. This is a most unattractive woman in every respect. She asks brusquely for the essential details, which Martha and I provide. She records them very carefully and very slowly in her large tome, as if the world and her job depended on it. Possibly her job does. It is swelteringly hot in this cramped, stark office, and I can't wait for this endurance test to end. She asks me to sign the book to authenticate the details. I do so. This has been such a trying but necessary exercise. We get up to leave and the woman barely says goodbye. This is yet another low point of the time I have had to spend in Angostura.

We return to the town centre (such as it is) and visit other civic offices. In the course of this day, a sea of faces representing officialdom passes in front of my eyes, but they don't register with me at all. "Sign here." "Sign there." "Put your passport number there." "Give your home address here." And so on and so on. On each occasion I do as I am bidden. I do not question anything. Every request they make, I comply with. It is so alien to my nature, not to be controlling my own life, and to have no input into any decision affecting what is going to happen to me. But the circumstances are such that I have no option but to hand everything over to others. I feel powerless to do anything. To me, the quicker I am in and out of each office, the sooner I will see Victoria and Caroline.

The visits to the civic offices completed, we return to the hotel, and Martha and I sit on the same sofa in the lounge. Martha tells me that there is nothing else to be done now. The good news is that I am definitely booked on the afternoon flight to Buenos Aires, but Martha cannot really appreciate, when she says, "There is nothing else to be done," that there is one thing I still have to do, which I am absolutely dreading. It had only come into my mind when I knew I was definitely returning to Buenos Aires today. Now it is totally dominating my thinking, and the prospect of it is something I find completely devastating. The one thing I still have to do is retrace my steps of yesterday and make exactly the same journey in reverse, with all its horrendous memories. Every inch of the way.

I shall remember exactly what was happening yesterday at each stage of the journey. Not just at the scene of the accident, but the entire day. The happiness we shared on the journey before the accident; the check-in at the airport; Kate asking me, "Can I sit by the window?"; her contretemps about excess baggage; and so on. It will be another nightmare, and I won't even have Martha's company, reassurance and support. She will be on her way to Neuquén to carry out her vital duties on my behalf. I can't even think how I will feel as I pass the scene of the accident, when I pass Kilometre Post 34. It does not bear contemplation. But I can't avoid the scene of the accident – there is only one road back to Bariloche. The one we took yesterday. I start to become completely obsessed with what is going to be the most difficult and emotional journey I will ever undertake. But I have to face this nightmare if I am to see my two daughters. And I have to.

Then, in the midst of what I believe to be the prospect of a real horror, I start to worry about the most stupid, inconsequential and unimportant thing imaginable. Possibly it is the brain trying to find an escape route, trying yet again to find a way of coping. I now begin to agonise about luggage. Why? Because, when I fly out of Bariloche, there will now only be one passenger, me, with all my luggage plus Kate's. They will try to charge me excess baggage. How absolutely ludicrous! My wife has been killed in the most tragic circumstances and I am worried, seriously worried, about the cost of excess baggage. At this stage, although I don't realise it now, I have temporarily lost my mind. It has to concentrate on irrelevant detail. Not satisfied with the grotesque nature of my worry, I start to build it up even further in my mind. "Kate would never have paid excess baggage. I just can't let her down. For her sake, and in her memory, I shall refuse to pay it. Even if they won't let me on the plane. Yes, that's what Kate would have done. I must do the same. I shall refuse. They can do their worst." I become very angry at this prospect I have built up in my mind out of nothing. I even start to shake with rage. I am now totally 'lost'. Lost in every way.

Indeed, so lost in thought, I have forgotten that Martha is still sitting next to me, talking somewhat animatedly. And then she says, "I have to leave you now, as I must collect my motorcycle and start my journey to Neuquén." I thank her once again for undertaking this vital task. Martha tells me that a driver and a man called Jose from the tour company will be coming to the hotel fairly soon to take me to Bariloche. Martha wishes me a safe journey (never have those words been more meaningful than now), she rises from the sofa, I kiss her hand, she smiles understandingly and leaves. How I wish she was coming with me. I need her support so much.

Soon afterwards, two men appear at the entrance to the hotel. One of them approaches me and introduces himself as Jose. He explains in limited English that he is to take me to Bariloche Airport. He tells me that a car is waiting outside and that he will arrange for all the luggage to be placed in the boot. I see the other man busying himself and I am aware of activity near the hotel exit, but I deliberately avoid looking there. Jose asks me whether I am ready to leave and, when I indicate that I am, he asks me to follow him. We walk out of the hotel and some distance away I see the second man putting the luggage in a very smart black limousine. I follow Jose, but for the first time in my adult life, I don't bother to check that all the luggage has been safely stowed. I don't want to see that luggage ever again. We walk to the car. I say nothing. My mind is too full of so many thoughts; I am still worried about being charged for excess baggage. I leave the hotel behind me forever. I know I shall never return to it. That would be impossible.

The journey I am so dreading – the journey which will be the worst I ever have to make – is about to begin.

CHAPTER 32

JOURNEY

"Long Day's Journey into Night"
EUGENE O'NEILL

"Will the day's journey take the whole long day?
From morn to night, my friend."
Up-Hill, 1862
CHRISTINA ROSSETTI

As I continue my walk towards the car, I realise that I am shaking. Not with pain, as fortunately that is now subsiding. Nor am I shaking with the fear of getting into a car. I realise afterwards that at no time was I frightened of going on a car journey, although that was the cause of yesterday's horror. Will I be able to survive passing the scene of the accident at Kilometre Post 34? What if the police are there? What if there is a crowd of onlookers there?

We reach the car. It has seemed to be an endless walk because of my fears. In reality it is just a few metres. The driver has a suitably sympathetic expression on his face as he opens the rear nearside door for me. Oh no! My mind may be confused, but I have already worked out that that will be the side of the car which will be closer to the scene of the accident. What if it gave a clear view of the scene of the disaster, with various people busying themselves with the aftermath of what happened? So, having resolved in advance that I will sit on the offside of the car, I walk round and open the rear offside door. But, as I get into the car, my overriding thought is still, how will I be able to cope when we pass Kilometre Post 34?

I settle into my seat. This time, some twenty-four hours too late, I put on my seat belt. It is such an appalling moment. A terrible thought. If only … if only … But nothing will turn back the clock. I still haven't really absorbed what has happened in the last twenty-four hours. I am now going to experience something that nobody should have to endure. My eyes fill with tears. We set off. I turn my head away from Jose, who is totally silent. I go on crying as I look out of the car window at the passing countryside. I don't remember anything I see on the first part of the journey. Except the kilometre posts mercilessly counting down, kilometre by kilometre, the distance before we pass my nemesis. Kilometre Post 137 passes, then 136, then 135, and so on. Each time, I subtract 34 from the number on the post so that I know how far it is before we reach my own personal hell. Each and every time I think, as I engage in my horrible arithmetical exercise, still that far to go? It can't be.

The question will not go away. How will I cope? I don't know. 87 … 86 … 85. But somehow or other I will have to cope with it. It is going to be there. No avoiding it. I start to tremble. My heart is racing. I am making this ordeal worse than it need be. Even worse than I imagined. Will I totally break down and collapse into a torrent of tears? I decide there is only one way to deal with this situation – assuming that I am capable of dealing with anything at the moment. I shall watch all the kilometre posts until we get to 35, and then I will look away to my left, away from the accident scene on the right. I will continue to look to the left for quite a while until I am sure in my own mind that the car has passed the place where our two lives came to an end. Yes, that's what I will do. And having come up with my plan, I feel less emotional – although my heart is still beating very fast. Yes, I have found the solution. My first plan worked brilliantly this morning, and so will this one, my second of the day.

In the car there is silence. Neither the driver nor Jose really speaks any English and they do not converse in Spanish. I feel they must know what I am going through. Occasionally, Jose looks at me with a slight smile, both understanding and sensitive. 72 … 71 … 70. Just hold on. It will be alright if you keep to your plan. Just calm down. 63 … 62 … 61. I am still counting each one, but I shall stop, definitely stop, at 35.

My somewhat steadier emotion after I decided on my plan is now evaporating. I am getting very upset. I look away from Jose. I look out of the window and cry. And then, as we round a bend, with an open, straight section of road ahead, I see Kilometre Post 35. This is it. I look very firmly away to my left. Doing that, or, more accurately, the prospect of doing that, has been my lifeline for most of the journey. It has made it possible to survive the ordeal, and survival is the only touchstone I have now.

We pass Kilometre Post 35. I see it on the left-hand side of the road. We, of course, are on the right-hand side of the road, so we are even closer to the scene of the accident. I am being really tested now. I keep to my resolution. But then suddenly I snap. Despite everything I have promised myself, I cannot resist the temptation to look to the right. I fail my own self-imposed test. Some evil, cruel, controlling force dictates I look to the right. When it comes to the crunch, I have no will, no power to resist. So look I do, not knowing what I will see. Possibly the crushed, battered wreck of the car. Possibly a police car. Possibly a policeman taking photographs or measurements. Or maybe just a police tape cordoning off the scene. There might even (horrible thought) be a crowd of onlookers gawping at the site of merciless death.

Before I look, a vision flashes through my mind, as it has done so many times in the past day. Kate lying on her back on the slope, the strip of skin torn from her forehead, the eye plucked out and pushed towards her ear, her lips parting once as if she was going to speak, and her diaphragm moving inwards, but only the once. An absolutely horrific sight of cruel, devastating injury and total mayhem. But of sound there was none. No shout, no scream, no cry. Just a small gurgle. That vision will always haunt me.

So I turn to look at the place where Kate's life was lost and mine was destroyed. There will never be a more significant place in the world to me. It is where my world stopped. So I look. What do I see? Nothing! Absolutely nothing! It is as though the most momentous event of my life had never happened. There is the grass bank, there is the shingle, and there is the row of trees where the car eventually came to rest. No sign of the car. It must have been taken away by the police. No pieces of metal. Not even a sign of disturbance. Just nothing. It is like any other stretch of this fateful road. I can't believe that something so dramatic could occur and within twenty-four hours there is no sign or evidence of it. Life is taken and there is nothing to show it ever existed. I am shocked. I am devastated. It is not that I want to wallow in the horrendous event that occurred, but the fact that this piece of countryside is like any other – as though the accident and Kate's death were a figment of my imagination. It almost seems as though it was a dream – or rather a nightmare – from which I might now wake up. Except I won't.

The car slows down for traffic ahead and I am tempted to ask the driver to stop so that I can look once again at the scene of Kate's death. But what would be the point? I would merely be torturing myself, and inevitably there would be more tears. So the thought leaves my head almost as soon as it enters it. I say nothing. The car speeds away from the scene of the accident. I am lost in thought. I look to the left, away from the scene, and gaze into the middle distance. And I weep copiously. I am thinking that Kate is no more, and the place where she was evicted from this world wants no further part of her cruel death. At least she is not suffering, but this empty place has inflicted more suffering on me.

But I have faced down – just – the worst demon of this drive. The anticipation of it had instilled real fear in me and I had become an emotional wreck, not knowing what I would see and how I would react. My overall reaction is not what I expected – amazed that such a devastating event could occur and yet there was no sign of it twenty-four hours later. I don't know what I did expect, but it wasn't that. Is life so meaningless? Is it so transient? Is it of no consequence? Is it to be discarded or cut off with no sign that it ever existed? I ponder these questions as I look out of the window of the speeding car and I realise that the answer to all of them, and to a million similar ones, is of course yes. But it has been brought home to me in the most brutal and cruel way. I realise also that the incredibly emotional build-up to passing Kilometre Post 34 has totally drained me. I feel very, very tired. I just want to sleep now.

The rest of the car journey is of no consequence and the kilometre posts have none of the significance that they did on the countdown to Number 34. Near the airport we pass the beautiful lake that Kate was so happy and excited to see yesterday. It was, we thought, a view which foreshadowed the amazing things to come. Was that only twenty-four hours ago? It feels as though it was a lifetime ago – and it was.

And so, eventually, we arrive at Bariloche Airport. Yet more memories of yesterday. I get out of the car and, led by Jose, go to the check-in desk. There, waiting, I am to be surrounded by luggage again. Kate's luggage stares me out. It torments me. I look away. Jose speaks quietly to the check-in clerk. Her expression changes immediately from a normal one to that of a sad, understanding countenance. She looks concerned and the concern must be for me. As for my earlier ludicrous worries about having to pay for excess baggage, there is no problem. It is all checked through without query, no doubt because of the words Jose has had with the check-in clerk. She continues to look most understanding. She tells me that I will be upgraded to First Class – something that on other occasions would have pleased me no end. But not today. What does it matter? What does anything matter? She tells me that they will board me first and seat me on the plane before anyone else is allowed to enter the aircraft. She is obviously a caring person, who is doing everything she can to help me. I appreciate her kindness and sympathy. I ask Jose whether Kate's coffin is definitely on the plane. I am distraught at the prospect that it might not be. He seems to understand my distress and says the coffin has definitely been loaded. Later we are joined by the other representatives of the travel company who have done so much on my behalf. I have only one question for them, "Is my wife's coffin on the plane?" They assure me that it definitely is, but I am so worried I ask them again. And again. I have to know she is with me. I simply couldn't cope if she were left behind. Just before I leave them, to be shown to the Departure Lounge, I ask the same question again, just in case. They have infinite patience and confirm, yet again, that Kate will be with me.

I am escorted into the Departure Lounge and, as I am the first person to arrive there, I sit entirely alone. I think to myself that, apart from being alone in the bedroom at the Hotel Corrientes, this is the first time I have been without company since the accident. This is the start of the rest of my journey through life, when I will have to 'go it alone'. It is another depressing thought, but over the coming months and years I will have to accept that 'going it alone' is what fate has determined I will have to endure.

To the people who came into the lounge subsequently I must have cut a very lonely figure. They would have seen me hunched over, staring at the floor, deep in thought, yet really unable to think, sobbing softly. The closer I sit by the exit door for boarding the plane, the closer I feel to Buenos Aires and to Victoria and Caroline. So I shuffle along the row of seats to the one which is right next to the exit. The Departure Lounge door opens. A stewardess comes in and walks over to me. She obviously knows I am the passenger who is to be treated with great consideration. She asks me to follow her to the plane. I rise to my feet somewhat unsteadily. She takes my arm. I walk with her. Slowly. The other passengers remain where they are. She supports me as I walk up the aircraft steps. Then the thought hits me again that this is the return leg of the flight I took yesterday with Kate, when she was so full of excitement about what was ahead.

Inside the plane one of the cabin crew takes me by the arm and leads me to my seat. I slump down where they indicate. It is a window seat. The seat next to me is, and will remain, empty. A window seat and an empty seat next to it – could anything have been more evocative to turn the knife in the wound? The window seat. I hear Kate's voice asking, "Can I sit next to the window to get the view of the city [Buenos Aires]?" The empty seat mocks me, and the person who sat there yesterday now lies in a coffin in the hold. I start to sob again. The whole flight, I think about Kate in a wooden box, a short distance away from me, all life extinguished. The thought is too much for me and I gaze out of the aircraft window, trying to distract myself – totally pointless. On the flight, although it may seem strange, I think that Kate is with me, albeit in a box. That is some consolation. At least I can escort her back to London. She may not be at my side, but we are flying home together.

I have no recollection of arriving in Buenos Aires or being taken to the hotel – not the one Kate and I stayed in, that would have been a nightmare to end all nightmares. My only thought is about Victoria and Caroline. How soon will I see them? Representatives of the tour company meet me at the hotel and assure me that, even though the flight has been delayed, Victoria and Caroline should reach the hotel in about an hour's time. I am comforted by thinking that I only had to spend one day in Angostura and now our planes have arrived almost at the same time in Buenos Aires. I have only an hour to wait before we are reunited. I am so very, very grateful for that. A long delay, spending the time alone, would have been so very hard to bear. The tour company representatives talk to me, no doubt trying to keep my mind occupied with sympathetic considerations. And, true to her word, Martha turns up at the hotel a little while later, clutching the promised official documents that she went all the way to Neuquén to collect for me. I fall upon her, thanking her so much for making it possible for me, Victoria, Caroline and, vitally, Kate to leave the country with all the necessary formalities completed. She has done the most wonderful job and has been tireless in ensuring that every effort will be made to help me endure this dreadful nightmare. She promised to be with me the whole time I was in Argentina and she has – except for when she went to Neuquén as my saviour. Now she has but one last task to perform and it is clearly causing her some distress. And then I see why. From a large carrier bag she takes out Kate's handbag, which I had not seen since we were inside the car, and slowly, carefully, and with obvious emotion, she hands it to me. There are tears in her eyes. This is one of the most poignant and heart-rending moments in my life. Martha realises the pain this is causing me – how much the sight of that handbag is destroying me. She knows I am suffering so much. But she knows, and I know, she has to do it. In fact, I want her to because, as it was Kate's most personal possession, I feel it is reuniting me with her. By taking Kate's handbag from Martha, I feel Kate and I are together again. In the months to come, that handbag, as far as I am concerned, IS Kate. I take it everywhere with me, and if it is with me, Kate is with me. It is my friend, my comforter; by stroking that smooth shiny leather, I can face life – just.

I have never opened the handbag. I want to keep it entire, as a whole, undefiled, undamaged by the events of 4 January 2009. One doesn't have to be a psychiatrist to understand the subconscious way my mind is working.

As I stand at the hotel reception desk, I realise I need to wash and change, and that will fill in the time until Victoria and Caroline arrive. I tell the concierge to inform me as soon as they know when my daughters have reached the hotel. I must be there to see them at the first opportunity. Believing I have done everything I can, I say goodbye to Martha for the time being and go to my bedroom.

A little while later, Reception phones me to say Victoria and Caroline are close to the hotel. I go down to Reception and, almost as soon as I arrive there, they are coming through the entrance doors. It is wonderful that within an hour of my arrival they are with me. But they look so tired, so exhausted, like waifs who have been blown in from the street. My heart goes out to them; they have had the most terrible journey. They have had to fly via Frankfurt, and both there and in London the plane's departure was delayed by heavy snowfalls. As I discover subsequently, to add to their misery, the airline has lost Victoria's luggage. The journey for them has been horrendous, but what matters to all three of us is that we are together now. We fall into each other's arms, as though nobody else in the world matters or indeed exists.

And to us at that moment they don't. At last I have my beloved daughters, albeit tired and exhausted, with me. All three of us need each other so much. Again, I cannot hold back my emotions and I burst into floods of tears in the main lobby of the hotel. In twenty-four hours I have cried so much. Is there no end to my tears? Not yet, obviously. As far as I can take it in, everyone in the lobby appears to be looking at us. It doesn't matter. Nothing matters except we are together. We stand there hugging and kissing each other for a long time. I have never felt more emotional with them in my entire life. This is the moment that has kept me going, kept me more or less sane, in the last twenty-four hours. Nobody has ever needed someone as much as I need them now. As much as I want to be with them now.

The emotional greeting subsides but does not end. We exchange stories, but I want to hear from them how they feel, what has happened to them, what they want to do, and indeed what I can do for them after their appalling journey. I must have asked them so many questions, but I cannot remember one of them. Nor can I remember any of their answers. All that I can remember is that their journey was long, difficult and incredibly tiring. And as for me, I knew that the most horrific journey of my life was over; indeed, I was aware that my life as I knew it was also over. But – and this was a huge 'but' – I had been reunited with my two children, my adored daughters. So adored that my last words to Kate as she lay dying in my arms on that accursed hillside were to thank her for giving me Victoria and Caroline. Ever since, I have been greatly comforted by the thought that they were my last words to the wife I also adored. I live in the hope that she heard them; please God that she did because at that moment I felt that I had brought the four of us together in that most wretched of places. That family was no more, and I knew that I would have to reconcile my mind to the fact that we were now a unit of three, bereft of the person who had been at the very heart of all our lives. Even so, we could make that unit of three work, and we three agreed that evening over supper that we would do so in memory of, and as a tribute to, the amazing person who had created and nurtured our family with so much love for over thirty years. When I went to bed that night, I kept on thinking about the agreement we had made over supper, and then, although my mind was in total turmoil, I made the most important decision of my life. I decided that I would dedicate my life to keeping that unit of three intact. That would be the priority from now on, and nothing else mattered. It would give me so much to live for – there would be nothing else now – and Kate would have so approved. Her love for us and our love for each other would bind us together. Nothing that happened at Kilometre Post 34 could prevent that.

CHAPTER 33

I FIND 'GOD'

"Out of the night that covers me,
Black as the pit from pole to pole,
I thank whatever gods may be
For my unconquerable soul.

In the fell clutch of circumstance
I have not winced nor cried aloud.
Under the bludgeonings of chance
My head is bloody, but unbowed.

Beyond this place of wrath and tears
Looms but the Horror of the shade,
And yet the menace of the years
Finds and shall find me unafraid.

It matters not how strait the gate,
How charged with punishments the scroll,
I am the master of my fate,
I am the captain of my soul."

Invictus
WILLIAM ERNEST HENLEY (1849–1903)

They are lined up in a row. Like soldiers. I stand and stare at them, mesmerised by them. Those wretched cases. Their very presence has mocked me, terrorised me and destroyed me all week. Kate's luggage. Redundant now, but I feel compelled to take it back to London. Will I ever be free of this dreadful baggage?

It is the following morning and we are at the airport. We have to go. Back to London. Home. Time to bring to a close this cataclysmic stay in Argentina. But there is, and never will be, any way to bring to a close this apocalyptic episode in my life. Never.

We are huddled together in the Departure Lounge. Victoria tells me afterwards that I look dazed, confused and exhausted. I am. We board the plane. We are about to leave together – the unit of three, plus Kate in a coffin in the hold – our final flight together as a family. We arrive at Heathrow at 4 am. It is a bitterly cold January morning. A deep blanket of snow has smothered the entire airport. To my amazement, bearing in mind the atrocious conditions and the early hour, we see my brother and sister and their spouses waiting for us as we emerge from the Arrivals Hall. Walking through the front door of my home an hour or so later is surreal. I am home, but it is not home as it had been, and it never would be again.

Victoria and Caroline had decided to stay at home with me, and I was so grateful they did; the unit of three continued. In the dark, dark days, weeks and months that followed, I was in my own personal hell; days of pain, fear, loneliness, confusion, insecurity and a total inability to cope. Indeed, in Argentina a psychiatrist I had seen there had diagnosed post-traumatic stress disorder and had predicted many of the symptoms I was now experiencing. I was haunted by the fear of losing Victoria, Caroline, or indeed both of them. I was desperate for company, but fearful of not being able to appear normal when I was in such an emotionally fragile state. I was also affected in some unexpected ways; above all, I felt compelled to run long distances every day, always accompanied by my faithful little dog, Truffle. She was my constant companion and gave me great comfort at a time when I needed it most.

Then I discovered 'God'. And I was saved.

One of my closest friends is a psychiatrist and very soon after our return he referred me to his eminent colleague, Dr Islam, at The Priory in Roehampton. Once a week I went to see this wonderful human being. Strangely, I remember little of our conversations. What I do remember is that Dr Islam never gave me advice, he listened attentively, and he sensitively asked me the most penetrating questions. 'God' was my saviour. I revered him and was totally reliant on him. Without him there would have been darkness everywhere. The candle would have flickered and died; that is why

I referred to him as 'God', and it was through him that I found the strength and the will to go on. I became utterly dependent on my weekly visits to him, and when I left, I always felt better, often distinctly better, than when I had arrived. After some five months of seeing Dr Islam, I had improved so much that I was able to return to full-time practice at the Bar and was in court the following month.

Then epiphany. One week when I was due to see Dr Islam, I was feeling particularly depressed. I felt I could describe my future by reference to a metaphor which would appeal to Dr Islam, who is a very keen follower of cricket. So at the session that followed I told him that I felt like the nightwatchman in the cricket match that was my life. It was towards the end of the day, light was fading fast, and my side had lost another wicket. It was imperative that no further wickets of recognised batsmen were lost that night in the gathering gloom. So in goes the nightwatchman, a bowler with no batting pretensions, whose only role is to keep his wicket intact until stumps are drawn. He is not there to achieve anything, he is merely there to play out time.

I looked at Dr Islam and said with considerable emotion, "That is how I see the rest of my life." Dr Islam's response was immediate. It was so brilliant, particularly given that it was spontaneous, that I shall never forget it.

"But that is only a part of the story," he said. "The next day dawns; the sun rises and floods the pitch with the most glorious light. The nightwatchman returns to fulfil his real role in the match, as the most outstanding bowler. Throughout the day he bowls brilliantly and takes several critical wickets. His teammates are inspired by his vital contribution, his team wins and he is applauded off the pitch. Now you have the whole story." How amazing to come up with such an encouraging and thought-provoking conclusion to my metaphor, which had been completely and so cleverly turned on its head. It gave me so much hope for the future. How right he proved to be!

And to emphasise Dr Islam's stunning end to my metaphor, as I walked out of the entrance to The Priory, the clouds parted and the sun burst through them to bathe the beautiful gardens with the most dazzling light. Surely, I thought, the sudden arrival of the sun and the stunning vision that was now before me had to be a sign. So I decided to walk round the gardens, to digest the inwardness of what Dr Islam had said and absorb the whole uplifting experience. I thought

Above: With my new love, Sally, on her birthday, 2012

long and hard, and then the moment of my epiphany ... The way forward was so obvious and so very clear that it was like that shaft of sunlight piercing the clouds, illuminating everything so brilliantly. The completion by Dr Islam of my metaphor told me exactly what I now had to do. I would emulate the success of the bowler. I realised that through Dr Islam I would find the courage to create a second life. There and then, on that very spot, I became absolutely determined to do just that. That courage, that decision, that determination would all come together and I would be saved. I would create new interests, and develop existing ones, which I would find completely satisfying. I would do this with conviction and enthusiasm. My focus would be on the future, not the past. The past would only be there to the extent that I could build upon it in a meaningful way. The future would be there as an exciting challenge. My consultation with Dr Islam that afternoon had completely changed my view of my future and of life. My nightwatchman would be banished, forever replaced by the world-class bowler who could still achieve so much.

I finished my walk and got into my car. I drove very slowly out of the grounds – I had so much to ponder. I felt like a new man – and indeed I was! I reached the end of the driveway of The Priory and, after a little hesitation, I turned right to continue my journey, a journey now infused with so much hope and optimism.

Indeed, I did keep to the decision and the resolutions I made at my moment of epiphany. In due course I became involved in arts administration, the arts generally and opera in particular. I started visiting museums and art galleries. I took up new sporting activities, making many new friends in the process. But most important of all, I commenced writing my autobiography, and I found the process of writing the most fulfilling experience of my new life. All these activities gave, and still give, me the most enormous pleasure and complemented what until then had been the real focus of my life, namely, my professional work. And all of this found its origin in 'God's' completion of my metaphor.

So now I have reached a stage I would never have contemplated as possible. I do have a second life which is meaningful, full of purpose, deeply satisfying, and which makes me very happy. I am truly fortunate.

All of the above was originally written in 2013, when I was in a very optimistic mood. I could not have foreseen what was to befall me next. Essentially, disaster, but, with my track record, how could it be otherwise? Since 2014 I have had three operations for cancer, a diagnosed heart attack, two strokes, heart failure and then finally (or so far finally), three months of radiotherapy treatment. Indeed, I have almost died three times. As my GP said, "You have been to hell and back." I corrected him politely by saying more accurately, "I have been to hell, but I'm not sure about making it all the way back." However, when people see me now and hear what has happened to me, they say, "But you look so well!" The reason I have survived and look well, I have concluded, is that I am a fighter. I am determined to overcome whatever is thrown at me, even life-threatening conditions. I will not surrender. I will fight to the very last breath in my body. To me there is no other way.

Was I right to fight? The question answers itself. Of course I was right to fight against all the odds. And the reward proved – if proof be needed – to be fantastic. I have found the most wonderful woman, who has brought joy into my life. The woman, Sally, to whom this book is dedicated, has been with me every step of the dreadful path that I have had to tread in the most recent years. I regard myself as so very fortunate to have found her. And, having found her, I now know for certain that I shall never give up on life, whatever the odds. I am so very lucky to have her by my side. I have reached for and captured a real star.

Quotations feature at the beginning of every chapter in this autobiography, but in light of what I have said in the previous paragraph, I have saved till last what is possibly, in my circumstances now, the most poignant one of all. It is the title of a play by Shakespeare, *All's Well That Ends Well*. That's me. That's my life. And it's not over yet. I shall never stop reaching for the stars.

Above: My beloved Truffle, 2009